CONSULTING
TO
MANAGEMENT

CONSULTING
TO
MANAGEMENT

Larry E. Greiner

University of Southern California

Robert O. Metzger

Metzger & Associates

Prentice-Hall, Inc., Englewood Cliffs, New Jersey 07632

Library of Congress Cataloging in Publication Data

GREINER, LARRY E.
  Consulting to management.

  Includes bibliographies and index.
  1. Business consultants.   I. Metzger, Robert O.
II. Title.
HD69.C6G73   658.4'6   82-7582
ISBN   0-13-169128-7   AACR2

Editorial/production supervision and interior design by Steven Young
Cover design by Photo Plus Art
Manufacturing buyer: Ed O'Dougherty

Printed in the United States of America

10   9   8   7   6   5   4

ISBN 0-13-169128-7

Prentice-Hall International, Inc., *London*
Prentice-Hall of Australia Pty. Limited, *Sydney*
Prentice-Hall Canada Inc., *Toronto*
Prentice-Hall of India Private Limited, *New Delhi*
Prentice-Hall of Japan, Inc., *Tokyo*
Prentice-Hall of Southeast Asia Pte. Ltd., *Singapore*
Whitehall Books Limited, *Wellington, New Zealand*

Contents

7   Marketing Assignments   127

8   Financial Analyses and Studies   163

9   Organization and Systems Studies   188

10   Human Resource and Compensation Studies   203

11   Data-Gathering Methods: The Art of Inquiry   218

PART IV
Stages in Consulting   249

12   Defining Client Needs: How To Enter a Foreign
Culture   251

13   Diagnosing the Issues: How To Unravel the Problem   261

14   Implementing Change: How To Sell Your
Recommendations   269

15   How To Sell More Work—or Leave Gracefully   287

16   The Uniqueness of Each Client   299

PART V
Reflections on Consulting   309

17   Resolving Ethical Issues: You Can't Avoid Them   311

Preface

Worldwide, management consulting represents a $5 billion plus industry with more than half of those dollars being generated here in the United States. In the 1980s, national management consulting billings could well double, and several major firms will increase their individual billings to $100 million a year or more.

This next decade in America will be a very difficult one for most business enterprises. It has already started out being far more complex than the 1970s, witnessed by the deregulation of airlines, trucking, and financial institutions. After deep trauma in the automotive industry since 1979, "Detroit" has been attempting a comeback to regain sizable markets lost to imports. Chemical and pharmaceutical companies are already struggling in reaction to tough government regulations and the resultant lack of product development. Industry by industry, the turmoil and challenge go on. Also new industries such as biotechnology, home entertainment, and home computers are experiencing phenominal growth that is difficult to manage.

Throughout it all, management consultants will play an ever more important role in every aspect of American business ranging from strategic planning to productivity improvement. They will introduce new compensation plans to stimulate innovation and design "real-time" information systems to encourage cost control.

Yet very little has been written about management consulting. Even though some graduate business schools are now introducing courses in management consulting in response to student demand, there are no real textbooks on the subject. About the only source of information comes from periodicals, such as the *Wall Street Journal*, the *Harvard Business Review*, and *Business Week*, which publish occasional articles about the industry or a new service offered by consultants.

Most consultants begin their careers fresh out of an MBA program by joining a well established consulting firm, such as a McKinsey or a Booz Allen. They learn about consulting "on-the-job" under the tutelage of experienced client managers and partners. Aside from their MBA training, coupled with their imitating more seasoned senior mentors, nowhere have these fledgling consultants been exposed to the fundamentals of the profession. Independent consultants, without the benefits of a mentor/boss relationship, simply learn by doing.

Professional standards and certification processes within the industry are not universally accepted or enforced, as they are in law or medicine. Consequently, anyone can declare himself or herself to be a consultant. Numerous stories abound about how a team of young MBAs, still "wet behind the ears," learned at the client's expense by submitting a report that merely confirmed what the client already knew—that they were in trouble.

Yet, there are many fine, experienced consultants, both generalists and specialists, who bring an expert, objective, and sensitive viewpoint to their clients. These able consultants have learned to cut across political lines, to distinguish between symptoms and root causes, and to recommend and implement pragmatic solutions. Just how these effective consultants operate with their clients has not been codified in the skimpy literature.

In the fall of 1978, Professor Greiner created a new MBA course elective on management consulting at the University of Southern California. His decision was based on growing requests by second year MBA students for more information about management consulting as a career, as well as needs expressed by consulting firms for an MBA better educated in consulting skills. The course utilized a combination of guest consultants, lectures, readings, and a real consulting project. After two years, the course became one of the most popular MBA electives, and it required a waiting list for admission.

One of the early guest lecturers was Dr. Robert O. Metzger, the other author of this book, a former financial service industry CEO and now managing partner of his own national banking consulting firm. Together we decided to write this book after concluding that the evolving outline of the U.S.C. course had not been covered with such breadth in any prior publication on the profession. Each offering of the course had raised new issues that had not been anticipated previously. Guest consultants also demonstrated a richness in points of view that cautioned against a simplistic set of principles for the effective consultant.

As practicing consultants, we have drawn heavily on our combined experience of more than 25 years. One of us, Larry Greiner, is an academic and consultant, while Robert Metzger is a former executive turned consultant. Our continuous dialogue, drawing from these two different backgrounds, produced the kind of "creative tension" that we hope has resulted in a book with a balance between theory and practice, knowledge and skill, and perspective and technique.

Although the book has its origins in academia, we do not intend it as a textbook removed from the reality faced by consultants. Quite the contrary. The course and the book would not have had its impetus without demands and challenges made by those people who were antici-pating or living with a career in consulting. Perhaps the most guiding principle for us has been to write a book that we would have liked to have read ourselves as fledgling consultants, as well as a reference to refer to later as a source of confirmation and insight into our subsequent expe-riences as consultants. The book, in essence, is dedicated to consultants of all types, ages, backgrounds, and futures.

We also hope that the book will be read by managers—not because they plan to become consultants but because they are the ones who are in a unique position to exercise "quality control" over the profession. A more informed executive will be able to work more constructively with consultants. Our best consulting experiences have come more from work-ing with strong executives in healthy organizations than from weak managers in sick organizations.

Our gratitude goes to several people who have given generously of their support, encouragement, and love in a task that often got side-tracked by other demands. There is our publisher, Ted Jursek, who both cajoled and left us alone at the right times, while always keeping the faith; there is our production editor, Steve Young, who demonstrated his commitment to a quality product beyond our expectations while assur-ing that the rigorous production schedule was maintained; there are the many anonymous MBA students and consultants who participated un-knowingly in adding fresh insights; and, there are Judi Conway and Nancy Rench, our manuscript typists, who performed their skills as we wish we could as consultants. Most of all, there are our loved ones—for Bob, they are Dorothee, who gave so much of her time to proofing the drafts and galleys, and Joelle, who accepted so many weekends without her father and who cheered so loudly when told the book was finally finished. For Larry, they are Marta, Corinne, and Justine—all of whom gave smiles and shed tears over our ups and downs. Thank you, all, so much!

Larry E. Greiner, DBA
Robert O. Metzger, Ph.D., CMC

CONSULTING
TO
MANAGEMENT

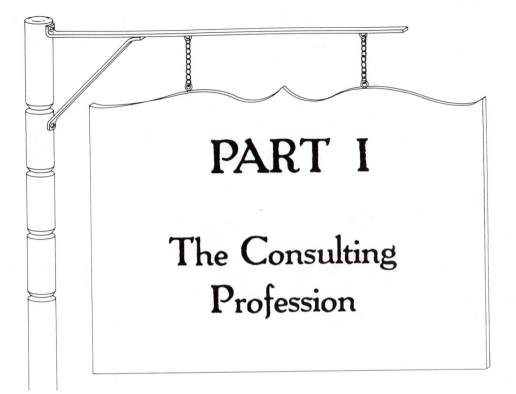

PART I

The Consulting Profession

In this part of the book, Chapters 1-3, we provide the reader with an overview of a major professional industry—the consulting profession—and the myriad of differences that abound in it. This perspective is paramount to understanding how any particular consultant or consulting firm fits in its relationship to the consultant. We introduce the reader to the size of the industry, the purposes of typical consulting firms, their size, and their similarities and differences. We also explore the vast array of differing types of consultants, be they generalist, specialist, process, content, diagnostic, change, custom, and package; their various approaches to working with clients; and their philosophies with respect to their roles. Finally, we examine the skills required and the background and experience necessary to pursue and excel at a career in the profession. This knowledge is fundamental if our readers are to select just what kind of consultant they would like to be and how best to utilize their strengths and experiences in their own and in their clients' best interests.

I

What Is Management Consulting?

Management consulting is an exciting growth industry that will not sit still for a clear definition. In the 1970s corporations and public agencies turned increasingly to consultants for advice, graduate schools produced more and more students who chose consulting as a career, many older executives opted to leave corporations to hang out their shingles as consultants, and a number of professors decided to enhance their careers (and incomes) by moonlighting as consultants. This trend continues.

Consider these statistics that attest to the rapid growth and development of the consulting industry:

1. *Explosion in Revenues.* Current estimates are that management consulting revenues are close to $3 billion annually in the United States alone. This compares with $2 billion in 1970 and less than $1 billion in 1960. The annual growth rate now is approximately 20%. Revenues from the private sector account for 75% of total billings, whereas the public sector has increased to a sizable 25%.

2. *Proliferation of Services.* Not only have revenues skyrocketed but so has the variety of "products" offered by consultants. Management consulting began in the early 1900s with an exclusive focus on industrial

engineering, but today there are approximately 115 different services being offered by management consultants.

3. *Growth in Professional Staff.*   To meet the growth in demand for consulting services, many new people have entered the industry to practice their skills as consultants. There are currently 40,000–50,000 full-time management consultants, which is three times the number existing in the mid-1960s. Estimates range as high as 70,000 if part-time consultants and internal consultants within corporations are included.

4. *Entry of New Firms.*   Consulting is an easy industry to enter; little is required in the way of capital, only a telephone number and a calling card. Currently, there are about 6,000 firms with two or more employees, 75% of which were founded after 1960 and 50% during the 1970s. Even the makeup of the ten largest firms has changed dramatically, with six of the top ten coming from the Big-8 accounting firms in 1980, compared with none in the 1960s.

Management consulting is obviously not a mature industry; it is still an adolescent venturing eagerly into the future. But this youthful spirit also brings numerous problems. Is it possible, in this explosive growth period, to formulate even a tentative definition of management consulting? What do consultants really do? What should be their qualifications? How can they be educated and trained? And how can they be regulated so that the incompetent ones don't mar the industry's reputation?

In this book we attempt to give some meaning to this young but important industry, yet we know that more will be said and understood at a later date when a greater level of maturity is reached. Management consulting is a complex, elusive industry and occupation, which unfortunately has raced ahead of an established body of knowledge and a codification of standards for excellence.

DEFINITIONS BY OTHER CONSULTANTS

There is no end of popular stereotypes for management consultants—admirers view them positively as "experts," "doctors," "innovators," and even "revolutionaries." Critics, on the other hand, see them negatively as "witch doctors," "charlatans," "unemployed executives," and "pop psychologists." None of these epithets does much justice to the role of a consultant, although there is probably some fragment of real experience behind each of them.

Let us look at how certain leading books and professional associations have attempted to define management consulting, once they have given serious consideration to its history and current state. We take these definitions from the few written sources available on management consulting, a list of which is included at the end of the chapter.

From *Management Consulting: A Guide to the Profession*

Management consulting is a professional service that helps managers to analyze and solve practical problems and transfer successful management practices from one enterprise to another.[1]

From *Association of Consulting Management Engineers*

Management consulting is the professional service performed by specially trained and experienced persons in helping managers identify and solve managerial and operating problems of the various institutions of our society; in recommending practical solutions to these problems; and helping to implement them when necessary. This professional service focuses on improving the managerial, operating, and economic performance of these institutions.[2]

From *Management Advisory Services Division, American Institute of Certified Public Accountants*

Professionals with broad and specific expertise who use their skills to help solve management problems, to assist in the planning process, and to provide objectivity and perspective.[3]

From *Institute of Management Consultants, United Kingdom*

The service provided by an independent and qualified person or persons in identifying and investigating problems concerned with policy, organization, procedures and methods; recommending appropriate action and helping to implement these recommendations.[4]

Several common features stand out across these definitions. These common features are examined below:

1. *Independent Orientation.* Words such as "perspective" and "objectivity" signal an independent stance by the consultant. The con-

---

[1]M. Kubr, ed., *Management Consulting: A Guide to the Profession* (Geneva: International Labor Organization, 1976).

[2]Advertising brochure, (New York: Association of Consulting Management Engineers, Inc.).

[3]Monroe S. Kutner, ed., *University Education for Management Consulting* (New York: MAS Division of the American Institute of Certified Public Accountants).

[4]M. Kubr, ed., *Management Consulting: A Guide to the Profession* (Geneva: International Labor Organization, 1976).

sultant does not automatically accept the problem and facts as given by the client, but stands apart from the client to form a separate appraisal.

2. *Special Training and Qualifications.* To make an independent evaluation and develop useful recommendations, management consultants must possess an inordinate amount of skill. This ability is derived from not only a combination of special training and practical experience, but also a high degree of personal integrity. The term "qualifications" implies certification by other professionals in the field.

3. *An Advisory Service.* Management consulting is a helping activity, not a direct performance of management duties. It is performed in cooperation with the client who bears final responsibility for hiring and using the consultant and accepting or rejecting their recommendations.

4. *Problem Identification and Analysis.* One principal activity of the consultant is to be problem oriented—that is, to address an issue of concern to the client, to look behind it to determine its validity, to reformulate the problem if necessary, and to identify its underlying causes.

5. *Problem Solving and Implementation.* A second major activity is to recommend solutions and even to help the client, when asked, in implementing solutions. Consultants are not hired to perpetuate the status quo.

We agree with all these criteria, yet still find them lacking in defining more precisely the nature of the consultant-client relationship. All four definitions, in our opinion, are either too ambiguous or too narrow in defining the client. Some omit reference to the client altogether; others refer to "managers" and "management." Our preference is to use the term "organization" to refer to the client, since we feel that allegiance to a sole individual or selected subgroup, such as management, may undermine the consultant's position of independence and objectivity.

Another missing ingredient is the contractual nature of the agreement between the consultant and client. In addition to the term "advisory service," we would like to add the words "contracted for" to imply a conscious agreement between the two parties that indeed a consulting arrangement is taking place. Such an agreement is usually for pay and in writing, although it is not required. We do believe that it takes at least mutual consent to lend legitimacy to an activity called management consulting. A person may believe that he or she is a consultant and act in this manner, but if the client thinks otherwise from the outset, then how can it be called consulting?

Finally, we are troubled, in at least two definitions, by the absence of the term "management" in referring to the types of problems undertaken for study by a consultant. We know of many types of consulting, but the modifier "management" gives it special meaning. Consulting on an engineering problem is not management consulting, nor is it the sale of a new computer or any proprietary product. While we believe that the consultant should avoid acting as a servant of management, we still see the consultant's focus as being on the management problems facing the client organization.

OUR DEFINITION

Now let us attempt a new definition, knowing full well that a few words are inadequate to capture the richness and complexity of a changing occupation. Our words do, however, draw some boundary lines around what management consulting is and is not:

> Management consulting is an advisory service contracted for and provided to organizations by specially trained and qualified persons who assist, in an objective and independent manner, the client organization to identify management problems, analyze such problems, recommend solutions to these problems, and help, when requested, in the implementation of solutions.

Given this definition, a few words are necessary to spell out what is *not* management consulting. Too many individuals and firms these days have identified themselves as management consultants, yet their actions seem far removed from the reality of our definition.

Some clear examples of nonmanagement consulting are technical engineering on new products or machinery, the continuous performance of actual management or employee duties, and the conduct of clerical functions. A management consultant is not an engineer, an executive, or a secretary.

Less clear examples are the conduct of training programs, the installation of computer systems, the performance of outside activities such as accounting or library research studies, the giving of informal advice to managers, and the "head-hunting" activities of executive searchers.

We prefer not to view these activities as management consulting, important as they may be, unless they have resulted from a broader analysis and plan prepared by a management consultant. Otherwise, such efforts accept the problem and facts as given by the client and are merely ancillary services for decisions already taken or predetermined by the actions of management.

Management consulting is not a product that is neatly packaged and sold at a fixed price. Rather, it is an open-ended activity in which the management problems and solutions are usually ill defined and where the client seeks greater clarity and advice through the consulting process. The consultant has the opportunity to bring his or her intellect to the systematic unraveling of the client's problem and then to apply creativity to the formulation of a sound solution.

WHY HIRE CONSULTANTS?

So far we have defined management consulting solely from the consultant's point of view. But what about the potential client's definition of consulting? Do they see it differently or put additional weight on certain factors that consultants overlook? No definition can be complete without considering the recipient of the service. It takes two to tango!

The following are the principal reasons given by clients for hiring consultants, as identified from various surveys. Consultants

1. Provide independence and unbiased judgment.
2. Present new ideas and a fresh approach.
3. Possess the ability to diagnose problems and evaluate solutions.
4. Perform tasks with technical skills infrequently needed.
5. Supplement present skills of staff and management.
6. Implement systems and train employees.

Reasons 1, 3, and 6 appear in our previous definitions, but reasons 2, 4, and 5 receive short shrift and deserve further comment. Clearly, the creative element is raised in reason 2; it is the injection of a new and talented person into the management process that clients see as valuable. Organizations become parochial, and this is recognized in the need for outside ideas derived from a consultant's unique training and experience across many organizations and industries. Few executives have seen as many different organizations as have experienced consultants.

A more mundane set of motives appears in reasons 4 and 5, that of adding temporary personnel to the client's existing resources. This suggests that consultants, from the client's viewpoint, can be regarded as a kind of glorified source of temporary help. Clients recognize that it would be too expensive to staff up with full-time employees as a means for handling all the problems and special tasks facing their organizations.

Our own experience suggests that there are also less conscious and politically motivated reasons for hiring consultants. One common motivation is to obtain confirmation for a tentative diagnosis already made by uncertain managers. A second reason is to undermine internal opposition within the executive ranks by using the consultant as the main proponent for change. A third is to protect vested interests from attack, such as the CEO who may be trying to relieve pressure from a meddlesome board of directors.

If we take all the client reasons cited into account, a second and less professional-sounding definition emerges of the management consultant:

> Management consulting is the temporary infusion of outside and credible talent to provide new ideas and additional personnel to the client organization, as well as to serve the special interests of those hiring the consultant.

MORE THAN A DEFINITION

At this point we should recognize that any definition of management consulting depends on the eye of the beholder. A consultant may arrive at the client's premises with a pristine and professional concept, only to be met by a client with more sinister motives. The consultant will often be torn between an ideal concept of consulting and the practical realities of each client situation.

Perhaps another and more realistic picture of management consulting emerges from consideration of the actual problem-solving process that will face the consultant. What are the appropriate data to gather and where can they be found? How accurate and relevant are they? How should they be analyzed to gain a better understanding of the client's problem? Is the client's problem real or perceived? Is there some other, more fundamental, issue in question? What is it that is really causing the client's concern? Why did the client hire a consultant? What are the strengths and weaknesses of the client organization? What alternative solutions are available to meet the client's needs? How should recommendations be presented to gain the client's acceptance? What is the best approach for implementing proposed changes?

These unanswered questions make it clear that no precise set of words can sum up adequately what is management consulting. If consulting was an established science and if the problems encountered could be answered neatly by this science, a more objective definition might be possible. For now we will stop this unending task of definition by stating in only a half-joking manner that

> Management consulting is an uncertain and evolving process conducted by a foreign intruder who muddles through by performing various problem-solving activities, while trying to maintain high professional standards and still attempting to meet the needs of the client.

SCOPE OF SERVICES

The roots of management consulting go back to the early 1900s when it had a dominant engineering orientation. The Industrial Revolution of the mid-1800s was followed by the advent of scientific management in

1910, as advocated by Frederick Taylor, H.L. Gantt, and Frank Gilbreth. These pioneers proposed the systematic use of job analysis, time standards, and incentive pay to bring greater rationality and fairness to the treatment of workers in exploitative owner-managed factories.

Management consulting maintained a technical focus until after World War II when war-oriented companies returned to the production of consumer goods. Consultants began to develop services to meet expanding needs for financial assistance, new product development, and the training of supervisors.

By the 1950s, management science and the computer had come of age. Many new and sophisticated techniques were available to consultants to bring to organizations, such as capital budgeting, marketing research, and computer software for data processing.

Still it was not until the 1960s and 1970s that management consulting began to take off as a growth industry. Rapid advances in computer technology made it possible to go beyond rudimentary inventory and accounting systems to introduce sophisticated information systems for assessing performance on a real-time basis. Strategic planning studies were spurred by intensified competition, newly emerging industries, worldwide markets, and inflation. Government regulation and social interest groups gave rise to environmental planning, product liability assessments, and affirmative action compliance. The birth of service industries, from fast-food chains to packaged vacations, required entirely new marketing strategies, personnel policies, and organizational structures.

Today we find management consulting spread across a wide variety of industries and services. The most complete listing was made in 1975 by Jerome H. Fuchs in his book, *Making the Most of Management Consulting Services*, where he classified 115 different specialties into 11 broad classifications:[5]

1. General management (organization planning, strategy, etc.)
2. Manufacturing (production control, facilities, etc.)
3. Personnel (management development, selection, etc.)
4. Marketing (sales forecasting, pricing, etc.)
5. Finance and accounting (cost accounting, valuation, etc.)
6. Procurement (purchasing, inventory control, etc.)
7. Research and development (project determination, etc.)
8. Packaging (machinery, design, testing, etc.)
9. Administration (office management, procedures, etc.)

[5]Jerome Fuchs, *Making the Most of Management Consulting Services* (New York: AMACOM, 1975).

10. International operations (licensing, tariffs, etc.)
11. Specialized services (recruiting, telecommunications, etc.)

Even this list is probably out of date; for example, one service not mentioned is "litigation support," which has burgeoned recently with the increase of lawsuits filed against companies. Management consultants are being used by lawyers to develop a sound defense for clients founded in economics, information retrieval, and marketing practices. Another newly emerging service is office automation and systems design.

Despite the proliferation of consulting services, a limited number of them still experience greater demand than do others. Moreover, some of the services listed by Fuchs, are verging, in our opinion, on other forms of consulting, such as engineering and accounting. In the 1980 *Directory of Management Consultants*, prepared by James H. Kennedy, editor of *Consultants News*, 583 consulting firms submitted the following list of their principal services:[6]

SERVICE	NUMBER OF FIRMS OFFERING
General management	219
Personnel	143
Marketing	126
Organization planning	113
Manufacturing	112
Management development	100
Strategic business planning	97
Administration	96
Finance and accounting	89
Marketing strategy and organization	82

We can see that "general management" consulting is by far the most dominant service provided. It focuses on top management concerns for a variety of issues, from acquisition strategies to an audit of management strengths and weaknesses. In a 1979 *Fortune* magazine article, it was estimated that strategic planning studies produced annual consulting revenues of $100 million.[7]

Interestingly, the more subjective areas of personnel and organization planning rank near the top. Clients are apparently finding their present organizational structures and employees so resistant to change that they are searching for new ideas and alternatives to cope with a

[6]James H. Kennedy, ed., *Directory of Management Consultants*, 1980.

[7]Walter Kiechel, III, "Playing by the Rules of the Corporate Strategy Game," *Fortune*, September 24, 1979.

turbulent and uncertain environment. The more quantitative area of "finance and accounting" is confined to a limited number of firms that specialize in this service; it also may be an area of competence that many client organizations already feel adept at performing.

TYPES OF FIRMS

To meet the expanding demand for a variety of services, the large, established consulting firms have diversified, whereas the consulting industry, as a whole, has spawned many new firms that specialize exclusively in a few disciplines, single industries, or local markets. It is clearly not a monolithic industry dominated by a few giants but rather a plethora of large and small firms operating at the national and local levels, all positioned to appeal to a certain kind of clientele.

Consulting firms can be divided into eight types of practices, each of which seeks to distinguish itself in a limited segment of the market:

1. National general management firms
2. National CPA firms with consulting units
3. Functionally specialized firms
4. Industry specialized firms
5. Public sector firms
6. Think tanks
7. Regional and local firms
8. Sole practitioners

The large general management consulting firms provide a range of services to meet the concerns of top managers, which include strategic planning, organization design, reward systems, control and information systems, and management development. Their offices are located in the largest cities in the United States and abroad, and their clients are concentrated among the *Fortune* 500 and large government agencies. Their consulting staffs tend to be composed of young, poised, and articulate graduates from major business schools. Among such consulting firms are three early pioneers in the industry—McKinsey & Company; Booz, Allen & Hamilton; and Cresap, McCormick & Paget—and some relative newcomers, such as Management Analysis Center and Temple, Barker and Sloane.

The fastest-growing consulting firms are the Big-8 CPA practices, which only recently vaulted into the top revenue ranks. Arthur Andersen, for example, now employs approximately 4,400 consultants worldwide located in over 75 offices. These firms have a "built-in" market provided by established audit clients. Their familiarity with the accounting side of a client makes it easier to suggest additional consulting work. The services provided by most CPA firms emphasize "quantitative" types of consulting on information systems, computer systems design and installation, and financial analysis of investments. Some accounting firms have elected to concentrate on certain industries such as banking or manufacturing; others have entered the executive search business for the purpose of finding controllers and financial experts for their clients.

Sharply critical of the Big-8 firms have been the general management firms and the leading professional organization for consulting firms, ACME (Association of Consulting Management Engineers). They see a "conflict of interest" in the performance of both accounting work and consulting projects for the same client. ACME goes so far as to exclude accounting firms from its membership. The accounting firms defend themselves by arguing that their consulting units are organized separately from the audit function, while emphasizing that they uphold high professional standards of independence and stressing that many of their consulting clients are not audit clients.

Functionally specialized firms have chosen to concentrate on a limited range of services. Here we find Hay Associates in compensation and human resource consulting, The Boston Consulting Group in strategic planning, The Alexander Proudfoot Company in manufacturing, and the Forum Corporation in training and management development. For these firms, intense specialization is required to develop an in-depth expertise of the highest quality. They see themselves as providing an expertise that is seldom available from a client's own internal staff resources.

A fourth type of consulting firm is one that concentrates on a few industries. These include Theodore Barry & Associates in utilities, Kurt Salmon Associates in apparel and textiles, and Kenneth Leventhal, a CPA firm, in real estate. Such consulting firms build a reputation for knowledge in the specific complexities of economics, marketing, finance, law, and technology facing a particular industry. These firms believe that knowledge can be developed and transferred more easily within an industry than across industries.

An industry-related but distinctly different type of management consulting is conducted by firms working mainly in the public sector. These include PRC (formerly Planning Resources Corporation), Radian, and Charles River Associates. Their livelihood comes from government contracts for studies of various social and economic issues as well as for assistance in the design and implementation of new programs. To be successful in the public sector, it takes an intimate acquaintance with the legislative and political process, funding procedures, and proposal writing in this sector. Many public sector consultants are former government employees.

Another segment is the burgeoning "think tank" market. It has arisen as clients desire futuristic studies, novel approaches to problem solving, and advanced technical advice that cannot be supplied easily by the more typical consulting firms. Such avant-garde firms include The Rand Corporation, SRI International (formerly the Stanford Research Institute), Abt Associates, and A.D. Little. They typically employ a large number of Ph.D.s who enjoy the challenge of research and innovation.

So far we have discussed large consulting firms with a national orientation, whose strategies can be discerned as slanted toward general management, functional disciplines, and industries. But there are many hundreds of small firms that limit themselves to regional and local markets. Their forte is intensively serving clients located near their offices, where they seek to build a close, personal, and continuing relationship, especially with smaller enterprises that are untouched by the marketing of the big consulting firms. Consultants for these local firms tend to be older and more experienced, often operating as "doctors on call," perhaps even on a yearly retainer fee.

Finally, there is the "loner" in management consulting, the sole practitioner. This is the individual who prefers not to work for someone else and shuns the responsibility of building a firm. There are thousands of such practitioners, some who do exceptionally well and others who squeak out a marginal living. Many perform consulting assignments on a part-time basis, as do academics in educational institutions. Their specialities vary enormously, from merger and acquisition analysis to management training. New business comes to them largely from personal contacts; their fees usually undercut those of the larger consulting firms with a higher overhead.

QUEST FOR PROFESSIONALISM

Management consulting is a recent occupation relative to the established professions of medicine, law, engineering, and accountancy. Moreover, the rapid growth of the consulting industry and the expansion of services provided makes it difficult to establish a clear concept of just who is the professional management consultant and what is professional about a consultant's behavior.

We are prepared to go so far as to call management consulting an emerging profession, but it clearly does not yet meet all the standards common to traditional professions. For that to happen, there has to be an established body of knowledge, educational requirements, testing procedures, an accepted accrediting body, and regulatory rules for governing conduct.

However, the seeds for all these elements have been sown and are bearing fruit. The IMC (Institute of Management Consultants) was established in 1968 to grant the designation of CMC (Certified Management Consultant) to those who

1. Spend at least half time in management consulting and work on a fee basis.
2. Have five years of management consulting experience, including one year of project responsibility.
3. Possess a college degree or equivalent.
4. Submit outlines of work performed.
5. Pass an oral examination.
6. Pass a check of client references.

While the IMC was slow in getting off the ground, it now boasts over 1,600 members with chapters in several cities. It has developed a standardized three-day saturation training course that has attracted over 1,000 consultants. One Big-8 firm, Touche Ross and Company, has indicated a commitment for all its consultants to achieve CMC certification. We remain hopeful that an even higher level of certifying standards will be reached, including a graduate degree akin to an MBA, a nationally administered written examination, a submitted sample of past work, and independently solicited recommendations from clients and professional colleagues.

Another professional group is ACME (Association of Consulting Management Engineers), which is the original association founded in 1929 to establish a body of knowledge and govern the ethical conduct of its members. Membership is limited to consulting firms, not individuals, and there are 65 members (although none are from the Big-8 and not all the major national firms are members). It publishes, surveys, and distributes information to member firms, and it supported the founding of the IMC.

Three other reputable professional associations exist for different types of management consultants. The AMC (Association of Management Consultants) was formed in 1959 for smaller firms and sole practitioners. The SPMC (Society of Professional Management Consultants), also founded in 1959, is similar in membership to AMC but has accrediting procedures that require five years of full-time consulting experience, submission of materials from past consulting engagements, and a check of references. The AIMC (Association of Internal Management Consultants) has 185 members who practice consulting as full-time staff employees of corporations and public agencies. It disseminates information and holds conferences to upgrade the skills of its members.

In 1977, all five of these associations formed COMCO (Council of Management Consulting Organizations) for the purpose of information exchange among their members. A future role for this conglomerate of associations will be to clarify and agree upon professional standards and to take responsibility for implementing them. Realistically, however, we expect that it will take several more decades before there is a single, universally accepted certification process required by local and state governments, as is the case with CPAs today.

THE CHALLENGE BEFORE US

What does all this professional activity signal to consultants in general? To us it means a growing concern for the quality and ethics of all management consultants. Only a small percentage of the total consulting population currently belongs to any of the associations mentioned. Left untouched are thousands of consultants who qualify simply by calling themselves management consultants. Is this self-appointed title sufficient? Hardly, we answer, and we hope that the reader will agree.

This book represents a small contribution toward the goal of achieving professionalism in management consulting. There is already a growing body of knowledge that relates uniquely to consulting. While it is still more an art than a science, there is enough accumulated experience, supplemented by a lot of borrowed theories and techniques from other fields, to begin to make sense out of this exciting and important occupation.

We urge the reader to join with us in not only reacting to what is said, but in feeling a motivation to contribute further. A sense of self-motivation and self-critique is at the heart of all professionals.

RECOMMENDED READINGS

Association of Consulting Management Engineers, *Professional Practices in Management Consulting.* New York: 1966.

Directory of Management Consultants. Fitzwilliam, N.H.: Consultants News, 1979.

FUCHS, JEROME, *Making the Most of Management Consulting Services.* New York: AMACOM, 1975.

FUCHS, JEROME, *Management Consultants in Action.* New York: Hawthorne Books, 1975.

HIGDON, HAL, *The Business Healers.* New York: Random House, 1970.

HOLLANDER, STANLEY C., and STEVEN R. FLOSTER, *Management Consultants and Clients.* E. Lansing, Mich.: Michigan State University Business Studies, 1972.

KLEIN, HOWARD M., *Other People's Business—A Primer on Management Consultants.* New York: Mason/Charter, 1978.

KUBR, M., ed., *Management Consulting: A Guide to the Profession.* Geneva: International Labour Office, 1976.

LIPPITT, GORDON, and RONALD LIPPITT, *The Consulting Process in Action.* La Jolla, Calif.: University Associates, 1978.

"The New Shape of Management Consulting," *Business Week,* May 21, 1979.

SHAY, PHILLIP W., *How To Get the Best Results From Management Consultants.* New York: Association of Consulting Management Engineers, 1974.

SUMMERS, EDWARD L., and Kenneth E. KNIGHT, *Management Advisory Services by CPAs.* New York: American Institute of Certified Public Accountants, 1976.

WOLF, WILLIAM B., *Management and Consulting: An Introduction to James O. McKinsey.* Ithaca, N.Y.: New York State School of Industrial & Labor Relations, Cornell University, 1978.

2

Consultants
Types and Roles

The term "management consultant" has an authoritative ring to it, as if it is one clearly defined and well-understood role. Nothing could be farther from the truth. There exists a myriad of consultant types and roles for them to perform. Just as the field of medicine has its general practitioners and plastic surgeons, so does management consulting.

This chapter describes a variety of consultant types and roles: generalist versus specialist, process versus content, diagnostic versus implementation, custom versus packaged, internal versus external, and large versus small firm consultants.

Consultants should make a choice among these various alternatives; they cannot be all things to all people. The choice you make depends upon a careful assessment of (1) what you feel most comfortable with in terms of your personality, knowledge, and experience; (2) the client's preference for an approach that matches its working style; and (3) the nature of the client problem you are attempting to analyze and solve.

Ideally, you should seek a good "fit" among all three conditions—a consultant who goes off in one direction while the client demands another approach is doomed to perform ineffectively. For example, if a client has an EDP problem that requires specialist expertise for which it does not have a trained staff, you cannot take a generalist approach where you nondirectively motivate the client into rediscovering the problem and solving it internally.

GENERALIST VERSUS
SPECIALIST CONSULTING

Generalists are the *diagnosticians* of the profession. They sell and accept assignments on the assumption that there are certain management fundamentals required to run any business successfully, whether the client is manufacturing widgets or selling life insurance. Such fundamentals include strategic planning, organization, marketing, production, financial control, compensation, and communications. If any of these basic management disciplines break down, the client will have serious problems.

Generalists possess knowledge about all these functional business areas, usually through MBA training and executive experience, from which they are presumably equipped to tackle a broad range of client problems. For the generalist consultant, it is the proven basic principles of sound management that make the difference between success and failure, not the finely tuned elegance of a computer system or the statistical esoterica of a financial calculation.

Specialists, on the other hand, believe that we live in a complex world where management knowledge and techniques are changing and advancing rapidly. They point out to the generalists that no consultant can know everything there is to know about a specialized topic, such as compensation and fringe benefit plans, unless they are experts at it. Those who do specialize, usually through personal fascination and lengthy training, consider themselves better prepared to resolve a complicated compensation problem with all its nuances than any generalist skimming over the surface.

The generalist consultant, of course, counters the specialist orientation by asking, "Are you really dealing with a compensation problem? How do you know that the compensation issue isn't just a symptom of a far deeper problem? Doesn't your bias as a compensation consultant limit you to an exclusive focus on the client's reward system? And even if a new compensation program is justified, will it really solve the underlying client problem?"

We have exaggerated the extremes of this argument to indicate the validity and limitations of each orientation. The generalist may indeed discover a deeper problem beneath the espoused problem but still not be able to provide in-depth expertise to design a technical solution. On the other hand, the specialist may do a superior job in analyzing the "trees" but become lost in the "forest."

How does each type of consultant find his or her appropriate niche? Generalist consultants tend to be more effective on complex problems at the top management level where a comprehensive diagnosis is necessary before rushing into solutions. Conversely, if the client is relatively clear about the problem and if the problem is confined to a technical discipline, such as asset valuation, then a financial specialist can likely provide far better assistance. It is when each type of consultant tends to go beyond his or her strengths, or when the client calls in the wrong type of consultant for the problem, that we find a troubling mismatch.

Both types of consultant need to appreciate the value of the other. Generalists can go only so far; then they must call in a specialist. On the other hand, specialists need to sense when the client's problem goes beyond their discipline, bring that awareness to the client's attention, and recommend a generalist diagnosis before proceeding further.

PROCESS VERSUS CONTENT CONSULTING

Process consultants are the psychiatrists of the consulting trade, whereas content consultants are the specialist surgeons. The process consultant offers no specific answers but rather asks lots of questions. A typical conversation between a process consultant and the client might proceed as follows:

Process Consultant:	What seems to be the problem?
Client:	I'm not sure. Morale is terrible.
Process Consultant:	What makes you think that?
Client:	Absenteeism is up, and so is turnover.
Process Consultant:	Why do you think it's up?
Client:	Our personnel statistics show it without question.
Process Consultant:	Why do you think so many people are leaving?
Client:	I don't really know. Perhaps our salaries are too low.
Process Consultant:	Have people complained about their salaries?
Client:	No, not really.
Process Consultant:	Then what else might explain it?

And on and on it goes. As in the field of psychoanalysis, the nondirective process consultant believes that only the client can help himself or herself to solve the problem. Thus, the client is led through a self-examination and self-healing process where the consultant asks penetrating questions without giving a personal evaluation or offering solutions. A basic assumption is that far greater knowledge of the problem and its solution resides within the client, not the consultant.

For the process consultant, no outsider can know or learn enough about the client organization in such a short time to be in a position to analyze and solve complex problems. Instead, the client itself must take major responsibility for problem identification and solution formulation.

If the process approach is the Freudian side of consulting, the *content* consultant draws from General George Patton. The content consultant tells the client what is wrong and then advises a strategic move. The same conversation we began earlier with the process consultant might proceed as follows with the content consultant:

Content Consultant:	What seems to be the problem?
Client:	I'm not sure. Morale is terrible.
Content Consultant:	What makes you say that?
Client:	Absenteeism is up, and so is turnover.
Content Consultant:	That is usually a sign of noncompetitive salary scales. I will analyze your salary scales in light of your competition and the local labor market, and if I am right, I will implement a new wage system to resolve the problem. When can I meet with your personnel director, before or after lunch?

The content consultant takes direct action to verify the causes of a problem and then writes a report to support a set of specific recommendations. Content consultants believe that they are better able to see the "forest" for the "trees" because they are independent and objective outsiders. They have witnessed too many clients' getting tangled up politically in the superficial symptoms of a far deeper problem.

Advocates of content consulting believe that they possess a greater breadth of experience and depth of knowledge to select from a wide variety of solutions to best fit the client's needs. They see themselves as more skilled at formulating solutions than the client, who is in the business of producing widgets at a profit, not designing new wage schemes.

Critics of content consulting point to all the failures that occur when the client either does not agree with the consultant's definition of the problem or is not involved in the planning of recommended changes. Content consultants can easily become overbearing and thus isolated from their clients, thereby leaving clients in a state of dependency in which they neither understand the problem nor feel ownership over the solution. Hence, we have the consultant's eloquent report that gathers dust in a client's bookcase.

On the other hand, content consultants are quick to criticize process consultants for their abdication of responsibility to the client. They believe that few clients have sufficient insight or knowledge to solve problems by themselves—otherwise, why call in a consultant? For example, how can a client be expected to step back objectively from its traditional career and promotion policies to design the most up-to-date and appropriate career development system?

Our position is that extremes of either approach are rare and not likely to be effective. Most clients are not interested in hiring a psychiatrist to "shrink" them, nor are they receptive to a professional lecture. Generally, we see more content consultants in the field because clients are too busy with daily fire-fighting to engage in a lot of reflection. However, good content consultants must be empathetic and willing to involve the client at frequent intervals throughout the diagnostic and solution stages.

We do know, however, some very effective process consultants whose clients prefer to participate actively in the consulting process. Such consultants and clients have grown comfortable over many years of working together and using each other as sounding boards. The process consultant must be highly trained in the fields of psychology and group dynamics, be willing to bite his or her tongue frequently, and be extremely adept at offering the right question at the right time. Clients of process consultants tend to be informal organizations where their key executives feel a lot of trust for one another and are willing to confront and discuss their differences openly.

DIAGNOSTIC VERSUS IMPLEMENTATION CONSULTING

Another way of contrasting different modes of consulting is between those who concentrate on diagnosis and those who focus on implementing change. It is the difference between analyzers and doers.

The *diagnosticians* are adept at producing an X ray of the problem. They penetrate beneath the symptoms, identify the causes, produce a summary of the "real" problem, and recommend a course of action. However, they often stop at this point by refusing to get their hands dirty with the long and arduous process of seeing recommended changes through to fruition. Instead, they prefer to move on to another client for another analytical project.

Many of the large general management consulting firms emphasize the diagnostic approach. Typically they are hired by large corporations that may indeed prefer to implement their own changes or seek another viewpoint to compare with their own analysis. Evidence produced by the consultant is then used by the client to overcome resistance or to reinforce actions already contemplated before ever hiring a consultant.

Consulting firms that employ a diagnostic approach believe that it represents a more efficient and appropriate use of their younger staff. Many of their consultants are bright but inexperienced MBAs who are long on analytical skills but short on training for warfare in the trenches. Getting involved in implementation can be a bloody and time-consuming process where there are frequently no heroes.

Change-oriented consultants are critical of this antiseptic approach used by diagnostic consultants. They believe that "true" consulting is never done until the client has been moved off the status quo permanently. They point to the millions of pounds of diagnostic reports that have gone the way of all paper products. For them it is a major responsibility to help the client in actually implementing their recommendations.

Consulting firms that embrace implementation strategies tend to be more involved in EDP systems and hardware or in human resources consulting, such as management development and executive search. These projects lend themselves to implementation, such as installing a new computerized information system, in locating a key executive, or in conducting a management training program. These consultants tend to be "hands-on" people who are specialist technicians.

Critics of the implementers contend that they are often more enamored with their tools than with a thoughtful understanding of the client's problem. In doing so, the implementing consultant can easily acquire an "employee mentality" that usurps responsibility from the client's employees. Hostility may build toward implementing consultants who are insensitive toward training their replacements within the client firm.

We see the need for both approaches, although a closer link between analysis and change is desirable among all consultants. Many diagnosticians walk away from their clients before at least going far enough to see their proposed changes begin to take fruit, whereas implementers need to step back from their hardware to see if the changes they are pursuing are really in the client's best interests.

CUSTOM VERSUS
PACKAGED SOLUTIONS

Wide differences prevail in the manner in which consultants provide solutions to their clients. The major approach for years has been custom-designed solutions that are tailor-made to solve each client's particular problem. Here the solution is a "one-of-a-kind" product. How else, the *custom* consultants argue, can a consultant solve a client's problem without giving full recognition to its unique needs and management goals? For example, if the client situation requires a more decentralized structure, the consultant must consider if sufficient executive capability exists within the company to fill an increase in management positions.

Competing with the tailor-made approach has been the recent growth of packaged programs. These standardized solutions are geared more toward resolving generic types of problems across many clients. Most common are EDP packages to improve management information systems, training programs for developing managerial talent, and strategic planning methods to reorient the path of a company.

Even some of the major consulting firms that once believed in custom solutions have unconsciously become wedded to the same solutions tried over and over again with apparent success—such as dividing up the organization into profit centers.

Much controversy obviously surrounds these two different approaches to formulating solutions. The custom advocates are quick to criticize the "retail marketing" of packaged solutions. They believe that clients cannot be fitted to solutions; rather solutions must be fitted to clients. They worry about clients who buy neatly packaged solutions with lots of promises, only to wake up later with a hangover.

The *package* consultants respond that custom solutions are extremely costly and not subject to proof through continuous application. Why, they ask, should a well-designed compensation system for one client not be applicable to many others? How many times does one have to redesign the wheel? They decry custom solutions that are sold for three times the price of a packaged solution, and therefore ask if clients are being bilked unnecessarily.

Our own preference still lies with custom solutions. We see certain packages applicable to technical solutions, such as inventory control and data processing. But most problems faced by management consultants are not yet so standardized. Moreover, the research evidence on the value of packaged solutions is still scanty and hardly as positive as their proponents claim. The future will probably see more substantial packaged solutions being designed, but in ways that are adaptable to each client's needs.

INTERNAL VERSUS
EXTERNAL CONSULTANTS

As organizations become larger and more diversified in their product lines, they naturally become more complex in their management practices. And, as Murphy's law would predict, these large complex organizations experience more management problems than do smaller organizations. Thus, we find that most of the *Fortune* 500 companies have turned increasingly to hire their own full-time, in-house consultants as members of their corporate staff groups. It is more cost efficient since three internal consultants at $55,000 annual salary each can be hired for the cost of a single McKinsey consultant at $800 per day for a full year.

But the issue of external versus internal consulting is not merely a question of corporate size and profitability. Why do large companies continue to retain outside consultants?

External consultants contend that it is an issue of objectivity because *internal* consultants lose perspective out of loyalty and constant exposure to a single organization. Moreover, insiders rarely have easy access to the CEO, since they are subject to the chain of command and politics that affect all full-time employees. What internal consultant, the outside consultants ask, is going to stick his or her neck out when salary review time is approaching?

Internal consultants retort that their extensive knowledge of the company is far greater than that which can be obtained by an outside consultant from a limited scope of investigation. These insiders already know the political terrain and the hidden problems that can escape outside eyes. Another advantage of internal consultants, besides their lower cost, is their constant availability—they are "doctors on call" who can work on more problems continuously than an outside interloper confined to a single project and a travel schedule.

We see value in both roles, especially in larger companies. External consultants will never be replaced because their independent viewpoint is needed. Furthermore, there are far too many problems faced by large companies than can be staffed up for with a cadre of internal consultants.

Nevertheless, we have observed significant benefits accruing from the judicious use of internal consultants assigned directly to the office of the president. The key rests with the CEO who must relish knowing the truth, no matter whose nose gets bent out of shape in the executive dining room. The internal consultant carries a heavy professional responsibility to "tell it like it is," even if it means the unemployment lines.

LARGE VERSUS SMALL
CONSULTING FIRMS

Much recognition has been given by the business press to large consulting firms—the McKinseys, the Booz, Allens, the ADLs—and recently to all the Big-8 accounting firms. They receive credit for reviving companies, introducing new practices, and providing additional executive blood to tired corporations. These elite consulting firms are loaded with talent, provide a wide range of services, and adhere to high professional standards.

But all is not rosy with the monoliths of the consulting industry. They prefer large projects with big clients, and their fees are high for services that are not always delivered with the utmost quality. In these established firms, once a senior partner has made the sale, the actual work is usually performed by a less experienced staff of MBAs, who may unfortunately learn at the client's expense. Their analytical work, if supervised properly, can be first rate, but they rarely stick around for the difficult job of implementing their recommendations. A client who wants close personal attention from a big consulting firm may find that he or she is dealing with a bureaucracy that reacts as slowly and impersonally as many large organizations.

That is why the consulting industry is also populated with hundreds of small firms and thousands of independent consultants. These local and regional firms take on smaller projects with the aim of providing more personal and continuous service. Experienced professionals are assigned to the job, men and women who are likely to see a project through to its implementation. Smaller firms are able to provide a long-lasting and close personal relationship with their clients, thus enabling the consultant to know the organization in-depth and act as a continuous sounding board. The fees of small firm consultants are lower, too, since they don't have a national network of plush offices and a large clerical staff to charge off as overhead.

However, there are limits to small firm consulting. They cannot provide a wide variety of services with the same quality as can big firms, nor do they have sufficient staff to take on major jobs. For example, in 1980, AT&T announced that it was hiring consultants to review the entire AT&T organization, a project that no four-person firm in Kansas City could possibly undertake and do justice to.

Large firms, because they have offices worldwide, will use personnel from all their offices to serve quickly those corporations with widespread operations and immediate needs. They are also more apt to employ industry and discipline specialists who possess the latest knowledge on a variety of topics. Finally, hiring a large firm can be less risky from a quality standpoint because the large firm has an established reputation to uphold.

CHOOSING THE RIGHT CLIENT

Much is made of clients choosing the right consultant, but little is said about the consultant's responsibility in this decision. For the sake of landing a contract, should the consultant present himself or herself as a jack of all trades? Some clients will no doubt see through this facade, especially when obvious deficiencies exist. They know, for example, that a small firm cannot possibly handle a large AT&T organization study.

But few clients are sophisticated enough to detect subtle differences between a vast armada of hungry consultants. They often do not understand the difference between process and content consultants or generalists and specialists. They may expect hands-on implementation instead of a diagnostic report. Or they may want a packaged computer program instead of a costly information systems study. Only after a large expenditure of money on the wrong consultant, not to mention frustration, does the unsuspecting client find out about its mistakes.

So consultants bear a heavy responsibility for seeking an appropriate match between what they have to offer and what the client needs. Discuss your approach directly with the client and explain why it makes sense for solving the client's problem. If you detect that there is not a good match—that you don't have the approach that fits the client's situation—then you have a responsibility to make that difficult decision, inform the client, and bow out of the bidding process.

If you oversell a client, you will only do a poor job and the client will be unhappy. Besides, there is a client out there somewhere who does need and fit your services.

RECOMMENDED READINGS

GANESH, S.R., "Organizational Consultants: A Comparison of Styles," *Human Relations*, vol. 31, no. 1 (January 1978).

GINZBERG, MICHAEL J., "Finding an Adequate Measure of OR/MS Effectiveness," *Interfaces*, vol. 8, no. 4 (August 1978).

HERSHMAN, ARLENE, "Big Bucks in Bankruptcy," *Dun's Review*, vol. 106, no. 5 (November 1975).

HUNT, ALFRED, *The Management Consultant*. New York: Ronald Press, 1977.

KELLY, ROBERT O., "Should You Have an Internal Consultant?" *Harvard Business Review*, vol. 57, no. 6 (November/December 1979).

KLION, STANLEY R., "MAS Practice: Are the Critics Justified?" *Journal of Accountancy*, vol. 145, no. 6 (June 1978).

KOLB, DAVID A., and ALAN L. FROHMAN, "An Organization Development Approach to Consulting," *Sloan Management Review*, Fall 1970.

SCHEIN, EDGAR H., *Process Consultation: Its Role in Organization Development*. Reading, Mass.: Addison-Wesley, 1969.

SONG, NORMAN, "Use and Abuse of Management Consultants," *Canadian Chartered Accountant*, vol. 104, no. 2 (February 1974).

TICHY, NOEL M., "Agents of Planned Social Change: Congruence of Values, Cognitions and Actions," *Administrative Science Quarterly*, 19, no. 2 (1974), 164–82.

WOODWORTH, WARNER, and NELSON REED, "Witch Doctors, Messianics, Sorcerers, and OD Consultants: Parallels and Paradigms," *Organizational Dynamics*, Autumn 1979.

3

What Makes
an Effective Consultant?

Consulting is a human enterprise. Whether the specific problem being addressed by the consultant is a new accounting system or the need for strategic planning, the essence of consulting still centers on the human qualities of consultants interacting with human clients. No computer program or mathematical formula can replace a consultant for comprehending the varied symptoms of a client's problem, formulating an accurate diagnosis, and devising an imaginative solution.

As a result, the success or failure of a consulting project depends on the multi-faceted skills that a consultant brings to the client's situation. If the consultant is not perceptive, does not communicate with sensitivity, or lacks up-to-date knowledge, the client's problem will not be solved.

Too often we assume that consultants should have the same skills as successful executives. Perhaps that is why many executives attempt later in their careers to become consultants. But they are not one and the same; consultants lack the formal authority to implement their recommendations. Unlike executives, consultants do not have the direct command of a company's resources and employees. At the same time, consultants are expected to invent solutions that client executives are unable to develop. Being a consultant is, in our opinion, a more difficult, challenging, and frustrating role than is being an executive.

We also hear that consultants should be "professional," "self-confident," "brilliant," "credible," and "poised." But these terms belie the broad range of underlying skills that go into the making of an effective consultant.

This chapter highlights those critical skills, based on interviews with numerous consultants, as well as our own experience. Seven broad areas of competence are identified, within which there are many specific skills. The seven areas of competence are (1) diagnostic ability, (2) solution and implementation skills, (3) general and specialized knowledge in management and its related disciplines, (4) communication skills, (5) marketing and selling ability, (6) managerial skills, and (7) certain personality attributes conducive to consulting.

We conclude the chapter with comments on how to acquire and sharpen these different skills. Consultants are not created on a distant planet as Superman or Wonder Woman. While consultants are no doubt partly born, they are mostly bred through intensive training and broad experience. The remainder of this book will elaborate on the application of these skills in the consultant-client environment.

DIAGNOSTIC ABILITY

Consultants are detectives—master sleuths who must ferret out the evidence, read behind the clues, and put their fingers on the culprit. They are problem finders as much as problem solvers. The client's problem is rarely what is stated in the beginning of a project.

Most important is the *quality of objectivity*. Consultants cannot believe every opinion expressed to them by client employees. Nor can they take sides with likable executives. They must possess a mentality of independence that permits them to step back from the proverbial trees to see the forest.

Another diagnostic skill is one of *intense curiosity*. Consultants must be nosy—delving behind symptoms and superficial explanations. They are puzzle solvers who must love the challenge of a messy and ill-defined problem. The bulk of a client's problem lies beneath the tip of the iceberg.

A third attribute is *conceptual and analytical*, which is the art of being able to see a pattern running through diverse pieces of evidence. Most client problems rarely have simple explanations; instead, they are shot through with a complex set of hidden causes. Being able to formulate a clear and succinct definition of a messy problem without writing 20 pages to explain it is a rare conceptual and analytical skill. Accurate diagnosis is a prelude to effective solutions.

Finally, ability at *inductive reasoning* is the diagnostic hallmark of effective consultants. They must treat each situation as if it is new and unique, not as an exact replica of their last engagement. Deduction from past experience can force invalid explanations upon a client. Each client's problem has nuances that escape textbook examples.

SOLUTION SKILLS

To identify a client's problem without helping to solve it is a consulting project only half completed. Solutions do not appear automatically just because the client's problem has been diagnosed accurately. Consultants must also complement their analytical skills with an ability to create answers that the client will accept and implement.

Imagination is an intangible but essential skill for all consultants. Creative solutions are required because clients would have solved their problems by themselves if traditional know-how were the only ingredient. Needed is a quality of consultant vision and idealism to bring out the best in a client.

But effective consultants cannot just be creative dreamers. They must keep their feet on the ground and be able to recognize what is achievable. Clients will reject an idealistic solution if they cannot see their way to implement it. A great deal of patience and a dash of compromise are necessary to move a hesitant client toward an acceptable solution.

Courage is a special quality for consultants to possess as they propose a change program. Clients become mired in the status quo because they and their employees prefer a known past to an unknown future. Resistance to change is inevitable. Consultants must stand up for their recommendations in the face of potshots from nervous senior executives or an arrogant CEO.

Teaching ability will also come in handy. While consultants are not professors, they must often train their clients to act differently if a change is actually to occur. Simply telling the client to adopt a new accounting system is insufficient without its employees knowing how to operate the system on a daily basis. It frequently takes "hands-on" teaching to make a real difference.

KNOWLEDGE

Consultants must be in the forefront of knowledge in their fields of expertise. Book knowledge is not reserved solely for academicians. Clients expect consultants to be up to date, even ahead of their own staff experts.

Why hire a consultant who is expounding the virtues of a traditional management technique that is regarded as passé by a client?

One essential area of knowledge is *management theory supported by scholarly research findings.* Too many clients (and even consultants) subscribe to myths that have been dispelled by previous research studies. For example, the canons of classical management (e.g., pyramidal organization structures) have been found to have only limited applicability to stable marketplaces and simple technologies. Therefore, consultants need to keep up with the academic literature or they will be purveyors of myths.

Applied techniques in the administrative sciences are another invaluable form of knowledge. All specialist areas in consulting require sophisticated expertise in such topics as modeling, questionnaire design, and statistics. Sloppy questions and crude statistics can lead to the wrong conclusions, to say nothing of reduced credibility in the eyes of a client.

Consultants need to be informed and articulate about all the popular management techniques. If a client asks about the merits of "management by objectives" as a goal-setting technique, you cannot beg off with a "Let me check at the library and get back to you later."

Most effective consultants possess generalist knowledge across many fields, especially in the basics of marketing, finance, production, personnel, and accounting. This aids them not only in seeing the "big picture" but also in conversing with executives on terms they understand.

The aspiring consultant should also choose one or two specialized areas for in-depth knowledge. One of these areas is normally a functional discipline, such as personnel and human resources management; the other area is typically a topical problem of concern to many clients, such as compensation systems.

You will be much more valuable to a consulting firm if you have both generalist and specialist skills. A firm that builds a staff with expertise in a variety of disciplines and topics can offer a broader range of services to clients.

COMMUNICATION SKILLS

If there is one essential talent that underlies all the skills discussed thus far, it is the ability to communicate effectively with the client. Close rapport is pivotal in being able to sell a proposal, in gathering accurate data from interviews, and in gaining acceptance for recommended solutions.

Sensitive listening skills are cited repeatedly by consultants and clients alike as the "number 1" factor that differentiates between good and bad consultants. Being able to draw private data out of a reluctant client may determine whether a problem is seen superficially or in depth. Clients evaluate potential consultants for their willingness to listen carefully rather than impose their own value judgments. Consultants must be sponges, not lecturers, and listening is the key to soaking up a client's needs, opinions, and concerns.

Exceptional writing ability is vital for summing up how well the consultant has listened to and understood the client. The first test comes in the written proposal to solicit business from a prospective client. If your proposal is vague, organized poorly, ponderous, and riddled with misspellings and typos, you have lost a client before gaining one.

Another test of writing skill comes later, in the final report, where conclusions and recommendations are expressed to the client. Cogent and succinct statements that summarize weeks of data gathering are an art not easily mastered in a host of English courses. Recommendations that have concrete and pointed meaning without overwhelming the client are preferable to those that rely on general and abstract management principles.

Oral presentation skills are required at meetings where clients are given progress reports or a preview of the final written report. These verbal sessions provide the client with a rapid overview of the findings and recommendations as well as an opportunity to raise questions and express disagreement.

A great deal of preparation, and even a dress rehearsal, is necessary for an effective oral presentation, which may include the use of graphics, flip charts, handouts, and overhead transparencies. A sloppy oral presentation will turn off a client to the point of discounting the written report. You are "on stage" in oral presentations. A single inarticulate response to a simple question from the client can cast a dark cloud over the consultant's credibility.

Another communication need is a broad repertoire of *intervention skills*. Meetings with the client can bog down in details if the consultant doesn't act to clarify the real purpose of a meandering discussion. Heated arguments can break out between executives that will require your know-how at conflict resolution. Even a sense of humor can lend perspective to a grim discussion.

MARKETING AND SELLING

A popular misconception is that consultants don't need to sell their wares. Consultants like to assume that hungry clients will naturally search out their God-given talents. They forget that competition within the consulting industry is intense and that many clients hold a skeptical view of consultants.

Overall marketing responsibility in a consulting firm falls on the key partners who chart its direction. They must develop a marketing strategy that distinguishes the firm's strengths from those of its competition. Then they must publicize and promote the firm's desired image among potential clients. Keeping the firm visible and reputable in the marketplace is a prerequisite to being considered when clients pick up the telephone.

The selling of a proposal to a prospective client requires a keen sense of what is really troubling the client. Based on a few initial interviews, the consultant must prepare a proposal that persuades the client to buy his or her services over those of a competitor. The client's decision will hinge on how well the consultant has presented such factors as the problem, fees, workplan, and expected results.

Further selling is necessary for "add-on" work with an established client. Here is an excellent opportunity to identify new issues because of the consultant's familiarity with the client's situation. But don't expect the client to agree automatically to extend your contract; it will take more selling to convince the client that the new issue is valid and worthy of consultation. This sale will depend heavily on the quality of work you have provided for the first project.

MANAGERIAL ABILITY

Although consultants are supposed to be adept at the art of management, it does not necessarily mean that they practice what they preach. Heavy managerial responsibilities fall on consultants, especially as their consulting firms grow and diversify into a broader range of services.

The earliest management challenge comes in one's ability to lead a project team of consultants. Teamwork is essential when a diverse group of consulting talent is required to solve a complex client problem. Without skillful leadership, the consulting team can become divided against itself. The engagement manager must hold frequent and effective meetings, keep the project on schedule, maintain cost control, guide the report-writing stage, and arrange for effective oral presentations to the client.

Overall management of the consulting firm falls to the senior partners and the managing partner. They are accountable for assuring a bottom-line profit for the firm. One necessary skill is strategic planning for the firm, as it seeks an established niche in an amorphous marketplace. Another skill is to attract, train, evaluate, reward, and retain the better junior consultants. A third is to assure efficient accounting systems for recording project expenses and billing clients. A fourth is to establish high standards of quality control over projects. Finally, there is top management's leadership behavior in creating a firmwide climate that is positive, challenging, and motivating for all employees.

PERSONALITY CHARACTERISTICS

As with any profession, certain personality attributes "fit" better with the consulting job than do other characteristics. Not everyone is born to be a consultant. Salespeople must enjoy relating to people, surgeons must remain cool under stress, plumbers must have a flare for tools and pipes, and artists must possess a creative urge.

Consulting is a demanding and frustrating job that never ends. Just when one project ends, you are on a plane to another job. Or when you are congratulating yourself for a job well done, the client calls to complain. What underlying attitudes will allow the consultant not only to keep his or her sanity but to perform jobs with consistent excellence? The following are nine essential attitudes mentioned most frequently to us by other consultants.

1. *Ethical Standards.* Consulting is a big-stakes game that affects the vital interests of employees, investors, and customers. These vested interest groups will seek to win the consultant's favor. Thus, your ethics must remain scrupulous in performing a job that does not cater to one group or the other. If you slip in integrity, you can harm others and yourself. A consultant who promises too much or speaks with a forked tongue will soon be out of a job.

2. *Empathy and Trust.* Client employees are usually reluctant to reveal their private concerns and complaints to a complete stranger. They are especially suspicious of consultants hired by their senior managers. To bridge this gap of inherent mistrust, consultants need to communicate empathy (not sympathy) for others, to be understanding and respectful of different points of view. They must be seen as trustworthy and unwilling to reveal names of confidants or distort information.

3. *Positive Thinking.* Clients react negatively to cynical and sarcastic behavior from consultants. An "upbeat" attitude is essential for the client to feel confidence in the consultant's recommendations. The client will also need positive reinforcement for taking uncertain steps into unchartered waters. Even in the selling of consulting services, the consultant must remain hopeful after 99 turndowns for that single sale just around the corner.

4. *Self-motivation.* Each consulting engagement requires daily adjustment to the vagaries of the client's situation. You cannot wait for instructions from the home office every time the client deviates from plan. Personal initiative is essential to react rapidly. Clients expect their consultants to be their own masters. If a hunch occurs to you, check it out. When you have a hot lead, go after it.

5. *Team Player.* Rugged individualism belongs in the boxing arena, not in consulting. Close cooperation is required among consultants as they compare perceptions of a client's problem and also as they relate to the client's employees in determining a plan of action. Loners have no place in consulting; it is a people business.

6. *Self-fulfillment.* Despite high incomes associated with consulting, clients rarely show their gratitude. They take personal credit for the positive results, while blaming the consultant for all failures. Consultants must learn to feast off their own sense of accomplishment and shrug off their defeats. There are few "thank you's" in this profession.

7. *Mobility.* Airlines love consultants—"Have bag, will travel" is the consultant's motto. If you like a 9-to-5 job from Monday to Friday with dinner at home every night, don't choose consulting. Continuous travel, up to 60% of one's time, is not uncommon. Prepare yourself and your loved ones for this gypsy life.

8. *Energy.* Long hours, plastic hotel rooms, greasy meals, and demanding clients take a toll on a consultant's emotional and physical well-being. It is essential to be in top shape to survive the wear and tear. Much self-discipline is necessary for resisting 2,000-calorie dinners and late-night drinking bouts with the client. Good consultants can burn out without preventative self-care.

9. *Self-awareness.* Too much is at stake for a consultant to take out neurotic tendencies on the client. Consulting does not place you out in front, leading the client into battle. In reality, you are backstage, acting with intelligence and reflection. A low-key and thoughtful demeanor is what the client wants. Your public and private behavior is being scrutinized constantly by the client's gossip mill. All consultants must recognize their personal strengths and limits; knowing oneself is as vital as knowing one's client.

SKILL ACQUISITION

Where and how does one acquire the skills of an effective consultant? The multitude of required skills should make it clear that a short training program or sheer determination are insufficient. Even many years as a successful executive does not make an outstanding consultant.

First, there is formal education in a graduate school of business or public administration. It is not a coincidence that a large majority of consultants hold an MBA degree from an outstanding business school. This intensive training gives a generalist perspective across several disciplines, teaches the application of conceptual and analytical skills, and hones one's writing and verbal abilities. No other experience can present these basic consulting skills in so short a time.

Another need for education is in a specialized discipline or topical subject, such as finance or strategic planning. Without this deeper and focused knowledge, the generalist consultant may be regarded as a dilettante who is master of nothing. Specialized knowledge can be acquired in graduate school electives or MS and Ph.D. programs, periodic seminars sponsored by universities and professional associations, and staff assignments in major corporations.

Actual work experience beyond graduate school is essential in either a business or a public organization. Formal education needs to be tested against the hard knocks of real-world responsibility. A healthy mark is left on a consultant's developing analytical and behavioral skills by learning the intricacies of a particular business and industry, making difficult decisions, carrying out project assignments, rotating through a variety of business functions, and coping with organizational politics.

Finally, there is the invaluable learning that occurs on the job as a practicing consultant. Every beginning consultant is an apprentice, no matter what the prior experience or education. The best source of learning is to train under a senior consultant—to acquire a "role model" for how it is done. Seeking out a variety of assignments will be more useful than will a repetitious look at the same industry or a single type of problem. Informal feedback on your performance should be sought out frequently instead of waiting for an annual appraisal. A self-critical look at your own mistakes and successes will be more valuable than will hanging your head or beating your chest.

All consultants must recognize that learning is a never-ending process if one is to remain effective. Knowledge is changing too rapidly for consultants to become complacent. But only the individual consultant can take primary responsibility for this reeducative requirement. The best "pros" in consulting remain students throughout their careers.

RECOMMENDED READINGS

A Body of Knowledge: For The Accreditation of Management Consultants.-
    New York: Institute of Management Consultants, Inc., 1979.
BLOCK, PETER,   *A Guide To Flawless Consulting.* La Jolla, Calif.: University
    Associates 1981.

BOETTINGER, HENRY M., "New Directions for Management and Consultants," *The Conference Board Record*, vol. 12, no. 3 (March 1975).

BOWEN, DON L., "When and How to Use a Consultant: Guidelines for Public Managers," *Public Administration Review*, vol. 38, no. 5 (September/October 1978).

CROMER, ROBERT R., "The Professional: Technician as Consultant," *Data Management*, vol. 17, no. 6 (June 1979).

FERGUSON, CHARLES K., "Concerning the Nature of Human Systems and the Consultant's Role," *Journal of Applied Behavioral Science*, 4, no. 2 (1968), 179-93.

HODGSON, RICHARD C., "Consulting: A Model for Management Development," *Business Quarterly* (Canada), vol. 43, no. 2 (Summer 1978).

HOROVITZ, BRUCE, "Advice a CEO Likes To Get," *Industry Week*, vol. 203, no. 5 (November 26, 1979).

"The Man Who Fires Managing Directors," *International Management* (UK), vol. 34, no. 9 (September 1979).

MINER, JOHN B., "The Management Consultant First as a Source of High-Level Managerial Talent," *Academy of Management Journal*, vol. 16, no. 2 (June 1973).

Personal Qualification of Management Consultants. New York: Association of Consulting Management Engineers, 1971.

PART II

The Marketing of Consultant Services

Foremost in any multibillion-dollar industry is an understanding of the marketing of its products or services. This is particularly critical to the consulting industry, for no matter how inspired or brilliant a consultant might be, until a client is obtained, that consultant cannot practice his or her skills. Further, there is the need to know what fee to charge, how to write a proposal or contract, and how to get the prospect to agree to start the project. Chapters 4 and 5 explore the basic marketing approaches used by successful consultants; in particular, detail is provided for those contemplating the starting-up of their own independent practice. We also break down the costs behind fees and demonstrate how they are used in preparing a bid to a prospect. Finally, we explore the various methods of payment that consultants might choose and discuss certain steps to assure that, in fact, you do get paid. While this is the shortest section of the book, it is one of the most important for both aspiring and practicing consultants.

4

Approaches to Marketing
How To Gain a Client

To the surprise and frustration of most consultants, marketing is the lifeblood of the industry. Consultants would rather consult than sell; after all, that is what drew them to the field. It is natural for them to assume that effective consulting skills, combined with a few satisfied clients, should lead to an endless stream of new clients. Therein lies the marketing failure of most consultants and consulting firms.

A RELUCTANT MARKETPLACE

For a prospective client to admit that a consultant is needed is a difficult decision. Many executives view this decision as a sign of self-defeat—that they themselves were unable to solve the problem. It is not easy for a vice president to go to his or her president with a request for outside assistance.

Another handicap is that many executives and their companies become so lost in the details of their operation that they fail to realize that they have problems. Their energies are so consumed with daily events and their minds so conditioned by traditional practices that smoldering problems and new opportunities evade them.

Or even if the prospective client recognizes a problem and admits to the possibility of using a consultant, it is still a big step before hiring one. A natural barrier is to question whether an outsider unfamiliar with the organization could make any more progress than the company could on its own. The benefits of consulting are not so clearly obvious or beneficial as seeking a medical doctor to prescribe penicillin for a bacterial infection.

Consequently, there is considerable suspicion among executives toward the value of consultants. For every manager who extolls the virtue of a particular consultant, there are many more who view them generally as "charlatans," "parasites," and "witch doctors." One anecdote of success can be matched by two horror stories, real or imagined.

Prospective clients are understandably confused by the vast marketplace of consultants. Rarely can they identify the particular kind of consultant they need. And even if they could, those qualities are hard to pinpoint among hundreds of consulting firms and thousands of consultants who present a "fuzzy" image at best. So why bother with consultants unless the pain is excruciating—and it seldom is.

THE MARKETING IMPERATIVE

Without successful marketing by the consultant, there is likely to be little business walking in your door. Prospective clients are often reluctant to approach the consultant, and when they do, the probabilities are slim that they will single you out from among a vast army of consultants. That is, unless you make a conscious and determined effort to bridge the gap.

Several strikes are against the consultant as a marketer. Not only is it distasteful for most consultants to stoop to selling, but time is limited because it takes away from the actual activity of consulting. Selling time cannot be billed to a client.

A carefully conceived marketing plan must, therefore, be designed and executed efficiently. And it will take self-discipline to escape the daily routine and seduction of consulting!

Foremost is for the consultant to realize that management consulting is an intangible service. There is no fancy package for the client to see, touch, hear, or smell. It cannot be sold like automobiles or deodorants; it cannot be farmed out to an advertising agency and promoted on television.

So what does the consultant do if traditional marketing techniques are irrelevant? There are two basic avenues for marketing an intangible service: the *direct* and the *indirect* approaches. Larger established consulting firms lean more toward the indirect approach, whereas smaller firms utilize direct methods in trying to outwit their larger competitors. The indirect approach concentrates on "image building," and the direct approach takes the consultant straight to the prospective client. Each strategy involves a great deal of ingenuity and skill.

INDIRECT MARKETING

Indirect marketing is largely the domain of the biggest and longest established consulting firms. Such premier firms as McKinsey & Company, Booz, Allen & Hamilton, and Arthur D. Little are sought out by *Fortune* 500 companies and government agencies to make proposals. These elitist consulting firms perceive little need to advertise or make "cold calls" on clients.

These firms strive for an image of high quality and a full range of consulting services. They want their quality image to be so pervasive in the market's consciousness that key decision makers in client organizations naturally select them before considering an unknown, though perhaps equally qualified, consultant.

Above all, the indirect approach is low key and subtle, to the point where the client does not realize that he or she is the "victim" of hidden persuasion. The market comes to the consulting firm because of its impeccable reputation, real or imagined. But that reputation has been planted consciously by the firm!

The indirect approach begins with a hiring decision for junior consultants. Typically, the new consultant is an MBA graduate at the top of his or her class from the elite business schools—Harvard, Stanford, Chicago, M.I.T., and Columbia. The starting salaries are exceptionally high, but the payoff can be rewarding to the firm. Clients want to know that they are getting the "best" and "latest" in management know-how; perhaps they themselves graduated from the same schools, and, of course, "great minds think alike."

Once the consulting firm is packed with talent, the campaign of subtle persuasion begins. First, they set themselves up in offices in the choicest skyscrapers in the middle of the financial community of major cities. They are just down the hall from their prospective clients.

Next, they infiltrate, at the firm's expense, community and social organizations where their future clients are likely to belong. There is not a Harvard Business School Club anywhere in the world whose membership is not heavily weighed with the staff of the local McKinsey & Company office. They also take active leadership in local Chambers of Commerce, the Rotary Club, charities, and social clubs. Consultants and prospects become "naturally" acquainted, so that, when a problem arises in the prospect's business, it is convenient and respectable to turn to "good ole Charlie," the managing partner of Cresap, McCormack and Paget, Inc.

Indirect marketing goes beyond community activities to present a solid image of expertise across a broad range of consulting services. Consultants are expected by their firms to make speeches to professional groups and to write articles in the *Harvard Business Review*. Seminars are arranged for local business leaders to hear about the latest knowledge on management subjects. And slick brochures are prepared to describe the variety of consulting services and the caliber of talent behind these products.

Within the consulting firm itself, considerable management attention is given to arranging, monitoring, and supporting the marketing function. Consultants are expected to file "contact" reports on whom they are meeting and wooing in the community. Market intelligence files are kept on local companies, their leaders, and problems facing their industries. Internal training sessions are held to update each consultant's knowledge, and substantial libraries are maintained for ready reference.

When a prospective client makes an inquiry, the full resources of the firm are marshalled to make an outstanding proposal and presentation to the client. Graphic artists are employed to prepare slides and diagrams. Experts on the client's industry are flown in from other offices. And "dry-run" presentations are held to eliminate the rough edges.

Large consulting firms have recently employed full-time marketing directors and organized into industry specializations. Marketing directors bring a special expertise that most consultants do not possess or feel inclined to develop. Industry specialization grows out of a recognition that management problems, government regulations, and market opportunities have become increasingly unique to specific industries. Clients are more likely to be impressed by a firm with a depth of industry knowledge, and a side benefit is referrals by client executives to their network of friends in the same industry.

One of the latest and most direct forms of indirect marketing is that of the *topical seminar*. Several of the Big-8 CPA firms and a number of established consulting organizations design and develop one- and two-day seminars for the general business public. The subjects range from the latest techniques in personnel management and worker productivity to developing new sources of debt and equity financing. Facilities are reserved at first-class hotels in six or eight major cities on consecutive weeks, and promotional fliers are mass-mailed to the personnel directors or the chief financial officers of all the major companies in each city. Those electing to attend pay from $100–300 per day, which is written off by their employer as a training expense. While the real purpose of the seminar is to expose key executives to the consulting firm so that those attending become prospective clients, the authors are aware of several firms that have had such financial success with their business development seminars that seminar income has become a major, consistent source of new revenue. The authors are aware also of several firms whose attempts to organize such seminars turned into financial disasters. Anticipating 100–150 participants, the partners showed up in a major city to find only 3 people in attendance. While they received full refunds of their deposits, the consulting firm was stuck with a huge bill from the hotel for conference facilities not used and for 150 lunches not served.

PITFALLS TO INDIRECT MARKETING

When one reviews the total billings of the top ten consulting firms in America and realizes that almost all the business has been generated through *indirect* marketing approaches, it would seem to carry the message that this approach is by far the best method by which to market consulting services.

Unfortunately, there are some obvious problems in a total reliance on indirect methods. There is an unspoken realization that indirect marketing requires a long time to build up subtle awareness and trusting relationships in the marketplace. This, in turn, implies a good deal of work-in-progress and a solid stable of existing clients to support the firm financially while the indirect marketing methods gradually bear fruit.

It costs an enormous amount of money to support the lengthy process of indirect marketing, and it requires the consulting firm to have a large number of consultants available to generate sufficient billings to support both themselves and their "nonproductive" colleagues who are spending large blocks of time in external committee meetings, writing articles, and giving speeches.

Other pitfalls to the indirect approach include high public exposure of individuals whose conduct may falter somewhere along the way or be damaged by political infighting in community organizations. It takes years to build a favorable image, but one "bad" incident can spread rapidly throughout the market grapevine.

DIRECT MARKETING

The reader should not be surprised that a reliance on indirect marketing can only be undertaken by the largest of consulting firms with economies of scale to support these costly activities. There are tenfold as many national consulting firms that are not in the top ten of billings and a hundredfold regional firms and a thousandfold individuals acting as independent consultants who have neither the time nor resources to rely on indirect methods. It is this majority of consultant organizations that use a *direct* marketing approach, and we will concentrate our comments on this mode for winning a client.

The direct approach recognizes that what is being marketed is an intangible personal service, much the same as life insurance. And just as with life insurance, the most proven method of marketing is direct sales. It is a method that requires contacting large numbers of people. For every twenty people contacted, five executive doors are opened. For every five executive suites entered, one sale is consummated. The direct approach is a "numbers game."

To understand direct marketing, we must deal with the principles of selling a personal service. At the risk of seeming to be writing a book, *How I Sold My First Ten Million of Life Insurance*, we must emphasize that the consulting profession is highly competitive, and unless one gains insight into some of the basic skills of direct selling, one will never get a client with whom to practice the profession.

To be successful in direct sales, the consultant requires straightforward skills in stamina, perseverance, and easy yet sincere talk. Direct sales is also a "people game," where the psychology of persuasion lies behind the "numbers game." It can be broken down into two categories, *cold calls* and *referrals*.

COLD CALLS

There are many individual styles and approaches to cold call marketing. Rather than list them superficially, we will expand on a particular approach that has proven useful to one author in beginning his consulting practice. This method requires that the following steps be taken:

- Develop a mailing list to the president or CEO of the prospective company (in the sample letter used in Exhibit 4–1, it is the chief hospital administrator.)[1]
- Develop a letter that outlines three or four key industry issues of likely concern to the executive.
- Mail out no more than *ten* letters each week, preferably on a Monday and, to keep down travel expenses, preferably to prospects geographically close to you.
- Never forget that the *one and only purpose* of the letter is to get that person's attention (your letter will accomplish that by its lucid, brief de-

---

[1] Exhibits can be found at the end of each chapter following Recommended Readings.

scription of the issues that the administrator most worries about) and that the letter is *not* intended to sell anything.

- Beginning the following Monday, call each of the letter's recipients for the *one and only purpose* of getting an appointment with that individual; the phone call is *not* intended to sell anything either.

- Remember that, on average, you will have to make five calls to each of the ten people before you reach them; most people are busy—not necessarily productive, but busy in meetings, seminars, traveling, sick, or on vacation. Don't get discouraged! However, don't send out more than ten letters each week since you will not be able to follow up effectively beyond 50 phone calls the following week.

Case in Point

One of the authors took the occasion of this chapter to reread some old notes from his first year in private practice. Over the first six months, 110 letters were sent out, 680 phone calls made, 28 appointments were developed, 7 people stood up the author, 21 people were interviewed, 15 proposals were solicited, and 3 new clients were obtained that subsequently generated over $175,000 in billings. That worked out to a value of $237.35 per phone call, despite the low "hit" rate.

WHO IS THE INITIAL "CLIENT"?

One of the key facts of life in consulting learned over the years is that the higher in the organization one goes for initial contact, the better the chances of obtaining a client. Wherever possible, the initial "client" should be the CEO, and any business development letters or phone calls should be sent to the top executive in the organization in question.

Key executives are more likely to have the authority to commit the company to a consulting contract without having to check "upstairs" or to run a proposal through a committee. If a prospect is left to "talk it over with Sam" or to review it with the administrative committee, the consultant is, in essence, asking the client to make the sale for him. It is not something that the client is well versed in doing; the prospect has heard only your one hour of presentation; he does not know how to answer specific questions about the proposal or how to handle objections from his peers or superiors.

Conversely, if the "client" is the CEO of the company, he or she is more able to engage your services on the spot and is more likely to authorize a larger contract than, say, an assistant vice president of marketing or a plant superintendent for production. Should you find that your initial contact lacks sufficient authority to authorize a contract, suggest strongly that you accompany this contact to any subsequent meetings with key executives.

INTERVIEWING
PROSPECTIVE CLIENTS

So you now have won an appointment with a prospect. Remember that you didn't sell anything in the letter except your fundamental knowledge of the industry, and you didn't sell anything on the telephone except a half-hour's time. And you will still not sell anything during the first 45 minutes of the half-hour interview you are granted.

What you are going to do once you are in the door is *interview*, not sell, the prospective client. Your mission is to gain as much knowledge about the company as you possibly can in a short period of time—to learn how your prospect thinks, what his or her values and priorities are, and, most important, what he or she feels are the problem issues, constraints, and opportunities facing the company.

The interview does not start with self-serving statements, such as "Here is what I can do for you as a consultant...". It is a delicate process, a mating ritual that is going to assure your success or failure—and you will only have a few minutes to make it work with a complete stranger who, it is guaranteed, will be reluctant to bare his or her soul, or company secrets, to a complete stranger.

To begin the process, thank the prospect for the time given to you. Executives' time is the most important, treasured item in their business world. They guard it jealously.

Next, take the opportunity to explain more about your firm and yourself. The prospective client is expecting you to do most of the talking anyway, so use that assumption to build the *image* you want to project. But be brief! Don't spend more than ten minutes explaining that your firm is a national (or local) consulting firm that specializes in certain industries or areas of technical expertise germane to the prospect. Reassure your prospective client of your general experience and the fact that your firm is an established, successful practice, even if you are talking exclusively about a one-person, independent operation. If you are on your own, that doesn't mean that you are not established. Talk a little about what you have been doing—your expertise.

The third step is to turn the tables. Explain that you know less about the prospect's company than what you have just explained about your own firm. Say, "I would like to ask you a few questions about your company so that I can have a better grasp of how our services might be useful to you."

At this point, a set of three key questions has proven useful to one author. These questions are asked to learn specifically which problems or constraints are foremost in the prospect's mind. To make a successful business development call, one cannot just propose some consulting work. The proposal must be relevant to the prospect's needs, real or perceived. The only way to know what these needs are is to ask

1. What are you most particularly pleased about in your company this year; what's going very well for you now; what is it about your company that is unique and distinguishes it from your competition?
2. What is not going as well? What are the two or three things that you are most concerned about at present?
3. What are some of the things that still need to be done but for lack of time, money, or management you just have not been able to address?

When asked with patience and empathy, these three questions will give you most of the information needed to put together a proposal.

The three questions are loaded psychologically. The first one gives the prospective client the opportunity to relax, to be expansive, and to talk about those things that please him or her. You may want to take a few notes or just sit quietly and listen. There is an old sales proverb that states, "Listen and you may learn something new; keep talking and you only espouse what you already know!"

Once the prospective client has relaxed and opened up a little to you, it is time to ask the second question. At this point, most prospects are willing to share more of their concerns and problems. If you have made a good impression so far, the prospect may even tell you some true concerns.

Finally, to prevent the conversation from becoming too tense or intrusive, ask the third question. It allows the prospective client to talk about his or her dreams, new plans or products, and projects left undone—things that could be exciting in the future if brought to fruition. This area often provides significant leads for the consultant; they are nonthreatening and important to the client.

At this point, you should have some basic knowledge of the company's strengths and recent successes, two or three of the most pressing issues facing the prospect, and the things that still need to be accomplished but the company has not been able to achieve on its own. The next and final step in the cold call is to ask if you may develop a proposal around some of the issues discussed (preparation of the actual proposal will be dealt with in the next chapter). Indicate that the proposal can serve as a concrete source for the executive to determine if there is indeed a basis for further discussion.

PITFALLS TO DIRECT MARKETING

Just as there are problems with indirect marketing so, too, are there constraints in direct marketing. It is not for the faint of heart or the individual with high ego-gratification needs. For every successful contact and eventual acceptance by a prospect, there are 10 or 20 or as many as 50 rejections. Prospects hang up on you, fail to remember that they agreed to an appointment, steal your ideas to solve their own problems, or use the interview as a forum for expressing their own views on how to manage without the aid of consultants. It is an ego-bruising, self-confidence-eroding process that is tolerated only by the most resilient of consultant psyches.

Another major pitfall to the direct sale of consultant services and one alluded to earlier, is the fact that you are asking an executive to bare his or her "corporate soul" to a complete stranger. Few executives are willing to do this under any circumstances. They may clam up or see you as invading their privacy. So be prepared for rejection, or better yet, have the skill and sensitivity not to probe beyond the client's limits of exposure.

Finally, the consultant may fall into the trap of placing sales ahead of expertise when asked by the client to submit a proposal on an issue where he or she has little knowledge or experience. Too many greedy consultants will prepare the proposal and make a sale, only to end up doing unprofessional work. There is a fine line of courage here—to believe in oneself to do a competent job or to turn down an assignment that would hurt one's own reputation and the reputation of consultants in general.

It is the authors' experience that consultant egos frequently exceed their ability to deliver. Know yourself well, and be realistic and ethical about your limits. Self-confidence is essential to a consultant, but over-confidence and slick selling approaches will betray you.

MAPPING THE MARKETPLACE

Unless new business contacts, whether through indirect or direct methods, are channeled and concentrated toward one specific market at a time, much effort can be wasted. Few consultants are able to make several dozen contacts across five or six different industries simultaneously and generate new clients from such a diffuse search.

The best way in which to develop business is to understand, as thoroughly as possible, the business issues of a client's marketplace. That effort takes time and substantial energy. To dissipate effort over several markets leads to insufficient knowledge of any one market and resultant failures as prospective clients see through a consultant's superficiality.

Let us define a marketplace as a specific industry environment (e.g., banking, insurance, shoe manufacturing, petrochemicals, whatever). To map this market requires that the consultant perform research to become familiar with the major issues facing that industry. The issues may be legislative, competitive, technical, or strategic. You should seek to identify three or four issues most prevalent in the mind of any CEO managing a company in that industry.

The second requirement to mapping a marketplace is using the knowledge gained in the research phase to hold an informal and exploratory conversation with managers in the industry selected. The purpose of these exploratory interviews, which can be made in personal visits or through telephone calls, is to test the findings of your research and to gain insight into other current industry issues not identified previously.

Case in Point

Recently it was suggested to the authors by a knowledgeable client that there was a ready market for their services in the gaming industry. In a subsequent telephone call to the vice president of a large hotel-casino group, it was learned that one of the critical problems facing the industry was management and supervisor training and development. It seems that, in a rush to open casinos in Atlantic City in the late 1970s, few people paid much attention to the New Jersey legislation that stipulated that all employees of those casinos must be residents of New Jersey for at least six months prior to their employment. This meant that experienced personnel could not be relocated directly from Las Vegas and, therefore, that local residents from New Jersey had to be recruited and trained.

This example of market research is exactly the kind of information needed to develop a marketing letter or phone call to casino management interested in expanding operations to New Jersey. Any consultant with supervisory training expertise and a desire to market it would have identified a good opportunity with such a phone call.

Mapping of the marketplace is an equally valid exercise for the large, established consulting firm. Periodic reviews to analyze where the firm's business has developed can often lead to insights as to how the firm's business can be expanded further. Analyses should be undertaken to determine the historical development of specific markets, what additional segments of those markets are still untapped, and what allied markets can be penetrated. For example, the Big-8 firms have recently extended their expertise with information systems into the design of telecommunications and word-processing systems.

KNOWING THE COMPETITION

Another important aspect in the marketing of consulting services is knowledge of one's competition. This information is vital for large or small firms because it provides an awareness of what one is facing in a bidding situation.

Large consulting firms with high overheads and large indirect business development expenses tend to bid higher on a given proposal than do small, local consulting firms. Knowledge that a McKinsey or Towers, Perrin, Foster and Crosby is bidding on the same job can aid a smaller firm in pricing its services competitively. It can help the independent consultant to know that he or she probably can bid a proposal a little higher than usual and still not have to worry about overbidding the contract. But be prepared to offer a service that these large firms cannot provide, such as close personal attention from beginning to end.

Competitive knowledge is also useful with respect to planning a market strategy for your own firm. If you know that the local Peat Marwick Mitchell & Co. office specializes in the petrochemical field, which is also a market you want to develop, then the local PM&M office is a good source for recruiting staff consultants or even partners with prior experience in petrochemicals. Don't attack the petrochemical market without these knowledgeable resources; otherwise, Peat Marwick Mitchell & Co. will be decidedly in front. Target only those industries where you have the resources or find special market niches in which your competition is weak.

Information on the competition is not easy to determine. Reading about the industry and noticing who is publishing articles about it can help, as can follow-up, exploratory interviews with industry managers. Much information can be gained informally through friends in consulting who are willing to swap intelligence. This suggests that you should place yourself in a network of local consultants out there; they do exist in all large communities.

It is critical that information gained about the competition is used *ethically*. No one ever found a path to "fame and fortune" through winning contracts based on derogatory remarks about the competition. To state that your firm is a better selection than Smith, Smith & Jones because they were recently thrown out of General Motors for incompetence is downright unethical, even if it is true. Don't do it!

What can be done is to capitalize on your firm's strengths in relation to a competitive firm. "They're a fine firm with a good reputation; however, because we are smaller, we believe that we can give you more personalized service" or "We are larger and have more people experienced in your industry available to work on the job."

No doctor ever won a patient by divulging the extent of his peers' malpractice suits; no lawyer ever won a client by telling prospects of his competitors' lost cases; and no professional consultant ever won a client by detracting from a competitor's reputation. Business is won by stressing your strengths, not your competitor's problems.

Case in Point

Several years ago, one of the authors had a two-year consulting relationship with a client that he gave up when he left a major consulting practice to start his own independent practice. No efforts were made by the author to proselytize the client. The consultants of the larger firm spent the first three months after his departure downgrading the author and the work he had done over the previous two years. The client became outraged at the implication that for two years the large firm had assigned to them a consultant who was now felt to be incompetent, especially when the client knew that the author had done beneficial, professional work. To make a long story short, the client dismissed the larger firm after three months, called the author, and gave him a contract.

YOUR IMAGE
IN THE MARKETPLACE

Another critical requirement to successful business development, one that ties in with the previous section, is that of your firm's public *image*. How should your firm be perceived by prospects and clients? Are you an industry specialist or a skills specialist? Is your practice a local one or a national one? Is it a full-service firm or a specialized one?

Typically, larger consulting firms pursue an image of "full services" to win over a range of clients with different needs or to secure a single client with a breadth of problems. Smaller firms and independent consultants tend to specialize in a few services or a certain "product," because they cannot support a full-service image economically, and it also gives them a focused selling point with clients.

Consultants change their image to suit their client's desires. If the client wants a local firm that understands the quirks of the local market, that feature is stressed. If the client requires national expertise, the consultant emphasizes prior experience with national firms or industrywide assignments. But don't promise what you can't fulfill.

It is important to develop a firm's image based on the resources you can bring to a client. If you have a great deal of compensation knowledge and experience and prefer working on compensation problems, then the image to develop is obviously one of outstanding work on compensation matters. Don't try to be all things to all people, especially in a smaller firm. Clients see through false images.

New images also emerge to the surprise of the consultant. A pleased client in one industry may provide a lead to another client in the same industry. And before long, the consultant has developed a strong industry specialization and reputation.

REFERRALS VERSUS
ADVERTISING

The easiest method of business development is to sit down and compile a list of everyone you know in an industry you have selected, no matter who they are. This is a direct approach to the referral method.

Case in Point

An executive secretary of one of the author's clients was so impressed with her boss's satisfaction with the author and the rapport that he had developed with her in the client's office that she mentioned one day that her brother was executive vice president of a firm in another industry in another part of the country. A few letters and phone calls later, the author had another new client. So who do you know?

The next step is to call every one of the names on your list to determine if any of the industry problems developed in your earlier research are an immediate issue in that person's company and, if so, obtain the name of the appropriate person to contact. Also ask if it is acceptable to use your contact's name. If he or she says "yes," you have yourself a referral. One good referral is often worth weeks or months of hard work using other marketing techniques, because it creates instant credibility.

A good referral-based letter might start

Dear Mr. Jones,

I am writing to you today at the suggestion of our mutual friend (or your marketing director or your colleague), Bruce Smothers. Bruce is aware of the work we have done for International Widgets, Inc., and he felt that we might be helpful to you in a similar way. . . .

This letter separates you immediately from the thousands of consultants of whom Mr. Jones has never heard and places you in a unique position of being a consultant who has helped International Widgets, which is known by good old Bruce Smothers and which has sufficiently impressed Bruce that he has suggested that you write to Mr. Jones. It usually is a sufficiently powerful edge to get in to see Mr. Jones.

An even better referral, of course, is from a satisfied client. One of the disciplines addressed later in the book is that of always asking existing clients for referrals to their peers. It is a never-ending exercise, one that today accounts for more than 80% of the authors' consulting practice.

The least desirable marketing methodology is direct advertising in the public media, which is associated more with consumer products. Executives are reluctant to do business with an unknown because they must share a great deal of confidential, sensitive data. To share that information with a complete stranger selected from the Yellow Pages is too preposterous for an executive to consider. You can expect the telephone to ring from an ad in the Yellow Pages, but it won't be prospective clients calling. It will be a lot of sales representatives trying to peddle everything from "key employee insurance" to fluorescent pencils.

A better way to "advertise" is through the indirect methods mentioned earlier, such as speeches, articles, and brochures that describe your practice. A credible image will also be supported by working out of a true office rather than your home, hiring a secretary instead of an answering service, and acquiring a set of quality business cards.

The best advertising will come indirectly by word of mouth from satisfied clients. Clients do not purchase consultants on impulse. They look for more solid evidence provided by trusted friends and fellow executives. So leave the advertising to your clients; it is free if you perform effectively.

RECOMMENDED READINGS

"Accountants Losing MAS Engagements Because of SEC," *Practical Accountant*, vol. 13, no. 2 (March 1980).

BROWN, STEPHEN W., and DONALD W. JACKSON, "On Choosing a Management Consultant," *Arizona Business*, vol. 22, no. 8 (October 1975).

KENNEDY, JAMES H., "Just Among Us Consultants," *Conference Board Record*, vol. 10, no. 5 (May 1973).

LEVITT, THEODORE, "Marketing Intangible Products and Product Intangibles," *Harvard Business Review*, May/June 1981.

McKENNA, JAMES K., JR., "Choosing and Using a Consulting Firm," *Infosystems*, vol. 19, no. 10 (October).

THACKRA, JOHN, "America's Management Lode," *Management Today* (UK), January 1978.

"HRD Consulting—Should You or Shouldn't You?" *Training & Development Journal*, vol. 34, no.4 (April 1980).

WILSON, AUBREY, *The Marketing of Professional Services*. London: McGraw Hill, 1972.

EXHIBIT 4-1 "Cold Call" Letter

CHARLES, CRANSTON, KATO & KENT
CONSULTANTS TO MANAGEMENT
123 PROGRESS AVENUE
GOTHAM CITY, U.S.A.

Dr. G. Izzy Nervous
Chief Administrator
Plague Memorial Hospital
Bubonic Boulevard
Death Valley, California

Dear Dr. Nervous,

I am writing to you today about a number of concerns our clients
have expressed to us with respect to the critical issues challenging
health care administration in today's environment. Specifically,
these are:

- accelerated government intrusion into health care resulting in a diversion of resources, time and energy
  away from operations and into dealing with regulations
  and bureaucracy;

- political and public pressure for hospital cost containment programs which require increasingly sophisticated
  skills in the management of operations, staff and finances;

- economic and political pressure to improve occupancy
  levels in order to maintain management flexibility in
  dealing with double digit inflation and regulatory cost
  containment programs;

- a shortage of nursing and other skilled personnel requiring
  innovative recruitment and retention methods to maintain a
  high quality of care and comply with accreditation standards;

- the increasing complexity of third party reimbursement
  resulting in the need to maximize reimbursement options
  to deal with the ramifications of cost containment; and,

- the increasing need for private donations requiring unique
  approaches to physician and community relations.

EXHIBIT 4-1   (cont'd)

Dr. G. Izzy Nervous   Page 2

In each of these areas, our firm has successfully assisted clients
in resolving or improving their situation. From our extensive
experience, we have developed programs designed to improve a
hospital's ability to cope in these critical areas. However, due
to the variations of a given hospital's policies and priorities,
every program is individually structured.

We are a national management consulting firm based in Southern
California. Among our areas of specialization are commercial
banking, public utilities and power engineering, human motivation
and leadership development and health care and hospital management.

What makes us unique in the hospital field is our pragmatic approach
to hospital management. This requires a recognition of key problem
areas and innovative approaches to problem solving designed to produce direct and quantifiable results. The practical effect is to
provide services which are cost beneficial in the short term while
developing and improving a client's long term viability as a
service organization.

I would like to take the liberty of calling you within the next
few days to determine a mutually convenient time to meet and discuss how our firm might be of assistance to you and your institution.

                         Respectfully,

                         Nick Charles
                         Client Director
                         Health Services

5

Proposals and Pricing
The Mechanics

Once a prospective client has indicated an interest in your services, it is time to develop a written proposal. This is a critical step that, if successful, not only will secure a new client but will serve as a basis for mutual understanding on how the engagement will be conducted. In essence, the proposal is both a marketing and a planning tool.

A good proposal, one that gives the consultant a fair chance of gaining a new client, requires three fundamental parts. It must have a *beginning*, which states why the proposal is being submitted and what work is to be performed; it needs a *middle*, which states the timing of the work, the responsibility for that work, and the cost of that work; and it needs an *ending*, which summarizes the expected benefits to the client company.

WRITTEN PROPOSALS

A detailed example of a written proposal appears in Exhibit 5-1 at the end of this chapter. Upon examining the exhibit, the reader will identify six important sections to a good proposal:

1.   The first section, entitled "Our Understanding of the Issues," permits the consultant to restate exactly his or her recollection of the key problems or issues voiced by the prospect in earlier interviews. This opening statement crystallizes for the prospective client those specific issues and concerns that the consultant will be addressing. It gives the client an opportunity to reflect on whether or not these issues are indeed ones the consultant should address. Many a good proposal has been killed because the consultant didn't listen or the prospect was not very articulate in the initial interview. If a misunderstanding has occurred, the sensitive consultant should treat this section as a basis for renegotiation rather than debating what was said in the first place.

2.   The next section, entitled "Our Proposal" or "The Proposal," states clearly what the consultant proposes to do. Here the consultant outlines the focus and anticipated product of his or her work. Will it examine the present planning system, and will this require an analysis of financial data? Will the project involve an oral presentation or will it culminate in a written report? What will be covered in the final report; will it include not only recommendations but a detailed implementation plan?

3.   A third section, entitled "Methodology," is required to permit the consultant to explain in some detail the specific steps to be taken to accomplish the work. This helps the client to understand how you are going to investigate the issue, such as through interviews or outside research. It also allows the client to anticipate types of support and cooperation required to assist the consultant's efforts. It may even prompt the client to suggest other areas of investigation that are unknown to the consultant.

4.   Another section, entitled "Timing and Responsibility," schedules the various stages of work, identifies the dates for interim and final reports, and names the consultants who will be assigned to the work. This section should include a statement on confidentiality and the proprietary rights over any reports and findings. Clients want to know if privileged information will be treated in confidence and if they are receiving the best talent of the consulting firm. The consultant should be "open" about how he or she tends to work and who will be doing the job, so there will be no surprises.

5.   A fifth section, entitled "Arrangements for Our Services," is needed to price the proposal and specify expense reimbursement methods, billing schedules, and details of any retainer. All fees and cost items should be set forth, along with a schedule of expected payments. This information should be made clear to the prospect so that misunderstandings do not arise in the future. Details of the pricing procedure are discussed later in this chapter.

6.   The proposal should conclude with a section entitled "Benefits" or "Results" that outlines the major outcomes to be expected from the

project. In this section it is very important for the prospect to understand and perceive that the project is an "investment" that can yield a four- or five-fold dividend. If the client merely thinks of consulting services as a *cost*, such as an advertising or training expense, then the consultant has failed to persuade the prospect to understand the real benefits of the project. However, the consultant should not promise more than can be delivered realistically for the proposed fee.

PRESENTATION FORMAT

Whether the written proposal is in letter form or bound separately with a cover letter is an issue of personal style and the scope of the project. Some technical contracts may be 30 to 100 pages, with PERT charts, exhibits, diagrams, and the like and packaged in a fancy binding; others can be as short as 3 or 4 pages and mailed as a letter.

The proposal must be written clearly, neatly typed and designed attractively. It must be error free if it is to be read as a professional document prepared by professionals. It is helpful, too, if resumés or abbreviated biographies are enclosed of those consultants who will be working on the job, along with relevant articles or marketing brochures about the consulting firm. Credibility and credentials will often make the difference.

The proposal should be followed up in a week to ten days with a telephone call to the prospective client to ask if it has been received and read, if there are any questions or concerns that can be discussed, and when a decision might be expected. Prepare yourself well before making the call; anticipate the client's questions. The call should give the consultant a sense of the proposal's early reception; a vague response by the client requires the consultant to probe further before hanging up. Clients do not call back quickly if they have a negative reaction.

ORAL PROPOSALS
AND PRESENTATIONS

Rarely will a client agree to a contract that is not in writing. However, it sometimes happens that an oral agreement is reached before a written document is prepared. This usually occurs when a consultant and client are already well acquainted. It can also happen when there is immediate "chemistry" between consultant and client. In either case, a handshake is not a substitute for written confirmation, which should always follow oral agreements.

There are occasions when a prospect will request, or the consultant may suggest, that the consultant make an oral presentation to other senior executives or a management committee in support of a written proposal. The oral presentation, if done well, can be a powerful tool in the sale of consultant services; it allows the client to see the consultant in action.

Base the oral presentation on the written proposal. State the nature of the problem or the issues as they are understood by the consultant, the work to be done, the consultant's methodology, and the expected benefits.

Visual aids should be used in the form of flip charts or overhead slides; they serve to focus the group's attention and help to highlight the key elements. The consultant should present each section briefly and succinctly, and the entire presentation should be completed before starting a discussion. Interruptions are usually ego trips; most questions will be answered if the presentation is allowed to continue.

Unless asked specifically, the consultant should try to avoid discussions of fees and costs in oral presentations before a group. It is better to negotiate these details with the individual to whom the written proposal is addressed. However, should the issue of cost come up in front of the group, it should be addressed firmly and convincingly, but without entering into price negotiations.

Final agreement should be based on a written document. Oral agreements can be easily forgotten or distorted by both parties, particularly if the client becomes dissatisfied with the consultant or if the consultant does not receive necessary support from the client.

PRICING PROPOSALS

We were originally going to title this section "Knowing Your Costs," but "Pricing Proposals" sounds more profitable, though less accurate. You must know your costs to place a value on your time and the time of personnel working with you. Time is the basic element in the pricing formula.

Many neophytes to consulting think that pricing decisions are based on some kind of mystical formula. We hear no end of such questions as "What's a good price for a compensation study?" or "What should I ask for an analysis of a company's purchasing procedures?" or "What do most firms charge for an EEO-Affirmative Action audit?"

These questions imply that there is some underground cartel of successful consulting firms that have a predetermined pricing schedule—that a strategic planning study is worth $30,000, compensation analyses should be offered at $32,500, and purchasing systems are valued at $17,250. Nothing could be farther from the truth.

Proposals are priced on the basis of what they will actually cost the consulting firm, plus a reasonable margin for profit, no more and no less! Therefore, to determine what a job will cost puts a burden on the consultant to understand and analyze his or her costs, just as if the consultant were performing a cost analysis for a client's firm.

Self-discipline is important in confining your projected costs and products to the limits of the proposal. By this we mean that, if you have not agreed to a written report of your findings, do not write one, or you will find a job costed out at $20,000 suddenly costing you $30,000. In short, do not give anything away free, either materials or man-hours. If a proposal to review the client's organization structure did not include the preparation of new position descriptions, do not volunteer this service. You don't have to be charitable toward the client, so long as you do high-quality work on what you have proposed.

KEY COST FACTORS

The calculation of costs is captured in the consultant's daily or hourly fee, and this fee is derived from four basic cost elements:

1. A salary or income the consultant expects to receive annually
2. The time available for actual consulting annually
3. Additional personal expenses for benefits, such as health insurance and pension
4. Office overhead expenses, such as rent, secretary, and telephone

Let us assume that Sam Jones is a one-person consulting firm with an office and a secretary. Sam would like to earn $60,000 per year in income. Theoretically, he has 2,080 hours available, which is 40 hours times 52 weeks. This would make his billing charge $28.85 per hour if he worked full time and had no other expenses ($60,000 ÷ 2,080 hours).

But Sam's life is not quite so simple. He also wants to take 4 weeks' vacation, and he estimates that he must spend at least 3 weeks per year on office administration. So 52 weeks has declined to 45 weeks available for consulting, and the billing charge has gone up to $33.33 per hour ($60,000 ÷ 1,800 hours).

Next comes the hardest fact of life for Sam Jones; he must also devote considerable time to developing new business, or he will wake up without additional clients when a current job is completed. A typical allowance is 25% of one's time for business development. So Sam's 45 weeks available for consulting is now reduced to 33¾ weeks, and his billing charge has increased to $44.44 per hour ($60,000 ÷ 1,350 hours).

Two additional expense charges must be added to arrive at a final billing rate. Let us assume that Sam's personal benefits for health insurance, life insurance, and pension amount to 30% of his salary, which is a typical figure. So his income must be $78,000 instead of $60,000, and the billing rate thereby increases to $57.77 per hour ($78,000 ÷ 1,350 hours).

A second major expense item is for office expenses, which we'll assume to be $25,000 annually ($600 per month for office rent, $1,000 for a secretary, and the remainder for utilities, supplies, printing, mail, and equipment). This brings the billing charge, at cost, to $76.30 per hour ($103,000 ÷ 1,350 hours).

We will also add 15% for a reasonable profit before taxes because Sam wants to reinvest in the growth of his business. All of this adds up to a final billing rate of $87.74 per hour ($118,450 ÷ 1,350 hours) or a daily rate of $700. Sam, is in essence, a $700-per-day consultant, if he expects to reach his financial objectives.

Once you have determined the "cost" of your time, never sell it for less. If you do, you'll not only sell yourself short, but you'll put yourself in a financial bind when the bills roll in for payment. More will be devoted to these issues in Chapter 19, when we discuss the problems of managing your own firm.

TIME CALCULATION

The second major step toward pricing a proposal is to estimate realistically how long it will take to perform the work in terms of man-days. Exhibit 5-2 at the end of this chapter gives an analysis of time requirements for a management audit.

The key point in calculating time is to break down the engagement into phases, such as interviews, outside research, report writing, and feedback presentations. Each of these phases should be assigned a realistic number of days. The total will then be multiplied against the consultant's daily rate to arrive at an overall cost for professional fees.

Time is easy to underestimate because we assume an infallible schedule that is planned and controlled exclusively by the consultants. That would be fine if consulting did not depend so heavily on the plans and schedules of others. Unfortunately, you are at the mercy of planes, weather, and the client's calendar. So leave room for slippage.

You must also weigh the total fees against the client's ability to pay and the expected value of the results to the client. Small clients with annual profits of a few hundred thousand dollars are not going to buy a $100,000 proposal to analyze their production line and quality controls, regardless of the benefits. If you see that your estimated time is running high, reappraise your methodology, cut back on days, and rewrite the proposal to bring costs in line with what the client can afford. Large clients can likely afford sizable fees, but only if they perceive a good return for their investment.

Finally, there are any number of formats to use in quoting your fees. The preferred method by the authors is a flat sum based on a calculation of actual costs for the proposed work. For example, in Exhibit 5-1, it is stated, "We estimate that our professional fees for this work will be $30,000–35,000." The actual calculation derived was $32,800; however, one should not overlook the reality of having to spend a few extra hours obtaining specific information or polishing the written report.

Try not to get pinned down to the nearest penny, but establish a range of likely fees. Avoid breaking the total fee down into daily rates per consultant when more than one consultant is involved on a project. Some clients will see a vast difference between the daily rates of partners versus senior consultants and may ask for senior consultants only. It is not worth the hassle to explain why one consultant is worth more than another. Simply show them the total number of consulting days and the overall fees.

PRICING GOVERNMENT AND TECHNICAL CONTRACTS

Certain types of clients require a detailed breakdown of the total fee, namely, government agencies and regulated industries such as public utilities or public hospitals. Government agencies are restricted to how much they can pay outside consultants, often no more than about $25 per hour or $200 per day. At the same time, there is a bureaucratic awareness that few consultants work for such paltry fees. As a result, the government often allows "overhead" charges equal to 100–200% of "professional fees," so that $200 per day becomes $400 per day, or more. Another method of making up for the difference between fees and government contract constraints is to bid a 100-hour job as a 300-hour job. Your client should be aware that this is what you are doing; otherwise, your ethics are questionable.

Engineering firms and public utilities are similar in their demands for a breakdown of consultant costs. These firms are conditioned to bidding on government contracts and are typically more comfortable with a detailed format. Public utilities also find themselves under the scrutiny of state utilities commissions whose individual members are inclined to question unusual expenditures such as consultant fees. These organizations may restrict the daily rate that can be proposed by outside consultants to approximately $500–600 per day per person. To recover the true cost of these contracts, consultant firms either show more personnel assigned to the job than is the case, or they bid 110–150% of the man-days required to perform the work proposed. Exhibit 5–3 is an example of a public utilities proposal where the actual rate for principals is $90 per hour, senior consultants $65 per hour, and secretarial support $15 per hour.

PAYMENT METHOD

Just as there are a variety of methods to display the costs of a consulting project to a prospective client, there are a number of methods by which payment can be made to the consultant. The most common method is to bill the client monthly for the actual work performed during the previous month, including travel expenses. This is especially valid as a payment methodology when performing extended contracts that require several months of continuous consulting time.

Another method to smooth out the consultant's cash flow in large but discontinuous contracts is to request a monthly retainer over the life of the contract. This is often acceptable to clients who want to simplify billing procedures for their own accounting departments. For example, on a $100,000 contract, instead of paying $25,000 in month 1 and $3,000 in month 2 as the work takes place, the client agrees to send a check for $8,333 every month for 12 months, regardless of whether or not any work has taken place during a particular month.

A third payment method, usually for short engagements of less than 90 days, is a one-time, lump-sum payment at the conclusion of the project. Here the consultant must be self-sufficient until payment is received.

It is useful to request a retainer before the start of any large project. Such retainers help to "commit" the client to the project, and the consultant benefits by covering start-up costs for visiting the client's location, developing questionnaires, and performing outside research. Retainers paid in advance are typically limited to 30% or less of the total contract price and are not sought on contracts of less than $25,000.

THE PERCENTAGE CONTRACT

Some consulting firms sell and receive contracts with fees based on a percentage of the expenses saved or additional profits earned. The percentage contract can be very lucrative. For example, if a consultant is hired by a major corporation to reduce operating expenses on the basis of 10% of the amount saved over the first 24 months, a savings of several million dollars can equate to an enormous fee over and above the actual cost of the work. For a $100,000 effort on the consultant's part, a fee of $400,000 might be earned.

The disadvantages are quite clear, too. Usually such contracts are negotiated with firms that are in serious financial trouble, and, even if the consultant is successful, the client may be "terminal," which means the consultant will never get paid. Another disadvantage is that the consultant may work for 6, 9, or 18 months for free. If the consulting firm doesn't have other sources of revenue, it can go "belly up" before the terminal client. A third problem is that the client may choose not to implement the consultant's recommendations, so where does that leave the consultant? Finally, there is the most difficult question of "proof." The authors have seen numerous client-consultant disagreements over the amount of savings or added earnings directly attributable to the consultant's efforts. Lawsuits have resulted from these conflicts, which can be costly and embarrassing.

Percentage contracts are big-dollar, high-risk proposals. They are definitely not for small consulting firms or the faint of heart. Much of the consulting industry considers such contracts as professionally unethical; they are banned by ACME and Big-8 accounting firms.

RETAINER CONTRACTS

Another method of payment is the monthly retainer, which occurs when a client wants to use a consultant to obtain general advice over a broad range of issues on a frequent basis and over a lengthy period of time. The client is not sure exactly what will come up that will require the consultant's counsel nor can the consultant cost out such future services with any specificity. To get around this problem of project uncertainty, both parties agree on a minimum number of hours per month or per calendar quarter, and the client agrees to pay the consultant so much a month for a specified period, usually a year at a time.

While the consultant on retainer may not work on the client's account every month, the consultant tracks his or her time on the account. At the end of the year, if there have been any excess hours spent over and above the amount of the retainer, the consultant will bill the difference.

A retainer arrangement is preferable for a client who wants continuous access to a consultant who knows the client and works well with its employees. It is acceptable to the consultant because it gives him or her a steady cash flow, whether he or she works or not. Independent consultants like to develop retainer relationships with three or four clients paying $1,000–3,000 a month each. This more than covers their overhead and provides a secure financial base from which the firm can be expanded.

ASSURING PROMPT PAYMENT

Years ago, when first starting in the consulting profession, the authors learned that you can have a signed agreement and a firm handshake, then send an invoice in triplicate, and still not get paid. For larger clients, private or public, it is not the client's satisfaction with the consultant but the organization's bureaucracy that determines how and when you get paid. Many a small consulting firm has been decimated financially trying to collect from bureaucratic clients. Horror stories abound of the invoice that took six months to get through "the system." And it is not just the government; it's any large firm with layers of approval procedures and endless paperwork.

However, there are certain things that a consultant can do to assure reasonably prompt and consistent payment of invoices. First, ask your client how consultant invoices are paid and who in the accounting department is responsible. Visit that person, if possible, and introduce yourself. Find out how the invoice should be sent, in duplicate or triplicate. To whom should it be addressed? Is there a contract or purchase order number assigned to the account? Are expenses to be documented? To what extent of detail? Who can be called in case of problems or delays? All this information is vital to assure prompt payment.

Remember to thank the person responsible when payment is received promptly. You'd be amazed at how seldom accountants in large organizations ever get a pat on the back. And, when they do, they become even faster check issuers.

RECOMMENDED READING

EWING, DAVID, *Writing for Results in Business, Government, the Sciences and the Professions*, (2nd ed.). New York: John Wiley & Sons, 1979.

EXHIBIT 5-1   Proposal Letter

CHARLES, CRANSTON, KATO & KENT
CONSULTANTS TO MANAGEMENT
123 PROGRESS AVENUE
GOTHAM CITY, U.S.A.

Mr. D. S. Astor
President
Flameout Federal Savings Bank
100 Broad Street
New York City, New York

Dear Mr. Astor,

It was a pleasure meeting with your Mr. L. O. Thargic and Mr. I. M. Craven and learning more about Flameout Federal. In response to your concerns with respect to the challenges and opportunities facing the bank in the months ahead, below please find our proposal to assist you and your management team.

Our Understanding of the Issues

It is our understanding that senior management recognizes the need to develop and sophisticate the financial planning, budgeting and monitoring capabilities of the bank and to expand these skills in management by getting division heads more involved in the financial planning for and monitoring of their areas of responsibility. In this way, senior management will be developing and training a second level of management in the bank in preparation for the management challenges facing a $750 Million - $1 Billion institution.

At the same time, there continues to be a broad range of major challenges facing the management team which require analysis and strategic plans so that they, too, can be overcome in the months ahead. These challenges include:

- Development and clarification of long range goals for the bank and development of short range specific objectives and strategies designed to achieve those goals;

- Consolidation of the bank's financial and human resources to achieve efficient operations and to achieve the bank's short and longer range financial and non-financial goals and objectives;

EXHIBIT 5-1   (cont'd)

Mr. D. S. Astor   Page 2

- The development of specific strategies and operating
  plans which will increase pre-tax profits further and
  stabilize the cost of money and reduce operating expenses;

- The development of new revenue opportunities and methods
  to improve existing revenue sources; and,

- The development of a management team with a strong capability for devoting more of their time to planning and
  managing the bank's business through the development of
  a strong second level of management throughout the bank,
  to which more responsibilities can be assigned.

Objectives of the Study

To assist senior management in addressing these issues, Charles,
Cranston, Kato & Kent proposes to review, analyze and provide
recommendations regarding Flameout Federal's operations including:
financial, savings, lending, operating expenses, administration,
marketing and service corporations.   This study will accomplish
the following:

- Assist in the development of clear long range goals and
  short range objectives for Flameout Federal;

- Identify the strengths and weaknesses, opportunities
  and constraints which affect the bank's ability to achieve
  its financial and non-financial goals and objectives;

- Develop realistic recommendations and strategies for
  achieving its goals and objectives and for resolving
  constraints;

- Assist Flameout Federal's senior management in establishing
  a general outline for a mid-range business plan through
  1983-85, and a detailed operating business plan and
  strategy for 1980-82; and,

- Develop a methodology for financial and strategic planning
  and the monitoring and control systems to assure that
  profit objectives can be planned and achieved.

Methodology

In order to accomplish these objectives we propose that the
following steps be taken:

- Review and evaluate the financial and other relevant
  data of the bank and its subsidiaries for the fiscal
  years ending 1976 and 1977, and monthly for fiscal
  years 1978 and 1979;

EXHIBIT 5-1   (cont'd)

Mr. D. S. Astor   Page 3

- Interview the president and other senior managers regarding the banks' operations, organization, historical
  developments, decision-making processes, roles and
  responsibilities;

- Review and evaluate information from questionnaires
  to be completed by approximately 30-35 senior and
  middle management and branch managers, regarding
  operational strengths, weaknesses, constraints, goals,
  objectives, operations and attitudes;

- Interview senior management and selected members of the
  Board in order to clarify responses and issues regarding
  the items listed above;

- Develop and present our findings, conclusions and
  recommendations;

- Conduct a two to three day retreat with senior management to review our major findings and recommendations
  and to assist in the planning of long and short range
  business goals, objectives and strategies; and,

- Develop a set of approximately 40 financial charts for
  management to use in planning financial objectives and
  monitoring progress toward those objectives.

Timing and Responsibility

We propose to begin this work in February and present our preliminary report by the end of May, with a final report and
management retreat in late June, 1980.

One of the partners of the firm will be assigned the responsibility for managing all of the work proposed and he and his
staff will report directly to you. All of the analyses, findings,
reports and the financial planning charts are the sole property
of Flameout Federal and are not available to any outside third
party under any circumstances.

Arrangements for Our Services

For this work we estimate our professional fees will be $30,000-
$35,000, plus out-of-pocket expenses directly related with this
project, i.e., travel, lodging, and report preparation. We
estimate that these out-of-pocket expenses will be approximately
20% of professional fees.

Professional fees and expenses will be billed and are payable
monthly as they are incurred.

EXHIBIT 5-1 (cont'd)

Mr. D. S. Astor   Page 4

Benefits

This work will provide Flameout Federal with:

- An improved ability to plan and prioritize the bank's financial and non-financial objectives;

- Recommendations for the improvement of short term earnings;

- Specific business plans for the next 12-15 months, stressing the further improvement of the bank's net income;

- Recommendations to assist Flameout Federal in resolving its current constraints regarding savings, lending, administration, marketing and service corporations;

- Recommendations to assist the bank in defining its marketing activities in the savings and lending areas;

- Recommendations for reducing its operating expenses, cost of money, improving revenues, and the overall efficiency of operations; and,

- Recommendations for developing a strong second level of management throughout the bank.

We look forward to the opportunity to service Flameout Federal and your management team, and to participate in the challenges which lie ahead. We will be calling you in the next few weeks to answer any questions you might have regarding this proposal; and, certainly, we would be prepared to meet with you or your Board of Directors if you believe it would be helpful prior to our beginning this project. We look forward to seeing you again in the near future.

                          Respectfully,

                          Lamont Cranston

                          Lamont Cranston
                          for CHARLES, CRANSTON, KATO & KENT

EXHIBIT 5-2   Project Planning Notes To Develop Proposal Fee

Work Sheet For Flameout Federal

PHASE I - PROCEDURES

STEP	WEEK	PROCEDURE	MEN	DAYS	LOCATION
1	I	Gather all necessary documents (see appendix A)	1M	1/2	Client (1st visit)
2	I	Interview c.e.o. & c.f.o. re: accounting methods, role of boards, committees decision process & organization (see appendix B)	1M	1/2	Client
3	I	Interview lending & savings officers re: lending & savings operations - how are things currently done, why & by whom, where	1M	1	Client
4	II	Analyze financial data & develop kardexes (see appendix C)	1A	10	Office
5	II	Develop any further financial issues re: accounting or data and send letter to c.f.o. via c.e.o.	1A	1/2	Office
6	II	Meet with cartographer to develop paper mock-up charts, set scales & colors	1M 1C	1/2 1/2	Office
7	II	Review & analyze notes from c.e.o. & c.f.o. discussions and all documentation collected (see appendix A)	2M	2	Office
8	III	Cartography commences mock-up charts	1C	5	Office
9	III	Develop questionnaire	1M	1	Office
10	III	Questionnaire typed in draft form	1C	2	Office

EXHIBIT 5-2   **(cont'd)**

STEP	WEEK	PROCEDURE	MEN	DAYS	LOCATION
11	IV	Review draft with c.e.o., develop participants list, raise further questions or modifications to questionnaire, set up meeting with participants	1M	1	Client (2nd visit)
12	IV	Review preliminary chart mock-ups with c.e.o. & c.f.o., demonstrate usefulness, meet with participants & c.e.o. to explain questionnaire, get answers to step 5	1M	1	Client
13	V	Finalize questionnaire, print up and send out to participants (see appendix D)	1C	5	Office
14	V	Commence final plastic charts & order pegs for client installation	1C	15	Office
15	VI	Review & analyze kardexes & mock-up charts to obtain financial analysis	1M 1A	1 1	Office
16	VII	Send letter to c.e.o. to set up interview schedule in week IX	1M 1C	1/2 1/2	Office
17	VIII	Review & analyze returned questionnaires, develop issues and questions for first interviews	1M	3	Office
18	IX	Hold first interviews with questionnaire participants	2M	3	Client (3rd visit)
19	IX	Hold first full scale chart presentation to c.e.o., c.f.o. & others, sell usefulness of charts & monitoring	1M	1/2	Client
20	X	Review & analyze first interview results	1M	2	Office
21	X	Begin drafting Phase I report	1M 1C	1/2	Office

EXHIBIT 5-2   **(cont'd)**

STEP	WEEK	PROCEDURE	MEN	DAYS	LOCATION
22	X	Develop list of issues & additional questions for 2nd interviews	1M	1/2	Office
23	X	Send letter to c.e.o. reviewing work to date and setting up schedule of 2nd interviews	1M 1C	1/2 1/2	Office
24	XI	Review and edit draft of Phase I report & finish typing & make copies	1M 1C	1 3	Office
25	XII	2nd interviews	1M	2	Client (4th visit)
26	XII	Full day with president exploring issues and playing "what if," review direction of final report, test recommendations, sell monitoring & follow-on work, review draft report & schedule retreat	1M	1	Client
27	XIII	Finalize Phase I report & type & copy	1M 1C	2 5	Office
28	XIII	Prepare retreat schedule & Material	1M 1C	2 2	Office
29	XIV	Send letter re: issues to c.e.o., schedule of retreat week & any other material	1M 1C	1/2 1	Office
30	XIV	Update charts with very latest data, final chart corrections	1C	2	Office
31	XV	Meet with c.e.o. to sell follow-on work, review charts & issues & agree on desired results of retreat, review final Phase I report, distribute report to retreat participants	2M	1	Client (5th visit)
32	XV	Hold 2-1/2 day retreat	2M	2-1/2	Client

EXHIBIT 5-2 **(cont'd)**

STEP	WEEK	PROCEDURE	MEN	DAYS	LOCATION
33	XV	Review retreat with c.e.o. reaffirm sale of Phase II work	2M	1/2	Client
34	XVI	Prepare follow-on letter to c.e.o. on retreat results, goals, objectives, action assignments and proposal on Phase II work	1M 1C	3 3	Office

SUMMARY

41 professional man days:	$29,140
(41 x 8 x $88)	
12.5 accountant man days:	1,500
(12.5 x 8 x $15)	
22.5 cartographic man days:	2,160
(22.5 x 8 x $12)	
TOTAL FEES:	$32,800
22 clerical man days:	$ 2,112
(22 x 8 x $12)	
cartography supplies:	750
(20 roles of tape, 30 plastics, ink, paper mock-ups, metal pins chart case & amortization of office cartography equipment)	
4 trips to client	3,055
(7 airfares, 21 man-hotel nights, meals, rental car, parking, mileage and telephone)	
Printing	500
(printing, binding & shipping 25 questionnaires and 10 Phase I reports)	

EXHIBIT 5-2 **(cont'd)**

Photocopies $ 100

    (letters, notes, questionnaire
    and report drafts)

Telephone calls   100

TOTAL EXPENSES $ 6,617

Expenses as % of fees: 20.2%

EXHIBIT 5-2   (cont'd)

APPENDIX A - DATA REQUIRED

1) All monthly financial board reports last 2 years

2) Year-end financial board reports 2 years prior to that

3) All monthly FHLB reports last 2 years

4) Year-end FHLB reports 2 years prior to that

5) All audit & supervisory notes and letters last 2 years

6) Copy of organization chart (if available)

7) Copies of all position or job descriptions (if available)

8) Copies of all minutes of all board meetings last 2 years

9) List of all committees, purpose of committee and names and positions of members

10) Copies of all minutes of all committee meetings last 2 years

11) Copy of latest annual budget (profit plan) for this year

12) Copy of any long range plan (if available)

13) Copy of any profit plan, budget or long range plan monitoring report (if available)

EXHIBIT 5-2 (cont'd)

PHASE I PROCEDURES

APPENDIX B - INITIAL ISSUES

1) For c.e.o.

   a) Organizational structure and why - since when?

   b) History of the institution - significant events

   c) Composition of and relationship with board - its role and posture

   d) Composition and role of executive, loan and other committees

   e) Planning process - long or short range, who participates, procedures

   f) Competition, market, demographics

   g) Relationship with FHLB and state authorities

   h) Merger history, plans and current negotiations

   i) Service corporations - performance, history and plans

   j) Role of senior officers, history and evaluations - concerns, hopes, plans

   k) Compensation, bonus plans and fringes

EXHIBIT 5-2 (cont'd)

2) <u>For chief financial officer</u>

   a) Accounting procedures and policy - any major changes last 3 years

   b) Role and relationship with auditors

   c) Role and output of EDP

   d) Financial reports - how many, how often, to whom, how used

   e) Securities/investment portfolio - strategy, how handled, by whom, results

   f) Budgeting procedure and monitoring process - how, when, by whom, results

   g) All non-operating earnings, expenses

   h) Accounting/finance staff - any CPA's - roles, responsibilities

   i) Borrowings, policy, cost, from whom

3) <u>For chief lending officer</u>

   a) Composition of loan portfolio; SFR, conventional, FHA-VA; commercial construction; consumer/property improvement, mobile home, student, other

   b) Other lending activities - savings loans, participations, out-of-state brokerage sales - purchases

   c) Market, rates, points, fees, competition, customer profiles

   d) Application process and procedures - by whom, where, volumes, capacity

   e) Loan processing - by whom, where, how many days, capacity

   f) Approval procedures - by whom, approval levels, timing, role of loan committee and board

   g) Loan servicing - by whom, how, delinquencies and collections, policy on assumptions, late charges, refinancing programs, portfolio accessibility, reports - by whom, how often, how used

   h) Appraisals - where, how, by whom, timing, capacity, costs vs. fees, who is MAI rated?

EXHIBIT 5-2   **(cont'd)**

(chief lending officer - cont.)

i)   Yields by type of loan and how calculated, how often

j)   Organization of division, capability of personnel, concerns, hopes, plans

4)   <u>For senior operations officer</u>

a)   Savings portfolio - cost of money, mix, types of accounts & CD's

b)   Customer profiles, average balance per account, number of accounts, location of customers

c)   Branches - how many, where, when, type, cost, branch manager roles, training, organization

d)   Operations supervisors - how many, roles, training

e)   Tellers - how many, where, roles, training, turnover, compensation

f)   Savers products, services - IRA/Keogh, save-by-mail, etc.

g)   Competition - who, how - results

h)   Savings administration - who, how, when, role

i)   Branch expansion plans - applications outstanding, application done by whom, timing, cost

j)   Role of marketing, research, analysis, advertising, promotions, premiums, etc.

k)   Staff - appraisal, capabilities, concerns, hopes, plans

EXHIBIT 5-3 Technical Proposal with Fees Altered

CHARLES, CRANSTON, KATO & KENT
CONSULTANTS TO MANAGEMENT
123 PROGRESS AVENUE
GOTHAM CITY, U.S.A.

Mr. I. N. Competent
Vice President
Puerto Rico Power Company
Brownout Boulevard
Meltdown, Puerto Rico

CONFIDENTIAL

Dear Mr. Competent,

As per your request, below is detailed our proposal to assist
PPC in the organization, staffing and management of Unit 4.

Our Understanding of the Issues

It is our understanding that Puerto Rico Power Company is about
to commence the management of the construction and start-up of
Unit 4. This is an especially critical project for PPC for the
following reasons:

- Unit 4 is a major undertaking relative to
  PPC's size and in consideration of the two
  projects scheduled to follow it;

- This is the first management of a major
  project for the project manager selected
  by PPC for the job;

- PPC is a relatively small power company
  with a small senior management team which
  is currently taxed by existing operations
  and projects so that it is not clear how
  and to what extent senior management can
  provide the new project manager with the
  support he requires;

- Unit 4 will be the first fixed price contract PPC has undertaken;

EXHIBIT 5-3 (cont'd)

Mr. I. N. Competent   Page 2

- Unit 4 will have financial participation
  from an outside third party, the Florida
  Water District;

- To adequately staff the project, PPC will
  have to hire significant numbers of
  engineers, auditors, accountants, etc.,
  from outside the company;

- The PPC personnel department, while an
  adequate administrator, does not have the
  experience or methodology required to hire
  and absorb the calibre and number of people
  needed to staff the project teams and the
  accounting team in the time limit set by
  the project manager;

- As a result of the points made above, PPC
  management will be forced to learn a much
  more complex and sophisticated set of
  project management, monitoring and control
  skills;

- The project manager, in turn, must learn how
  to resolve complex issues of effective,
  positive interface between the various
  project teams and between the project teams
  as a whole and the internal PPC organization,
  the outside A/E, Fluor, and the outside
  partners in Miami;

- This, in turn, requires PPC project management
  to learn new methods of financial and project
  budgeting, monitoring and controls; and,

- Most important for PPC is the fact that this
  project is a learning experience for all concerned in the longer range objective that PPC
  organize and prepare for the management of
  two future projects which will require "state
  of the art" project management in partnership
  with Miami Edison and others.

As a result of these factors, PPC has requested Charles, Cranston,
Kato & Kent to submit a proposal to assist PPC management in the
organization of the project, the training of the project's personnel and to assist the management of other PPC staff support
divisions with respect to their assistance to the project manager.

EXHIBIT 5-3 (cont'd)

Mr. I. N. Competent   Page 3

It is important to distinguish between the technical/functional aspects of assistance versus the organizational and human development aspects of assistance. To this end, we will address the human resource management side of the problem. It is our understanding that PPC has already received proposals from MAC, Theodore Barry, Arthur Anderson and others which address PPC's technical needs. However, without the human development part of the total assistance package, technical systems, in and of themselves, will not work effectively. There is an undeniable need for:

- Clarifying the roles, responsibilities and authorities, often shared by two or more managers, in matrix organizations and developing effective management and communications styles to assure successful project management and project completion;

- Developing broader understanding across the organization of human systems problems to be shared and mutually addressed, both internally in utility companies and at the interface between utilities and their engineering and design constructors;

- Developing throughout the management team a greater sensitivity for and understanding of group needs and the skills to effectively communicate those needs to the public utility support divisions in addition to strengthening and improving labor relations;

- Providing a process whereby project and home office personnel are able, as a group and as individuals, to more effectively identify problems; make decisions and resolve those problems; and, implement pragmatic solutions quickly and effectively.

Our Proposal

We, therefore, submit this supplementary proposal to assist PPC management in the following areas:

1.   The Fluor project management organization must be evaluated and proper equivalents within PPC recommended and developed; and, to this end, we will identify what are the project management requirements, the interfacing roles, responsibilities and authorities which should be represented.

EXHIBIT 5-3 (cont'd)

Mr. I. N. Competent   Page 4

2.   We will diagnose the internal operations of PPC, identify
        the needs of the project to the home office and vice
        versa and design a process to identify reporting relation-
        ships with authority and role clarifications appropriate
        to the work to be accomplished.

3.   We will analyze the information gathered from the
        organization and provide recommendations as how to more
        effectively and efficiently develop a total PPC team
        for Unit 4 as well as the future projects with Miami
        Edison and others.

4.   We will help implement the strategies developed with
        the PPC management groups by holding a series of
        training sessions and interfacing programs between
        departments within PPC and between PPC and Fluor as
        appropriate.

5.   We will provide a monitoring service to guarantee the
        implementation of strategies.

Charles, Cranston, Kato & Kent

CCK&K is well qualified to address these issues and assist PPC
management. Briefly, our experience over the past five (5)
years includes: working in similar situations with utilities
such as Salt River Project, Houston Lighting and Power, Southern
California Edison, and Colorado Ute. Our experience with A/E's
such as Fluor includes work with Bechtel, Fluor, Holmes & Narver,
Brown & Root, and Sterns-Roger. However, the effectiveness of
the personnel to be assigned to this project resides in the
fact that their expertise deals with the human resource management
of large complex projects.

Without an effective team working together as experienced personnel, sophisticated systems of control or equipment maintenance
can be far less than even 50% of their capabilities.

Methodology

To provide the assistance described in the proposal section
above, CCK&K would:

                Interview key personnel to identify those
                areas of concern which exist at all levels
                of the organization to provide the basis
                for further in-depth interviews to be
                conducted throughout the organization.
                (Interviews of Fluor personnel would be
                conducted only with their project manage-
                ment personnel.);

EXHIBIT 5-3   (cont'd)

Mr. I. N. Competent   Page 5

. Analyze all the data gathered from the
   interviews so that significant themes can
   be isolated and information categorized
   into meaningful work sections in preparation for subsequent work sessions and
   programs, and appropriate reports with
   recommendations would be written at this
   time for the departments or groups involved
   in the project;

. Design the meetings required to resolve the
   issues identified through the data analysis
   so that we could meet then with various
   teams of project and executive management
   and PPC support divisions/departments and
   to develop strategies for implementing the
   recommendations;

. Conduct work sessions to clarify and implement
   the concepts of project management, roles and
   responsibilities, reporting relationships and
   requirements within PPC and between PPC and
   Fluor;

. Monitor the processes of implementation by
   working closely with the project management
   team and the home office support groups
   so that the team will become more and more
   adept at dealing with their interface concerns.

In addition to this assistance, CCK&K would develop for PPC
project management a Project Management Manual. This manual
is used as a pragmatic guide to assist in effectively directing
major projects. It would cover every important management and
control aspect from engineering to procurement, personnel and
accounting, security and P.R., etc. Sample pages of a similarly
developed manual are attached to this proposal in Appendix B.

Timing and Responsibility

As the principal-in-charge for our public utilities clients, I
will personally take charge of the CCK&K team in the implementation of this work. In addition to the written reports and
recommendations outlined above, I also will make periodic verbal
reports to you and the project manager on the progress of our
work, new issues identified and the remedial action recommended.

The CCK&K team consists of a combination of four (4) personnel
with a broad range of experience in this field. The relevant
resumes are displayed as Appendix A of this proposal.

EXHIBIT 5-3 (cont'd)

Mr. I. N. Competent   Page 6

As to the timing of our work, if we were to commence in Mid-August our activity chart would appear as follows:

	August	September	October	November
Preliminary Interviews	⊢—⊣			
In-depth Interviews		⊢———⊣		
Data Analysis and Report Preparation			⊢———⊣	
Develop Recommendations			⊢—⊣	
Work Session: #1				⊢—⊣
#2				⊢—⊣
#3				⊢—⊣
#4				⊢—⊣

Arrangements For Our Services

Our professional fees for performing this work will be $50,519.50.
This amount is derived by calculating the hourly rate of the personnel assigned and the number of days they will be on the project
as follows:

Principals at $40 per hour x 30 man days	=	$ 9,600.00
Senior Consultants at $25 per hour x 40 man days	=	8,000.00
Clerical Personnel at $6 per hour x 15 man days	=	720.00
Total Personnel Costs		$18,320.00

In addition to these personnel costs, we will charge our overhead at the accepted industry rate of 112.5% of personnel
costs, together with our out-of-pocket expenses, at cost, incurred on the project. These out-of-pocket expenses include:
travel, lodgings and meals and are estimated at $5,000.
Finally, there is a start-up fee equivalent to 15% of the total
contract price.

EXHIBIT 5-3 (cont'd)

Mr. I. N. Competent   Page 7

In summary, then, the costs to PPC on this project will be as follows:

- personnel costs	$18,320.00
- overhead costs @ 112.5%	20,610.00
- out-of-pocket expenses	5,000.00
- 15% start-up fee	6,589.50
Total Cost	$50,519.50

Within 10 days of this contract being approved, PPC should remit the 15% start-up fee to CCK&K and at that time, CCK&K will begin work.

Both professional fees and expenses are billed and are payable monthly. There will be a 1.5% per month late charge for all monthly remittances mailed later than 30 days from the date of the invoice.

Benefits

It is our experience that the benefits to PPC as a result of CCK&K's work be as follows:

. PPC will understand the functional operations of the Fluor project management team;

. PPC will have designed an effective counterpart organization with which to monitor the work in progress;

. PPC will have clarified the roles, responsibilities and authorities of all key positions on the project teams of Fluor and PPC;

. Communication lines will have been established between the two organizations so that timely decisions can be made with adequate information;

. The management team will have a greater sensitivity for and understanding of the project team's group needs and the communication skills required to resolve human resource issues before they become critical;

. PPC will have evaluated their internal support systems with respect to the efficiency and support required by a complex construction project;

EXHIBIT 5-3 (cont'd)

Mr. I. N. Competent   Page 8

- A process will be developed by which project and home office personnel can more effectively identify problems, make decisions, resolve those problems and implement pragmatic solutions quickly and effectively;

- PPC will have developed those critical project management skills required to monitor an A/E in this and future large projects requiring more and more sophisticated organization, reporting and tracking in addition to having its own project management manual;

- PPC will have provided the managerial framework in which other types of project and financial control tools and systems can function effectively;

- PPC will have been able to hire key personnel for the positions designed specifically for the work in progress; and,

- PPC executive management will be supported at the project level and internally with competent personnel who have been trained to manage their affairs effectively and to monitor Fluor's responsibilities against a project management "checklist."

Summary

This is a cornerstone project for Puerto Rico Power. It is a first for the company in a number of areas: the first fixed cost project, the largest undertaken to date, the first project with outside partners, etc.

As a result, it is crucial to PPC that the project team is properly organized, supported, managed and that it interface effectively at all points within the matrix. This proposal has addressed these issues in some detail both to explain how such a project must be approached to assure success and to assist PPC management as it prepares for the project.

CCK&K looks forward to the challenge of assuring PPC's success in this project. I will call you in the coming week to answer any questions you may have.

Sincerely,

Clark Kent

Clark Kent
for CHARLES, CRANSTON, KATO & KENT

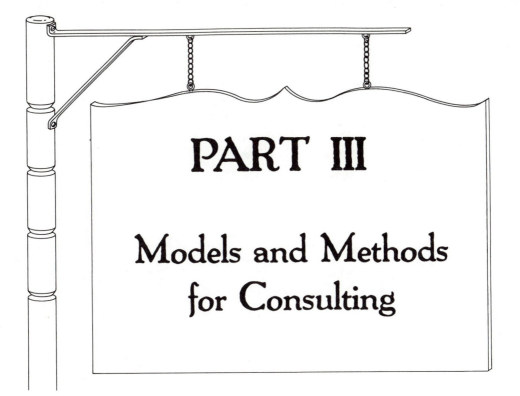

PART III

Models and Methods for Consulting

The next five chapters take the reader through a broad range of issues and model approaches typical to consulting assignments. They provide the reader with both a conceptual and pragmatic framework within which to address the most common types of consulting projects. While consultants need to determine an organized approach and thought process best suited to a specific client problem, they should be fully aware of the knowledge already available. Those areas, and ones which we will discuss, include strategic planning, financial analyses, marketing assignments, organization and systems studies, and compensation and human resources development. We have not included highly specialized, technical assignments such as production line and engineering analyses or data-processing programming, as these are relatively narrow fields of technical expertise that comprise only a small part of the total consulting industry. To conclude this section, we devote a chapter to the all-critical issue of data gathering methods. Without sound skills in this area, the consultant cannot obtain the information required to identify the issues or recommend meaningful solutions.

6

Strategic Planning Studies

The successful performance of a strategic planning assignment is the acid test for any generalist management consultant. It is the most difficult challenge facing even the most skilled planning expert.

In strategic planning, the consultant must be able to analyze all facets of a client's business from a financial, manufacturing, marketing, personnel, and organizational viewpoint, not to mention an in-depth understanding of the client's industry and competition.

If that isn't enough, this comprehensive analysis must be performed in a way that crystallizes the key strategic issues and choices facing the client and then proposes realistic recommendations. To change the strategic direction of any corporation is a herculean task, equivalent to turning a giant oil tanker in heavy seas.

Strategic planning is also rewarding work because it addresses the very essence, direction, and purpose of a client's enterprise, which, in turn, influences the future careers of its employees and the financial prospects of its owners. Strategic planning is the heady stuff for which MBA programs were created.

This chapter begins with the key elements of analysis to be considered in strategic planning, both inside and outside the client's organization. It then describes several analytical models commonly used by consultants to identify the underlying strategic issues. It closes with a description of a particular planning approach that the authors have found useful over the years.

PURPOSE AND BENEFITS FROM STRATEGIC PLANNING

Strategic planning is not detailed budgeting, it is not the extrapolation of last year's numbers, and it is not esoteric thinking about the economy in the year 2000. Rather, it is imaginative work that reduces great complexity to the simplicity of a workable plan. The aim of strategic planning assignments is threefold:

- To clarify environmental opportunities and constraints facing the client organization.
- To match these environmental factors against the internal strengths and weaknesses of the client company.
- To determine appropriate future objectives and implementation steps required to attain them.

Clarification of corporate purpose and direction is the paramount benefit of a strategic planning study. It helps not only organizations that have failed previously to develop strategic plans but even those that are long experienced in planning discipline. Strategic planning serves to

1. Test short- and midterm plans against long-term corporate objectives. It goes far beyond a myopic approach that projects last year into next year.
2. Help senior managers to focus on corporate problems and external constraints in an atmosphere of reflection and creativity, rather than succumbing to a siege mentality of day-to-day operating decisions.
3. Assist managers to evaluate a wide range of issues that are not addressed normally on a weekly or monthly basis (e.g., the economy, export markets, product life cycles, new R&D issues, capital expenditures, future personnel requirements, and executive succession planning).

Strategic planning is a foreign discipline to many small- or medium-sized companies. It is a complex intellectual exercise rarely learned or mastered by self-taught entrepreneurs. Even when the CEO knows personally where to take the organization over the next five years, he or she seldom has the time or resources available to turn dreams into reality.

In larger companies more accustomed to strategic planning, the top management is frequently looking for objective feedback on its present plans as well as for new ideas on how to implement these plans more effectively.

CONSULTANT SKILLS REQUIRED

Strategic planning consulting demands broad business knowledge and analytical skills. The consultant should be intimately familiar with a client's industry, its legislative and regulatory constraints, the unique managerial skills required, recent R&D developments, and the marketing strategies of its competition.

However, the effective planning consultant is more than a backroom analyst with Dr. Strangelove qualities. There is the rare ability to work on a peer basis with senior executives who may believe that they know more about their company than the consultant. Skill in developing creative solutions to complex strategic issues is also required. Most difficult is the ability to confront senior managers with hard facts and bad news while leading them to new insights. Once consensus is gained, there is the rare skill of translating intellectual understanding into concrete recommendations that still retain the emotional commitment of senior leadership.

ELEMENTS OF STRATEGIC ANALYSIS

Initially the planning consultant should review the client's environment in ten key areas: legislative, economic, industry, competitive, technological, community, managerial, organization and information systems, labor, and financial. Six of these areas represent a broad scan of the client's external environment; the remaining four deal with the internal strengths and weaknesses of the client company.

Legislative Forces

Every company must be alert continually to local, state, and federal regulations governing its industry. Equally important is the monitoring of proposed legislation, which may place new constraints on the way in which a company does business.

What is the impact of current legislation at federal, state, and local levels with respect to the business and its products? Are these statutes a constraint (paperwork to prove compliance) or an opportunity (export tax exemptions)? What legislation might be enacted and how will it affect the company? What impact might these regulations have on capital adequacy? What can the company do realistically to affect the future of such legislation?

A recent case in point is the Depository Institution's Deregulation Act of 1980. This legislation permits both commercial banks and savings and loan associations throughout the country to offer interest-bearing checking or NOW accounts for the first time in over 50 years. As a result, savings and loan associations have been forced to recruit and hire bank operations personnel familiar with checking accounts, while the commercial banks are faced with paying interest on what were previously "free" core deposits. To both industries this new legislation is a very expensive and market-threatening experience. Institutions that anticipated this change and planned for it were in a much better position in January 1981 than were those that believed in an unchanging future.

Economic Trends

The monitoring of economic trends can reveal a great deal to a company with respect to future orders, realistic inventory levels, price changes, cost of new debt servicing, and new wage demands.

How have recent economic trends impacted the business? What is management's best guess as to the economy over the next few years? How might this economic projection affect the industry and business? Does the economy really affect the business at all? This question is especially valid for small companies that can sometimes pick up one or two percentage points of market share and thus double or triple their sales when major competitors are affected negatively.

A recent example of negative economic trends and their impacts occurred in the 1979–1980 recession when interest rates soared and made the issuance of new mortgages extremely difficult, virtually shutting down the entire housing construction industry for a period of more than 18 months. Builders who foresaw this and planned accordingly stayed in business; those that did not failed financially.

Industry Growth Rate

Every industry is different in its growth rate and its vulnerability to new competition. Entire industries wane, such as the hat business, and totally new ones emerge, such as home computers. The client's products should be reviewed for what management is doing and plans to do about them in this dynamic context.

What is the state of the company's industry? Is it growing, stagnating, or declining? What specific factors determine the sale of products; is it price, quality, delivery, or service? Are opportunities present for developing new products and services to generate additional sources of earnings, or should certain products be phased out to reduce losses? Does the company expect to be in its present industry ten years from now? What other industries are allied with or complement the company's businesses, and how might they be entered? What is the state of R&D in the industry, as well as the client's own R&D efforts?

As a current example of an industry revolution, we have seen the introduction of home computers, where a number of small computer companies recognized that they would have difficulty competing with IBM and Honeywell in the large-computer hardware market. So they developed inexpensive retail models that could be sold to individuals for use in their homes or atop office desks.

Competitive Position

Many companies ignore their competition because "business is good," only to wake up one day to realize that they have been overtaken. A scan of competing products puts the client's products within a framework of relative vulnerability.

Who are the company's major competitors? What are their relative market shares? Who has been increasing or losing share of market? How can market share be enhanced? For very large, dominant companies, how might current market share be maintained? What products have matured and what new products are in development? What new, unexplored markets exist; exports, for example? What does the company anticipate from its competitors in the future, and what will be their likely impact? What other potential competition might be entering the industry?

A classic case in this area is the downturn in the U.S. automotive industry. As the price of fuel soared and as the quality of American-made automobiles declined, the Japanese saw their opportunity and took more than 20% of the American automobile market away from Detroit.

Technological Development

This analysis follows closely the scan of the client's industry. It alerts a client to what it ought to be doing and highlights where future capital investments should go.

What new technological developments are impacting the industry? What priority does the client put on R&D? Do new production methodologies assure better quality or faster processes? How might these technological developments threaten the company or assist it? How could they be applied to this company and at what cost? Can the technology be leased or must there be significant capital investment in new plant and equipment?

A noteworthy case is the turbulent watch industry where small circuitry chips have virtually replaced the spring-driven watch, thus forcing a number of traditional Swiss and American companies out of business. The surviving traditional watchmakers have shifted to high-priced watches sold primarily as jewelry items.

Community Expectations

A company's relationship with its surrounding community has been historically important in terms of labor supply and access to raw materials or consumer markets. It is even more significant today, given environmental regulations, living costs, and a city's dependence on revenue from business taxation.

How is the company perceived by the community where it has its headquarters, its branches, and its plants? How does it want to be perceived? What role is the company playing in community affairs and activities? Are the client's executives willing to commit themselves to public service? How important is this level of involvement for the company and for the community? Is the community stable or growing and is it able to provide a steady source of labor? Or is it dying as younger generations move away? How attractive is the city for attracting executive talent? What is the trend in the area's cost of living?

There are any number of classic examples of these issues. In the past decade, due to hostile unionism and high energy bills in many Northeastern communities, a number of factories moved South to a milder climate and a cheaper labor force. Also, several *Fortune* 500 firms relocated their headquarters outside New York City in the 1970s due to the city's high cost of living, crime, and taxation. Some banks have moved their credit operations elsewhere due to local restrictive usary laws.

The next four areas address the internal environment of the client, where an assessment must be made concerning the human, financial, and organizational resources available to implement any changes in strategic direction.

Management Goals
and Capacities

A problem common to most strategic planning studies is the contradiction between management's stated goals and its actual performance. It is not unusual to discover a board of directors that has never clarified how the CEO is to be measured and rewarded. Too often owners demand growth and innovation from management but take too much out in bonuses and dividends, thereby leaving few financial resources for reinvestment.

What are the personal and corporate goals of senior management? How fast do they want to grow and in what ways? How well has management met previously stated goals? How hard is this management willing to work over the next ten years? What do the owners expect? How does management attract new employees or develop existing employees into an outstanding team of managers? Where will new executives come from, and what talents must they possess? What will happen to employee recruitment or retention in light of rapid, moderate, or no-growth strategies?

A few years ago a major detergent manufacturer reexamined its goals in the face of declining profits. Its top management was startled to learn that its implicit goal had always been one of sales volume pitted against Procter & Gamble. Its marketing strategy had focused exclusively on large advertising expenditures to hype sales. However, P&G with its immense resources always outwitted them. Consequently, top management decided to focus on products that were not in a head-to-head battle with P&G.

Organization Structure and Information

A central mechanism for implementing or blocking a company's strategic plans is its organization structure and reporting system for monitoring progress. The client may have a perfectly sound strategy, but the company has not been organized properly to carry out its plans. Or sometimes the information system may be so inadequate that top management is unable to determine which products are making or losing money.

Is the client organized to reach its markets efficiently? Does sufficient authority rest with those managers who must react rapidly to changing events? How helpful are various staff functions in supporting line management? Are there proper controls for expenditures? Is the communication system set up to keep key managers fully informed and involved in major decisions? Does information or performance results reach the appropriate managers in a timely manner and in an understandable form? To what extent is the information system geared more to short-term results at the expense of measuring longer-term and anticipated future problems?

Japanese firms, for example, are widely recognized for their ability to coordinate diverse businesses and to move assets between them.

Communication on company performance is widely shared, and strategic decisions are exposed to extensive deliberation to achieve consensus and commitment. Their flexibility in organization and problem solving gives them an edge over rigid bureaucracies that inhale their own exhaust.

Labor Trends and Attitudes

Management's relations with the union must be analyzed carefully and strengthened if a company is to meet its objectives. If a nonunion shop exists, management must be aware of what is needed to preserve that independence, and companies located outside major labor markets must anticipate their future skill needs and the cost of attracting talent away from other labor markets. Possible strikes and excessive wage demands can bring a company to a standstill.

Is the current labor force adequate both in size and competence? Is labor readily available? What is the employee turnover rate? Is labor organized, and if so, is it strike–prone? What current skills are required versus what future skills will be required? What is happening in labor-management relations in other similar and allied industries? Are new plants to be constructed in states with right-to-work laws? How acceptable to labor is new technology on the production line? What kinds of wage demands does management anticipate in the future? What kind of fringe benefits?

Financial Conditions

No scan would be complete without a thorough review of the financial status of the company, its financial needs, and the inevitable conflict between the financial expectations of the owners, management, and bankers.

What fundamental returns on equity do the shareholders require? How might this affect reinvestment in plant, equipment, or R&D? What are the financial policies with respect to debt-equity ratios and leveraging? How has current profitability compared with peer companies and industries? Is the dividend policy supportive of both shareholder and management requirements? What is the profitability by product line and geographic area of business?

Recently, one of the authors consulted with a large partnership that was concerned about lack of growth in revenues. The firm's management believed that the problem lay in an absence of marketing expertise. However, the real problem stemmed from the partners' greed in paying themselves too much at the expense of needed investments in new employees and product improvements.

FRAMEWORK
FOR ANALYSIS

There are two basic ways that consultants analyze the major planning issues facing a client: the *Inside/Out* and the *Outside/In* approaches. The Inside/Out approach centers around the notion that the consultant and management should place greater weight on the company's internal strengths and weaknesses so that they might be used to seek opportunities that support the strengths of the company and avoid its weaknesses.

The Outside/In approach takes a detailed look at the external environment (the economy, competition, and markets), so that external opportunities and threats can be specifically identified. Let us begin with the various types of Inside/Out approaches.

Gap Model

The Stanford Research Institute (SRI) several years ago developed a planning model known today as the *gap approach*. It focuses the client's ambitions by portraying its earnings objectives five, seven, or ten years out and then extrapolates the company's historical earnings trend to the same point. There invariably will be a gap between where the client wants to be and where its current operations and profits are taking the company. The planning process is the act of developing specific action steps to close the gap.

For example, if profits are currently growing at 5% per year, leading to $20 million pretax earnings seven years out, and management has stated that it should be earning $25 million pretax at the end of the seventh year, then the critical issue is to determine how the missing $5 million annual earnings can be captured before the seventh year.

Distinctive Competence Model

The business policy group at the Harvard Business School has developed an Inside/Out planning methodology that deals basically with a client's strengths, attempting to turn these virtues into new market opportunities. This approach requires the consultant to identify a client's strong points, along with its management's values, to pinpoint the client's "Distinctive Competence." What does the client do well that can be turned into a future advantage? Any new direction, of course, must be consistent with the values held by top managers.

For instance, if the client has an outstanding sales force and an extensive distribution network, then an additional new product might be easily "pushed" in the marketplace. Or if the client has a strong R&D group, it can be challenged to develop new products for a top management that has valued too long its old, established product line beyond rationality.

The Delphi Technique

Here the consultant pursues a broad range of macro issues of international and national purport with respect to the client's industry and markets, together with a list of detailed scenarios that might impact the company in any number of ways. The consultant then distributes the list of issues and asks individual managers to indicate their judgments on a seven-point scale as to the likelihood of each event's occurring (such as an international oil embargo), as well as the level of impact that such an incident would have on the company.

Everyone's questionnaire values are totaled and averaged to show the mean probability for each event. The consultant then distributes to the group its average scores, asking each manager if he or she would like to modify or change previous judgments on any of the issues. The result is a "growing consensus" on what events are most likely to affect the company and its strategic direction. Such a process, for instance, might have helped savings and loan associations to anticipate traumatic legislation that eventually allowed them to introduce checking accounts, but also permitted banks to pay interest on checking accounts.

Group Process Approaches

These models depend on heavy involvement by the client's managers in discussing and confronting strategic issues. The consultant acts more as a facilitator than as a content expert.

One of the best known group process approaches is the Mason–Mitroff *dialectic model* for surfacing management assumptions, followed by the creation of alternative strategies to be argued in front of the total management group. Mason and Mitroff use questionnaires and discussions to map out the diverse assumptions and opinions made by senior managers toward a variety of "stakeholders" in their environment. Through eliciting these different opinions and various alternate strategies, the consultant assists in an argumentative process. Senior management seeks to arrive at a consensus on the real issues and best alternatives.

STRENGTHS AND WEAKNESSES OF THE INSIDE/OUT APPROACH

The best results to be achieved from Inside/Out models occur when the working relationships of senior managers are close, candid, and mutually supportive. An open climate is necessary for a frank discussion of internal weaknesses that requires considerable hard, introspective analysis.

Inside/Out approaches are particularly useful when the client has not developed a sound strategic planning methodology. As mentioned earlier, many such companies are small and medium sized firms that are addressing strategic planning for the first time. For these managers to learn the rigors of strategic planning, a beginning self-analysis using an Inside/Out approach seems to be the best path.

Another argument for Inside/Out approaches is its value in causing a greater involvement by line managers in the planning process, an omission that occurs too often in the largest of companies where planning is delegated to a staff planning group. Sophisticated planning systems must also include the implementers.

The level of candor required for an Inside/Out approach can be undermined if the working relationships of the senior managers is already seriously strained. Perhaps the greatest deficiency of Inside/Out models is their overdependence on information provided solely by internal sources. Such data can be biased and myopic; hence, the consultant should be prepared to contribute his or her view of the outside world.

OUTSIDE/IN APPROACHES

A second set of methodologies, Outside/In models, places greater emphasis on the client's products and marketplace, with correspondingly less weight on internal considerations. Some of the better-known models are the *portfolio* approach, courtesy of the Boston Consulting Group (BCG), the *experience/curve* model via Arthur D. Little (ADL), and the *strategic business unit* model, compliments of McKinsey & Co. These models have been used with varying degrees of sophistication and success by some of the largest corporations in the world.

The Portfolio Model

This approach requires the consultant to develop a grid of boxes into which the client's various products or businesses are classified according to market share, profitability, and growth potential (see Figure 6-1 for the BCG classification scheme). Very simply, whatever ends up in the upper left-hand box is considered a "star" or "winner," and whatever ends up in the lower right-hand box is a "dog" or "loser." The upper right box is for "wildcats" with future potential but little current profitability, and the lower left box is for "cash cows" with high profitability but low growth potential. The "stars" should be exploited for some

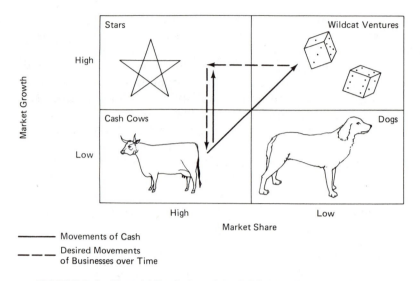

FIGURE 6-1   Pictorial Depiction of the BCG Classification Scheme

time to come, the "dogs" divested or shut down, and the "cash cows" used for feeding the "wildcats" and "stars."

The Experience Curve Model

This model works best with products whose manufacturing costs are a major part of total product cost. Simply stated, the experience curve is a method used to track the progress of the product from a high start-up cost and low earnings position toward an eventual standardized, routine, and low-cost production mode (see Figure 6-2). As production costs decline with higher volume, profitability is assumed to rise. This approach accepts a low margin currently to achieve a high margin in the future. Once maturity is reached, emphasis shifts to slowing the decline through product modification, and finally in the dying years, to milking the product for its last ounce of profit.

The Strategic Business
Unit Model

This model calls for the client to broaden its market concept for specific products as well as to add products that fit within the new concept. For example, AMF took its basic bowling equipment product and developed an approach that said, "We are really in the leisure-time industry." This led to diversification into all forms of sporting goods and

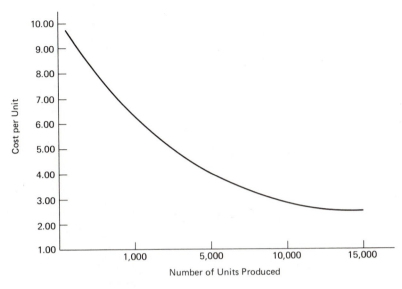

FIGURE 6-2   Experience Curve Model

equipment. The same approach has been used by United Airlines when it entered the freight hauling and hotel businesses and IBM as it moved into supplying an expanded range of office equipment for information and communications.

The PIMS Model

Some years ago, Strategic Planning Institute, formerly known as Strategic Resources Management, developed a computer modeling approach using marketing and financial data to determine the characteristics of a successful business in a given industry. The model is known as PIMS (profit impact of market strategy), and it has been used heavily by managements wanting to take a "what if" approach when reviewing projected changes to identify if their industry is sensitive to pricing variances or different types of promotions. Many major companies in a large number of industries subscribe to the PIMS program whereby they submit their company's financial and sales data to the PIMS model on a quarterly basis. The model, in turn, provides users with quarterly and annual industry statistics.

The Ansoff Model

Figure 6-3 shows a 57-variable model developed by Igor Ansoff. It may be the planning model to end all planning models. This approach

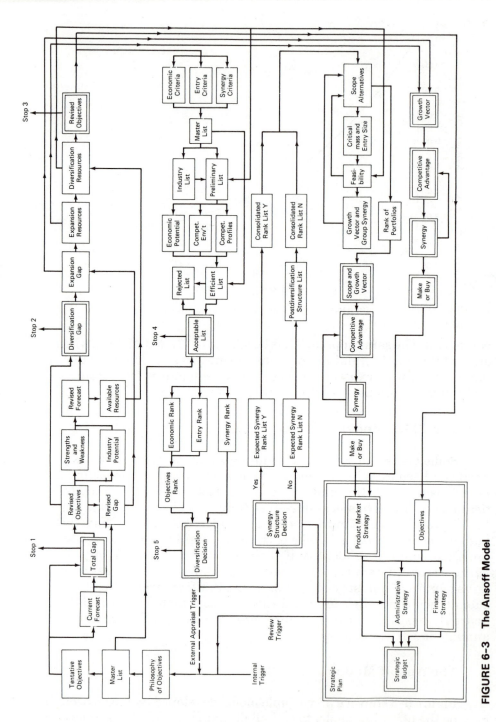

FIGURE 6-3 The Ansoff Model

Source: H. Igor Ansoff, *Corporate Strategy* (New York: McGraw-Hill Book Company, 1965).

requires management to walk through all the boxes in its decision-making process with respect to overall strategic objectives for each of its products and services. It is a complex and lengthy process that is more a checklist of critical questions to ask than a computer program for giving precise answers.

STRENGTHS AND WEAKNESSES OF OUTSIDE/IN APPROACHES

A recent *Fortune* magazine article entitled "Playing by the Rules of the Corporate Strategy Game," by Walter Kiechel III, reviewed many of the *Outside/In* models to cite horror stories from companies that tried them without achieving positive results.[1] Outside/In approaches are clearly not for everyone. While they are elegant, they can be extremely abstract and tend to oversimplify the issues in question. Such models can point out new marketing or financial opportunities, but there is little consideration for the inside strengths or weaknesses of the company and its management. Financial and marketing models do not test a company's ability to implement strategies that are different from past practices.

Outside/In approaches are probably most useful in companies whose planning is highly developed and whose financial information is sophisticated and that use the model not as an end but as a means to think differently and originally about their businesses.

OUR EXPERIENCE AND ADVICE

To the extent that the vast majority of companies do not know how to plan but survive from year to year, the need for strategic planning may seem questionable. Nevertheless, very few companies earn the profits they are capable of earning; still others stumble from crisis to crisis. It is easy for managers to overlook the fact that effective planning is a fundamental skill required by every organization.

Some managers can budget well without appreciating the need for long-range planning. Others are willing to address critical planning issues fearlessly but are not certain exactly what those issues are.

Many large companies go so far as to hire a full-time "corporate planner" to help their organizations. Unfortunately, the bright economists or young MBAs who act as "corporate planners" can easily be-

---

[1] Walter Kieshel, III, "Playing by the Rules of the Corporate Strategy Game," *Fortune*, September 24, 1979.

come trapped in the politics of the organization, especially when their immediate superior is someone other than the CEO. In such cases, they are doomed to failure. Because of the enormous impact that strategic planning can have on a company, the process must be started and supported fully by the CEO.

If, on the other hand, the consultant finds a CEO who is truly committed to strategic planning and who has the time and energy required for an intensive planning effort, a methodology that we use can be very helpful to small, medium-sized, and even larger companies. It is a group process model, primarily an Inside/Out approach according to Mason and Mitroff, that is particularly applicable to clients that do not have sophisticated, mature planning processes.

In our view, it is *not* the role of the consultant to plan for the client. The client must be led through a series of retreats and planning sessions to develop its own plan. The client must feel ownership. The consultant's role is to act as a resource in designing and moderating the planning sessions, and in providing new information to assure a more complete diagnosis by the executives.

As a first step, the consultant should prepare a complete analysis of the ten areas mentioned at the start of this chapter. This information should be scrutinized further in terms of the various models presented in the second section. No single model will provide "the answer," but one of them may be helpful for reducing the vast amount of scanning information to three or four critical issues.

At this point, the consultant is ready to involve the management in a series of presentations and probing discussions where it not only absorbs the knowledge provided by the consultant but goes beyond it to reach a level of consensus that will promote commitment to action. The following is a step by step account of how such sessions proceed.

Role of the Board of Directors

The board of directors is often an underutilized resource with respect to strategic planning, even though many of the directors are highly successful executives in their own, nonrelated companies. At an opening session with board members, we review our findings on the ten scanning issues discussed earlier in the chapter, and then we encourage a good deal of discussion and forward thinking.

For the most part, what we try to elicit from these board members is a broad range of opinions on future alternatives and performance parameters within which senior management can develop a more detailed long-range plan and strategy. Such sessions also help the directors to understand more about the pressures and burdens facing the CEO as well as the constraints under which senior management operates.

Invariably, out of such sessions comes a deeper understanding on the part of the individual board members as to what the corporation is really about, a greater respect for the CEO, and a clearer idea as to how the outside directors can help the company. Exhibit 6–1 is a summary report from one such meeting conducted by one of the authors.

Role of Senior Management

Once such a session with key board members has been completed, a similar but more pragmatic session can be held with senior management. The consultant should begin with the same report given to the board, after which the management group is asked to reach its own conclusions before hearing a report on the board's conclusions. In this way, it can find areas of agreement and disagreement to test further with the board.

Assuming that there is broad agreement on most issues (which is usually the case), the meeting can turn to formulating a specific plan of action. Long-range objectives should be developed in terms of financial goals, market targets, personnel needs, production requirements, and product development. Finally, a detailed plan of implementation is required that shows annual goals and assignments for those who must bring the plan to fruition. This last step is seldom completed at the retreat; rather, it is left for subsequent meetings of senior management, including discussions with the lower levels that will be affected.

Role of the Consultant

The most valuable role of the consultant in a group process approach to planning is that of facilitator. The consultant develops the agenda and subject matter to be covered. He or she assures that the discussion moves creatively toward the objectives of the retreat, steers discussion away from destructive political fights, but still encourages open debate. A strong attempt is made to assure that the less vocal are heard while the more aggressive do not dominate.

If the participants are well prepared, knowledgeable, and working together constructively, the consultant's role should be unobtrusive and not very participative. However, all too often, such sessions begin with long silences and irrelevant or paternalistic dissertations. Many senior managers, unsure of the role they should play or insecure in their being thrust up against new and threatening issues, look to the CEO to lead every discussion and resolve every issue. In such instances, it is the role of the consultant to be far more participative, to argue points for the sake of argument, and to ask various people for their opinions in an effort to break down political or emotional barriers to constructive, free thinking.

It is very difficult for one consultant to manage a retreat alone. The value of having more than one consultant present at these sessions is that, as one takes notes and monitors the agenda or discussion outline, the other is guiding the actual discussion, participating in the arguments, and watching the interactions between the participants.

Important is the need for good notes on what ideas and suggestions are made, by subject or area of responsibility. As these are documented by one consultant, the other can display the thoughts expressed on "flip chart" pages, which are then torn off and taped to the walls of the conference room. Following the sessions, the consultant should transcribe the notes into a memorandum to all participants that can be used later as an implementation guide and monitoring device to assure follow-up.

A further role of the consultant in strategic planning retreats is that of planner, matchmaker, conciliator, and arbiter. After the sessions break up in the evenings, it is the responsibility of the consultant to get opposing individuals together socially and apart from the group in an effort to resolve debilitating disagreements, to participate in follow-up conversations at dinner or over drinks as to what was discussed and decided that day, and to spend time alone with the client, usually the CEO, to ascertain if the meetings are up to his or her satisfaction. Intimate conversations with the CEO are important for relieving any tensions or frustrations that may have developed, as well as to do some coaching on his or her role in the next session. (That frequently means suggesting that the CEO shut up and let the other people talk.)

FOLLOW-UP

Once the goals and objectives of the company have been developed, the consultant can be of further assistance in assuring that the written and verbal conclusions from the session are, in fact, implemented. We begin with a top management meeting after the retreat to develop an "Action Assignment" list with agreed-to responsibilities for each member set within realistic time frames. Such a list is displayed as Exhibit 6–2.

Next, the consultant should work with each senior manager and his or her respective subordinates to infuse downward the goals and objectives and to return upward with a list of support and resource needs required to carry out these goals. The CEO, together with the senior officers, should then assign priorities and give support for those needs deemed essential.

This downward, upward, downward movement of ideas, plans, and needs provides a positive, dynamic set of interactions, which in turn gives a sense of purpose and direction to the company.

A consultant who is able to orchestrate these complex communications effectively has done a good job. He or she has revitalized and helped to create a supportive climate for everyone involved and has started the company off on a new road of accomplishment.

REPLANNING

Far too many clients think that, once they have a strategic plan, that's it! Yet market and economic factors change, as does the cast of executive characters. The only thing that should never change is the year-end objective, be it higher sales, greater profits, or the introduction of a new product. Interim factors leading up to that final objective can and do change, often several times during a fiscal year. Tactics are flexible, but objectives are sacred.

The consultant must help the client to comprehend what does change and what should not change. We recommend the use of quarterly review sessions where all the key managers give their input as to what is going well and what is problematic toward the achievement of annual objectives. From these observations, new tactics can be developed to still achieve year-end goals. It is this flexibility in tactics and inflexibility in objectives that are critical for moving a dynamic client off its historical path.

In addition to the quarterly review, the client should step back annually to review progress toward the long-term plan. Here it is legitimate to open up the overall strategic statement for reevaluation and even change. Are there any new developments in the client's external environment that demand a second look at the plan's viability? Did the first year go according to plan? If not, how can lost ground be made up in the second year? This type of preventive checkup should be conducted by the consultant until the management adopts it as a more routine habit.

RECOMMENDED READINGS

ANSOFF, H. IGOR, *Corporate Strategy: An Analytical Approach to Business Policy for Growth and Expansion.* New York: McGraw Hill, 1965.

BANKS, ROBERT O., and STEVEN C. WHEELWRIGHT, "Operations vs. Strategy: Trading Tomorrow for Today," *Harvard Business Review*, May/June 1979.

FELTON, SAMUEL M., JR., "Case of the Board and the Strategic Process," *Harvard Business Review*, July/August 1979.

HAMERMESH, RICHARD G.; M. JACK ANDERSON, JR.; and J. ELIZABETH

HARRIS, "Strategies for Low Market Share Businesses," *Harvard Business Review*, May/June 1978.

HAMERMESH, RICHARD G., and STEVEN B. SILK, "How to Compete in Stagnant Industries," *Harvard Business Review*, September/October 1979.

MASON, RICHARD O., and IAN I. MITROFF, *Challenging Strategic Planning Assumptions: Theory, Cases and Techniques*. New York: John Wiley & Sons, 1981.

McLEAN, EPHRAIM R., and GARY L. NEALE, "Computer-Based Planning Models Come of Age," *Harvard Business Review*, July/August 1980.

PAUL, RONALD N.; NEIL B. DONAVAN; and JAMES W. TAYLOR, "The Reality Gap in Strategic Planning," *Harvard Business Review*, May/June 1978.

PORTER, MICHAEL E., "How Competitive Forces Shape Strategy," *Harvard Business Review*, March/April 1979.

RAPPAPORT, ALFRED, "Strategic Analysis for More Profitable Acquisitions," *Harvard Business Review*, July/August 1979.

SCHENDEL, DAN E., and CHARLES W. HOFER, eds., *Strategic Management*. Boston: Little, Brown & Co., 1979.

STEINER, GEORGE A., *Strategic Planning*. New York: The Free Press, 1979.

THOMAS, DAN R. E., "Strategy Is Different in Service Businesses," *Harvard Business Review*, July/August 1978.

VANCIL, RICHARD, and PETER LORANGE, "Strategic Planning in Diversified Companies," *Harvard Business Review*, January/February 1975.

EXHIBIT 6-1 Consultants' Notes Following Up Board Policy Retreat

CHARLES, CRANSTON, KATO & KENT
CONSULTANTS TO MANAGEMENT
123 PROGRESS AVENUE
GOTHAM CITY, U.S.A.

Mr. N. O. Margin
President
The Bank of Disintermediation
Avarice Avenue
Depression, Delaware

CONFIDENTIAL

Dear N. O.,

Enclosed are the condensed notes from the Directors' Retreat.
These should be reviewed and amended as you see fit and copies
distributed to the members of the Board and selected members
of senior management. Please stress the confidentiality of
these notes.

The notes and the discussions held in Baltimore imply that there
is a great deal of follow-up work to be done. As a result, we
have developed a second, separate Action Assignments list for
you personally. It lists, in chronological order, the steps to
be taken as a result of the Retreat discussions and decisions.

At the same time, N. O., of these 20 odd Action Assignments,
there are several critical ones such as the development of a
performance bonus plan, a stock option plan, the drafting of a
detailed 5 year plan and the development of a detailed 1980
Profit Plan where we can be of great help to you and the bank
and should be intimately involved. I have placed an asterisk
next to these projects.

However, these projects will be time consuming and require a
great deal of work which would fall outside the limits of our
monthly fee agreement. On my next trip to Delaware, I would
like to discuss these projects with you.

Incidentally, it was a great Retreat!!

Best regards,

Nick Charles

Nick Charles
for CHARLES, CRANSTON, KATO & KENT

EXHIBIT 6-1   (cont'd)

CHARLES, CRANSTON, KATO & KENT

Consultants to Management

HIGHLY CONFIDENTIAL

The Bank of Disintermediation

Notes on the Director's
Long Range Planning Retreat

April, 1980

I.   LONG RANGE (5 YEAR) OBJECTIVES

By 1985:   Earnings Per Share: $10.00 Minimum
           Return on Average Assets: 1.00% Minimum
           Return on Equity: 17% Minimum
           Net Worth/Saving Ratio: 5.50% Minimum

II. STRATEGIES

A.   Financial

1.   To assure a stable work and planning environment
     and to protect morale at all levels in the bank,
     no tender offers will be entertained during the
     five year period of this plan.

2.   Based on this posture, it is assumed that no hostile
     offers will be made; however, in the event such an
     offer is made directly to shareholders, the President
     and C.E.O. is to form a task force to fight the offer.

3.   To reach the $10 per share earnings level, two things
     must occur. First, the bank will have to improve the
     "efficiency" of asset management as reflected by the
     Return on Average Assets. Second, the bank will have
     to expand, whenever feasible and realistic, its
     activities in the secondary loan markets and its real
     estate development activities.

4.   By so doing, the absolute growth rate of assets be-
     comes secondary. It is understood that the 20% per
     year growth rate will be difficult to maintain after
     1982 and an asset size of $100 Million plus; however,
     by "churning" assets more effectively, as conditions
     permit, profitability should improve.

EXHIBIT 6-1   (cont'd)

5. As a result, management should plan for continued rapid asset growth in the early years of the plan (1980-1982) and all profits should be reinvested in asset base expansion. It is recognized that a result of this will be a temporary weakening of the Equity to Deposit Ratio. In the later years of the plan (1983-1985) asset growth will be less important compared to improved profitability on an asset base larger than at present. In this way, while the improvement in Earnings Per Share may not be great in the early years of the plan, $10 per share is an acceptable objective by 1985, at which time the Equity to Deposit Ratio also will have improved.

6. At the same time, to strengthen the Board's ability to protect shareholders and the investment of their capital, the Board should expand its membership from 9 to 11. The two new members of the Board should be younger than the average age of the present Board and should have experience in evaluating real estate development and other similar investments. This added capability will, in turn, allow management the opportunity to research, develop and present additional development projects to the Board for approval.

7. Simultaneously, the following guidelines for management should apply to all proposed development projects:

    - The bank should stay within the statutory asset limitations at all times.

    - The project should have a turn-around time of not more than 18 months.

    - The project should have a premier location.

    - The bank is to obtain control (51%) of each project in the case of joint ventures.

    - The projects should be limited to the Dover "Metro" area.

    - Management is to assure accurate financial reporting on all projects proposed.

B. Marketing & P.R.

1. To support the financial objectives and the position of the Board, communications with the shareholders are to be improved. Specifically, a mid-year report should include a letter from the President or the Chairman outlining the Board's general philosophy.

2. The 1980 Annual Report is to be expanded both in financial and non-financial areas. It was felt that the best way to hold and improve shareholder loyalty is to keep shareholders well informed.

EXHIBIT 6-1   (cont'd)

3.   At the present time, the bank can best be defined as a
     small, Delaware institution with primarily ethnic sources
     of funds and primarily non-ethnic uses of funds.

4.   It is important for the bank to begin developing broader
     sources of funds and to develop a clearly identifiable
     image in the Delaware market as the fastest growing,
     most aggressive institution. It was felt that the bank's
     size and the implied safety of a larger institution is
     more appealing to the ethnic markets than the image of
     being an ethnic institution. In turn, the new image, as
     it develops, should provide the bank with a broader appeal
     to all segments of the Delaware market.

5.   This is in accordance with the bank's longer range
     strategy: to become a large Delaware institution.

6.   To support that position, all future branching is to be
     planned for and implemented in the greater "Metro" area
     of Dover, but not restricted to any one area such as the
     North East.

7.   Within three years or sooner, the bank is to establish
     its main branch and administrative offices in the down-
     town financial district. Realizing the difficulty in
     finding a good site, management should begin searching
     this year.

8.   At the same time, to support the planned profit levels,
     and to assure maximum return on assets, future branches,
     including the downtown main office site, should be leased
     whenever feasible.

9.   Further, management is to perform sale and lease-back
     analyses of two existing branches and present those
     findings to the Board by its July 1980 meeting.

10. The operating management of the bank must begin work on
     raising its image in the community through more involve-
     ment in community affairs, the United Way, Chamber of
     Commerce, etc. Further, the bank should consider hiring
     a well known "heavy" in the community to assist in busi-
     ness development and overall public relations, someone
     who could devote full-time to such activity.

C.   Deposit & Branch Operations

1.   As soon as possible, appropriate market research should
     be performed to evaluate existing branch markets and
     their potential, the overall effectiveness of the bank
     in its branch markets, the best opportunities for future
     branch locations, etc., and a report on the results of
     this research should be presented to the Board sometime
     later this year.

EXHIBIT 6-1 (cont'd)

2. As the branch savings solicitation force is developed, savings acquisition standards or goals should be set for each branch and the branch's viability should be measured against these standards.

3. To compete more effectively with the commercial banks and S&L's in Delaware, management should begin a program in product development commencing with a Telephone Funds Transfer (Cash Flow) service to attract commercial accounts.

4. The present feasibility for EFT products such as credit cards and telephone bill payment services should be tested with the DP Service Bureau, and if practical these products should be developed quickly also. Preliminary NOW account preparation should be made also.

5. The option on the adjacent land at 16th and Avarice Avenue should be used, if possible. That branch requires additional parking and drive-up facilities. An investment should be made to those ends.

6. During the present tight money situation, all members of the Board were urged to generate as much deposit activity for the bank as possible with their existing contacts.

D. <u>General & Administrative</u>

1. The Board recognizes the need to strengthen management further and an investment in addition, qualified personnel should continue to be made this year and next.

2. Further, to assure that the bank is able to retain and motivate its management and employees, the fringe benefits are to be reviewed and a proposal sent to the Board by the end of July 1980.

3. Management is to research the feasibility, also, of a performance based bonus program and a simple stock option plan for officers. These, too, should be presented to the Board sometime in 1980.

4. The monthly Board Report is to include a special page listing all development lots in inventory, sales, lot income and percentage of assets invested.

5. No change is to be made in the bank's current dividend policy.

6. Management is to develop a detailed 5 year plan before year-end 1980 for review by the Board.

7. The President is to develop and present to the Board proposed loan approval authority levels and operating and capital expenditure authority levels at the June meeting.

EXHIBIT 6-1 (cont'd)

8. The Board annually should schedule a full day meeting in January to review management's annual results of the prior year; and, to review and approve the profit plan for the year in question.

9. The Board annually should meet for 2 days in a Retreat environment to review basic strategies, long range plans and objectives and discuss indepth relevant issues for the future well-being of the bank.

E. Role of the Board

It was determined that the role of the Board of Directors should be as follows:

1. To assure the prudent investment of shareholder's capital.

2. To establish long range goals and financial objectives.

3. To review and approve the detailed annual profit plan as proposed by the Chief Executive Officer.

4. To review and evaluate annual performance results against long and short range objectives.

5. To establish senior management compensation and to review and approve stock options and bonuses as proposed by the Chief Executive Officer.

6. To review and approve overall compensation policy.

7. To review and approve loan approval and capital expenditure authority levels as proposed by the Chief Executive Officer.

8. To review and approve all routine loans on a statutory basis.

9. To appoint audit and salary review committees.

10. To develop additional business for the bank where feasible.

EXHIBIT 6-2   Consultants' Notes Following Up a Management Planning Retreat

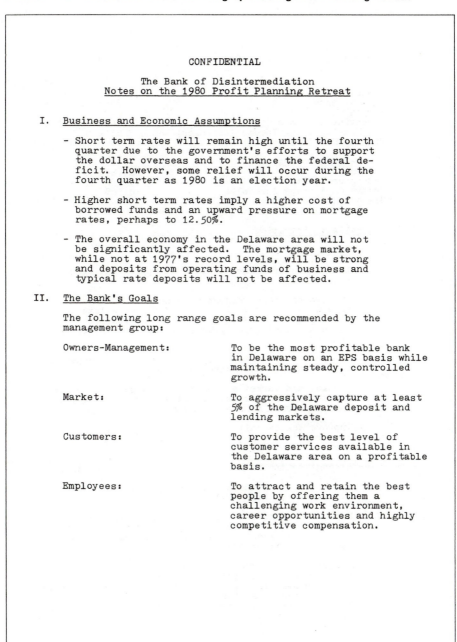

CONFIDENTIAL

The Bank of Disintermediation
Notes on the 1980 Profit Planning Retreat

I.   Business and Economic Assumptions

- Short term rates will remain high until the fourth
  quarter due to the government's efforts to support
  the dollar overseas and to finance the federal deficit. However, some relief will occur during the
  fourth quarter as 1980 is an election year.

- Higher short term rates imply a higher cost of
  borrowed funds and an upward pressure on mortgage
  rates, perhaps to 12.50%.

- The overall economy in the Delaware area will not
  be significantly affected. The mortgage market,
  while not at 1977's record levels, will be strong
  and deposits from operating funds of business and
  typical rate deposits will not be affected.

II. The Bank's Goals

The following long range goals are recommended by the
management group:

Owners-Management: To be the most profitable bank
                            in Delaware on an EPS basis while
                            maintaining steady, controlled
                            growth.

Market: To aggressively capture at least
                            5% of the Delaware deposit and
                            lending markets.

Customers: To provide the best level of
                            customer services available in
                            the Delaware area on a profitable
                            basis.

Employees: To attract and retain the best
                            people by offering them a
                            challenging work environment,
                            career opportunities and highly
                            competitive compensation.

EXHIBIT 6-2   (cont'd)

III.   Financial Objectives - 1980

	1980	1979
Gross Revenue ($000)	$5,884	$4,260
Cost of Money	3,836	2,681
Margin	2,048	1,579
Operating Expenses	(1,549)	(1,148)
Net Non-Operating Income (Expenses)	231	130
Pre-Tax Net Income	730	544
Tax Rate	33%	32.5%
After-Tax Earnings	489	367
Earnings Per Share	$4.24	$3.19
Return on Equity	16.75%	14.20%
Return on Average Assets	0.78%	0.76%
Net Asset Growth Rate	30.6%	29.2%

IV.   General Administration

A.   Strategies

- Maintain overall growth rate at approximately 30% per year.

- Improve earnings through more professional cash management and planning, expanded real estate lending and the development of an aggressive savings solicitation program throughout the branch network.

- Complete the staffing of the organization, especially in the savings and marketing areas.

- Develop and market at least one new savings service, telephone funds transfer, and one new lending product, property management loans.

- Improve the overall management skills through regular profit planning and monitoring meetings and greater delegation of authority.

- Strengthen the financial management and reporting capabilities through the recruitment of an experienced Chief Financial Officer (he is hired and will start in February).

- Expand the administrative support facilities to meet the requirements of a larger organization by locating and acquiring a new administrative headquarters for management.

- Review and evaluate overall management compensation and fringe benefit policies and procedures to assure that the bank is capable of attracting and retaining the best people available by offering them a challenging work environment and a highly competitive, performance oriented compensation program.

EXHIBIT 6-2 **(cont'd)**

B. <u>Action Assignments</u>

	Assignment	Whose Responsibility	Due Date
1.	Arrange commitments for additional borrowings from the Fed.	CEO	3 February
2.	Review loan packages for 1st Quarter loan purchases	CEO COO	3 February
3.	Obtain Board approval of the 1980 Profit Plan	CEO	15 February
4.	Review and evaluate potential of Commercial loan programs	CEO	15 February
5.	Recruit and hire a Senior Vice President, Operations	CEO	28 February
6.	Plan and organize annual stockholder's meeting	CEO	28 February
7.	Draft joint venture agreement outline for real estate development projects	CEO Sr. VP, Mortgage Lending	28 February
8.	File for branch office downtown	COO	28 February
9.	Calculate, prepare and mail dividend checks to stockholders	COO	15 March
10.	Develop and produce 1979 Annual Report	CEO	31 March
11.	Select site for new administrative headquarters	CEO	31 March
12.	Submit application for approval of new headquarters to the Fed.	CEO	31 March
13.	Locate secondary site for new headquarters should first choice be unavailable	CEO	31 March
14.	Apply for data communication lines for new headquarters	COO	31 March
15.	Hold Annual Shareholders meeting	CEO	30 April
16.	Organize and conduct first of the new quarterly employees meetings	COO	30 April
17.	Sell off the Broadway lot profitably	CEO	30 April

EXHIBIT 6-2   (cont'd)

Assignment	Whose Responsibility	Due Date
18. Organize and conduct Long Range Planning Retreat with Board of Directors	CEO	15 May
19. Organize and plan move to new headquarters offices	COO	30 May
20. Implement move to new administrative headquarters	COO	15 June
21. Determine solution for problem branch - redecorate or relocate	COO	30 June
22. Draft overall management compensation and fringe benefits policy and program for Board approval	CEO	31 July
23. Finalize overall organization structure and all position descriptions for Board approval	CEO COO	31 July
24. Review first six months 1980 performance against plan and replan where appropriate	CEO COO	31 July

V.   Operating Division

   A.   Strategies

     - Under the guidance of the new Senior Operations Officer, recruit and hire or promote from within, two and possibly three branch managers and reorganize the functions of all branch personnel to assure maximum efficiency and effective utilization of the branch network.

     - Develop a Telephone Funds Transfer or Cash Flow program as quickly as possible.

     - Reduce media advertising and direct the marketing budget toward product development, branch promotions and traffic builders, basic market research, branch employee training programs and the development of effective sales material and literature.

     - Aggressively penetrate the commercial deposits market in Delaware to obtain low cost, stable deposits on a consistent basis.

     - Increase net savings deposits to $57.5 MM from $45.5 MM by year-end.

EXHIBIT 6-2 (cont'd)

B. Action Assignments

Assignment	Whose Responsibility	Due Date
1. Develop and finalize position descriptions for the new organization of the Operations Division.	COO	31 January
2. Meet with all existing Branch Managers to review new organization of branch personnel and their functions and the overall 1980 strategies.	COO	15 February
3. Review and modify existing check cashing and withdrawal policies and procedures.	CEO COO	28 February
4. Appoint a Savings Administration	COO, Senior Operations Officer	15 March
5. Recruit and hire a secretary for the new Senior Operations Office.	Senior Operations Officer	15 March
6. Identify and recruit or promote two Branch Managers.	COO, Senior Operations Officer	31 March
7. Recruit or promote one new Branch Operations Manager.	Senior Operations Officer	15 April
8. Develop and implement Cash Flow product, operating procedures and marketing material.	COO, Senior Operations Officer	30 April
9. Review and evaluate viability of VISA or Interbank membership for merchant deposits.	COO, Senior Operations Officer	30 April
10. Review and revise, where appropriate, all existing marketing material.	COO, Senior Operations Officer	30 June
11. Develop and implement one new branch promotion scheme.	Senior Operations Officer	30 September
12. Develop new marketing material and brochures where needed.	Senior Operations Officer	30 September

EXHIBIT 6-2 (cont'd)

	Assignment	Whose Responsibility	Due Date
13.	Develop and implement cross selling training program for loan officers.	Senior Operations Officer	30 September
14.	Develop and implement branch personnel customer sensitivity training program.	Senior Operations Officer	30 September
15.	Develop and implement overall branch and savings division policy and procedures guide.	Senior Operations Officer, Savings Administration	30 September
16.	Develop overall plan and schedule for additional products and services development for 1981.	Senior Operations Officer	15 October
17.	Develop overall 1981 Marketing Plan and Budget.	Senior Operations Officer	15 November
18.	Present results of overall preliminary market research	Senior Operations Officer	30 November

VI. Lending Division

A. Strategies

- Expand real estate lending in government programs and in the $100,000 + single family residences.

- Sell $14,000,000 of loans on a minimum of break even to provide additional lending resources during 1980.

- Develop and market property improvement loan services to existing customers.

- Purchase $5,000,000 of loans from other institutions where profitable.

- Participate in commercial and construction loans in the Delaware market.

- Originate a total of $40 MM in new real estate loans.

- Expand lending services to the brokers and realtors by developing loan application services in the branches.

- Expand the training and accelerate the development of new loan officers.

- Review and clarify the functions and organization of the Loan Committee.

EXHIBIT 6-2 (cont'd)

B. Action Assignments

Assignment	Whose Responsibility	Due Date
1. Organize and promote broker/dealer contacts in the Town & Country area.	Senior Loan Officer	31 January and on-going
2. Develop and implement lending programs for the County and expand lending to the Avarice Avenue area.	Senior Loan Officer	15 February and on-going
3. Appoint a Loan Officer for the downtown area.	Senior Loan Officer	15 February
4. Develop and implement Loan Officer call standards and monitoring and evaluation procedures.	Senior Loan Officer	15 February
5. Review and restructure membership, role and authority of the Loan Committee and develop regularly scheduled meeting cycle.	CEO, COO, Senior Loan Officer	28 February
6. Complete reprogramming of the loan DP hardware.	Senior Loan Officer	28 February
7. Develop and implement consumer lending policy, procedures, documentation, forms, marketing program and promotional material.	Senior Loan Officer	28 February
8. Identify and appoint a second downtown Loan Officer.	Senior Loan Officer	15 March
9. Develop overall training program and schedule for all new loan officers.	Senior Loan Officer	31 March
10. Resolve the company car issue for the Appraisal Department.	Senior Loan Officer	31 March
11. Develop and implement VRM program and documentation for non-owner occupied property loans.	CCO, Senior Loan Officer	31 March
12. Develop appropriate construction inspection and draw down policy and procedures.	COO, Senior Loan Officer	31 March
13. Develop and distribute Facts Sheet program for brokers.	Senior Loan Officer	31 March

EXHIBIT 6-2   (cont'd)

	Assignment	Whose Responsibility	Due Date
14.	Hire and train one additional loan administrator.	Senior Loan Officer	31 March
15.	Identify broker needs with respect to broker services after the move to new head-quarters.	Senior Loan Officer	31 May
16.	Develop and implement loan application training program for branch personnel.	Senior Loan Officer	30 September
17.	Develop overall strategies and preliminary plans for Loan Division for 1981.	COO, Senior Loan Officer	31 October

VII. Finance Division

A. Strategies

- Strengthen overall financial reporting and accounting systems and methodology.

- Improve overall management reports.

- Develop systematic cash flow planning.

- Develop formalized investment management procedures.

- Review and revise overall liquidity policy and practices.

- Develop overall borrowings policy and practices.

- Borrow an additional $8 MM, of which $4.5 MM will be repaid by year-end 1980.

- Maintain an average yield on securities and cash of 10.0% during 1980.

- Reduce excess liquidity gradually from 10% to 7% by year-end 1980.

- Strengthen and develop overall the accounting personnel at the bank.

EXHIBIT 6-2   **(cont'd)**

B.   Action Assignments

Assignment	Whose Responsibility	Due Date
1. Debrief auditors.	CFO	1 February
2. Finalize 5 year financial extrapolation for Fed.	COO, CFO	1 February
3. Finalize 1980 Profit Plan and Cash Flow Forecast.	CEO, COO, CFO	13 February
4. Develop policy, procedures and methodology for Cash Flow and Investments Committee.	COO, CFO	28 February
5. Appoint Cash Flow and Investment Committee members.	CEO, CFO	28 February
6. Develop and implement Consumer Lending accounting and collection and billing procedures and policies.	CFO	28 February
7. Review all current accounting procedures and revise all accrual, deferment and depreciation methodologies and systems where appropriate.	CFO	31 March
8. Review and evaluate all accounting personnel and further personnel needs.	CFO	31 March
9. Develop and implement purchasing policy and procedures.	CFO	31 March
10. Evaluate and modify where appropriate all accounts payable policies and procedures.	CFO	31 March
11. Budget the costs and capital expenditure implications of the administrative headquarters move.	CFO	31 March
12. Review financial alternatives to the problem branch relocation and potential sale and lease back of other branch offices.	CEO CFO	30 April
13. Review and modify Real Estate Development Accounting procedures.	CFO	30 June
14. Review and modify all management and Board reports to coincide with the charts.	CFO	30 June

EXHIBIT 6-2 (cont'd)

	Assignment	Whose Responsibility	Due Date
15.	Develop annual operations and capital expenditures budgeting and planning methodologies and procedures.	CFO	30 September
16.	Review and modify where appropriate all DP/Finance interfaces and reports for overall and branch accounting.	CFO	30 September
17.	Prepare preliminary budget forecasts for 1981.	CFO	31 October

VIII. Operating Expense

The following estimates and assumptions were made with respect to operating expense in 1980:

Item	1980	1979	Assumptions
Marketing ($000's):	75	79	Shift from media advertising to sales material and promotions, new product development and market research.
Occupancy:	340	245	Includes expense projected to move one branch office and open new administrative headquarters.
General:	275	313	General inflation and expanded activities.
Miscellaneous Operating:	200	175	General inflation and expanded activities.
Payroll and Fringes:	659	439	(Includes 11 new people and three replacements and an average salary increase of 6% + during 1980.)
Total Operating Expense:	1,549	1,141	
As % of Gross Revenue:	26.3%	26.9%	

7

Marketing Assignments

Clients can design great products, but if they cannot reach their customers, or if potential buyers remain unconvinced to buy, then all is for naught. Marketing is an essential business discipline that tests the company's product or service against the customers' willingness to buy at a price that is not only acceptable to them but also generates an acceptable profit to the company.

Too many clients do not understand that marketing is a sophisticated, complex, and multifaceted business discipline. Effective marketing goes beyond mere selling techniques to include advertising, market planning, consumer research, product safety, packaging, distribution, pricing, and customer service.

It is the consultant's job to understand the basics of all these marketing techniques and to arrange them so that they reinforce each other in the marketplace. A well-coordinated marketing program that distinguishes successfully the client's product from the competition is the hallmark of successful companies.

TYPES OF MARKETING CONSULTANTS

Marketing assignments divide themselves rather clearly between the generalist diagnostician and the specialist implementer. The generalist provides an overview of the client's total marketing program to identify hidden problems and to chart a new set of marketing goals backed up by an integrated marketing plan. The specialist consultant, on the other hand, implements specific solutions in narrowly defined areas. Specialists are technicians who are highly skilled in such diverse areas as designing a new package or writing creative copy for advertising.

The following is a list of various activities performed by specialist consultants, none of which a generalist can ever master, although an awareness of them is essential for giving sound advice to a client on where to go next.

Market Research Services

- Consumer attitude studies
- Telephone and mail questionnaires
- Focus group research
- Market share analyses
- Competitive and industry studies
- Raw material supplier analyses
- Advertising impact
- New product test markets

Advertising Services

- Media selection and design
- Promotions
- Displays—from windows to shelves to branch offices
- Samples usage and distribution
- Premium program development
- Flyers and brochures design

Public Relations and Image Services

- Company names and logos
- Corporate image and message communications
- Government relations
- Industry, employee, and customer images

Sales and Sales Management Services

- Market definitions—local, regional, national
- Direct or indirect distribution

- Employee contests
- Sales force compensation
- Sales administration and information systems

Product R&D Services

- Packaging
- Pricing
- Design
- Safety
- Patents and licensing

In this chapter, we focus on the generalist approach to marketing assignments. A comprehensive and penetrating analysis by the generalist focuses the issues for managers and sets guidelines for detailed specialist work. Without this guidance the specialist may concentrate only on the symptoms of a deeper marketing problem. Clearly, some clients need a new image and logo design, but a superficial change in image will not motivate customers to buy a product that is unwanted or felt to be too expensive.

SYMPTOMS OF MARKETING PROBLEMS

The first classic symptom is declining market share. Clients begin to panic when a once-successful product loses its foothold in the market. Sometimes this decline is so gradual that it goes unnoticed until annual sales figures are published for the industry six to nine months after the fact. Also, the client can easily be deceived when unit sales are setting record highs, yet its relative percentage of industry sales may be slipping.

Slippage in market share, even when noticed quickly, offers no clue to determining the root cause of the problem. It could be due to high turnover in the sales force, poor product quality, the wrong media for advertising, or, the scariest problem of all, a competitor has built a better mouse trap!

Another common symptom is declining profits, even when sales are holding steady. The deeper cause of profit erosion, too, can be elusive. It may happen because of a gradual increase in the cost of raw materials without an accompanying increase in the price of the product. Or it may result from products returned by unhappy customers. The most ominous cause is market saturation, where it is costing more and more to attract the last remaining customer to the product.

A third set of symptoms appears with more subtlety, before numbers on the P&L statement confirm the problem. These signs usually appear in the form of "grumblings" from executives, sales personnel, or customers. It may be a sales manager's frustration with missed sales targets, or it may be an upsurge in customer returns, or it may be the best salesperson quitting. An alert consultant will pick up on these signs of frustration and probe behind them.

Case in Point

A client who manufactured a highly successful medical instrument suddenly began to detect signs of discontent from a previously motivated sales force. Several sales people had asked for transfers and others had requested an increase in their base salaries. One of the authors determined that the incentive scheme for sales personnel had begun to backfire. When the product was new, sales commissions were very high. Later, after the cream had been skimmed off the market, sales became more difficult, and commissions began to slip. The solution to the problem was exceptionally difficult to effect. An entirely new sales force had to be hired and trained— one that was motivated less by money and more by contact with medical professionals.

THE MARKETING AUDIT

Symptoms experienced by clients can, as noted previously, have a myriad of causes. Just how should the generalist begin probing to find the root problem?

We prefer to use a broad approach called the *marketing audit*, which looks at all facets of the client's marketing program. The audit can be sold as a "package" to the client as a means for assessing its total marketing effort, or the audit may be used by the consultant as an informal checklist when trying to dig behind superficial symptoms. Its value lies in a comprehensive investigation that leaves no stone unturned. Exhibit 7-1 presents a systematic approach to a marketing audit, prepared by Professor L. E. Gill of the University of Southern California. Typical questions guiding such an audit include

- Is there a true marketing strategy, understood fully and communicated throughout the company?
- Is there a long-range marketing plan and is marketing included in major planning decisions?
- Does the client have a sound understanding of who the customers are, and, more important, who are not customers and why? Has the client performed a target market analysis?
- Has the client identified all its possible markets and estimated their potential?

- Can the client objectively compare what it is doing with the products and services of competitors?
- Has the client tested the validity and competitiveness of its pricing?
- Does the client use the most appropriate advertising media to reach the customer?
- Is the advertising message imaginative and clear; does it differentiate successfully the product from the competition?
- Are advertising and other promotional methods tested for cost effectiveness and results?
- Is the product designed and packaged in a way that will attract the customer?
- Is the product distributed in the most efficient, cost-effective manner? Are there any distribution channel conflicts?
- Do the selling skills required to market the product exist in the company and, if not, what training and development is required to achieve the necessary skill levels?
- Is the sales force well managed in terms of control, evaluation, and coaching? Does the compensation system motivate and reward high performance?
- How much customer service is needed versus what is applied and at what cost?
- Does the client use market research, does it ask the right questions to the appropriate audiences, and how is research data used?
- Is the client aware of product obsolescence and is there effective R&D work toward new products? Has a product life-cycle study been done?

These questions are related to four key areas of investigation that must concern the generalist consultant continually. The client's total marketing program should be examined for its

1. Overall marketing strategy
2. Product features
3. Delivery systems to reach the customer
4. Customer buying characteristics

The first area to investigate is marketing strategy, which centers on the client's plans and objectives for establishing a successful niche in the marketplace. What is the client's basic posture in the market—is it as a follower or as a leader? Does this strategy call for high quality and high price, or is it striving toward large volume at a low price? How well has the marketing strategy been realized in past results? What is the actual profitability and market share on the product in question? Were these results above or below the plans of management? What future changes, if any, does management contemplate in its market strategy? What strategies are being pursued by the competition? What is the growth rate of the total market and its saturation level?

Next, the consultant should examine critically the product itself.

How well is it designed and packaged? What is its quality, reliability, and safety? How does it compare with similar products made by the competition? How is the product manufactured and what is its manufacturing cost? What warranties or guarantees does the client offer on the product? What R&D changes are being planned for the product, and what innovations are likely to come from the competition?

Third, a careful analysis should be made of the buyer for the product, both in terms of current purchasers and potential customers. How, where, and why do present customers purchase the product? What are their characteristics—by age, sex, location, and income? Do they buy on impulse or is the purchase planned? Are they satisfied with the product? What changes would they like to see made? What potential customers are not being reached? What are their characteristics and how is their buying motivation different from that of current customers?

Finally, there is the relative effectiveness of the delivery system being used by the client to reach the final customer. Is the product priced competitively? Is the right advertising media being used? What are the merchandising and promotion methods used to attract the potential buyer? Are distribution channels set up to move the product efficiently to the marketplace? Is the sales force managed and motivated properly by its leadership and compensation? Does an effective information system exist for processing orders and monitoring results?

The marketing audit helps not only to detect new problems but also to test for the "fit" between the four broad areas just discussed. For example, the client's product may be packaged attractively yet be overpriced. Or its customers may be asking for the product due to an effective advertising campaign, but the distribution system contains bottlenecks. Or the client's marketing strategy may be calling for growth targets that are unrealistic for a product recently made obsolete by a competitor's innovation. Exhibit 7–2 provides an example of an actual marketing audit prepared for a client by one of the authors.

DATA-GATHERING TECHNIQUES

To answer questions raised in the marketing audit, as well as in other types of marketing studies, the consultant must seek valid sources of data to describe and explain the client's problem.

One method is to perform a market research study through questionnaires and in-depth interviews. Except for major consumer goods companies, such as Procter & Gamble, few companies utilize sophisticated marketing research to learn the "facts" about their market or customers. Particularly relevant is a customer profile study that defines the demographic characteristics of the "average" customer, determines why they buy the product, and assesses their subsequent reactions to it. Without such information, the client is flying blind in its decisions about pricing, packaging, and advertising.

Case in Point

A bank was perplexed as to why its share of the mortgage lending market was shrinking. One of the authors, through a customer profile study, discovered that the "true" customer was not the home buyer but the real estate agent who guided the home buyer to a source of financing. Interviews with the real estate agents revealed that the bank, despite its fine institutional reputation, possessed the slowest loan approval system in town. Realtors were motivated to seek approval elsewhere to close the deal rapidly and receive their commissions. The study's findings helped the bank not only to identify its customers but to speed up its lending approval procedures.

A second technique is field observation; it requires the consultant to leave the client's headquarters and go sightseeing in the marketplace. After all, it is out there at the intersection between customer and product where top management's beliefs are either verified or refuted. Firsthand observation helps to determine what happens when the salesperson approaches a potential customer, or when the customer examines competing products on the store shelf.

Case in Point

One of the authors was hired by a bank to discover why, after enormous outlays in advertising, its new statewide service to cash customer's checks quickly and easily in any of its 115 branches was a complete flop. After pursuing a lot of deadends in interviews with top bank officials, the author decided to take a couple of days off to visit several branch offices. To his surprise, he found that there was no common logo, or color, or architecture to distinguish many of the branches, several of which had been acquired recently. Customers could not "see" the bank's branches and thus had no inkling as to just how convenient the new check-cashing service could be for them.

A third technique, conducted back at the client's headquarters, involves a close examination of its marketing information system. All too often the data to answer the problem at hand are buried under the client's nose in the form of past reports gathering dust in a file drawer. The consultant should analyze all available statistics on the product. Sales and profit information should be broken down not only by each product line but also by market territory and by expense items contributing to each product's total cost. The client may be enamored with total sales and profits without understanding that certain product lines are real losers.

Case in Point

A dress manufacturer was concerned about a slow growth rate in sales and profits, which was resulting in a decline in market share. Data supplied by the sales manager revealed that the bulk of customers were small specialty stores where each order size was small and consequently the cost of making that sale was high. In contrast, sales to a few major department store chains were much larger in order quantity, with greatly reduced selling expenses because of greater knowledge by the buyer and more rapid payment of invoices. The problem was solved by redirecting the sales force toward major department store chains. A mail-order system was introduced for smaller stores.

COMMON CLIENT MISTAKES

Over the years it has been possible for researchers and consultants to categorize the mistakes made most frequently by companies in their marketing programs. In turn, models and techniques have been developed for solving these problems as well as for educating the client on how to avoid similar miscues in the future.

1. *The Mix Problem.*   We have already alluded to this issue wherein the client focuses on one element in the marketing mix, such as advertising, which is expected to carry the full burden of a marketing program. In contrast, an effective program is built around a combination of elements called the marketing mix (product design, pricing, packaging, promotion, advertising, sales force management, and customer service). Each element is interwoven with the others to create a "reinforcing" effect on the customer's purchase decision. Every company will differ in its mix because of the uniqueness of its product and the particular niche it is trying to fill in the marketplace. The marketing mix for Wheaties is obviously different from the mix for Avis rental cars.

2. *The Segmentation Problem.*   Strong marketing programs are built around knowing exactly the personal characteristics of the ultimate buyer. Too many companies try to be all things to all people. Instead, it is important to segment the market into different buying groups and then to develop a special program or "mix" to reach each group. General Motors knows that the customer for a Chevette is unlikely to be the same customer for a Cadillac; the former is interested in price and economy, whereas the latter is concerned with comfort and luxury. The potential Chevette buyer may be an office worker commuting from the suburbs; the Cadillac customer could be a partner in a law firm or a real estate salesperson.

3. *The Product Life-Cycle Problem.*   Products are born, mature, and die, and each of these stages requires a different marketing strategy or "mix." Unfortunately, many clients do not realize the growth stage of

their product and as a result are holding onto obsolete strategies. A key concept in the beginning stage of a new product is to treat marketing expenses as an "investment," where costs may exceed immediate profits. Stingy clients who are trying to make an immediate profit from a new product are not likely to succeed over the longer term. On the other hand, when a product has saturated the market and is in its decline, management's attention should turn to price cutting and product refinements, such as "The *New* Ivory Soap at 10¢ Off."

4. *The Push-Pull Problem.* Certain products require a "hard sell" to push them in front of the consumer, whereas others are sought out by the consumer after a "soft sell." Clients waste a lot of marketing money without understanding whether their products require "push" or "pull" strategies. For example, a "push" product is soft drinks where constant advertising on radio is needed to remind the customer that active young people all drink X-Cola. Conversely, the purchaser of a computer is making a planned purchase where jingles on the radio are inappropriate. Here it becomes more critical to develop brochures with extensive information and to hire a professional sales force to contact the customer, answer questions, and demonstrate the product.

5. *The Psychological Set Problem.* Consumer research has demonstrated amply that customers have tunnel vision when making purchases. The prospective purchaser of a sailboat is more likely to read magazines on sailing than to look for a catamaran in *Vogue*. Clients should not suffer from the illusion that they can easily change the psychological set of potential customers. Instead, through market research, they should tailor a marketing campaign to fit the preexisting mentality of their consumers. Eyeglass frames, for example, will be selected from a display in an optical store, not from a TV advertisement. Or new rock records must be played on stations listened to by the under-25 crowd in large urban areas, not on pop music stations in the countryside.

6. *The Brand Extension Problem.* Many clients run into marketing problems because they do not stick with what they know best. Hence, they fail to capitalize on what the customer knows best about them. Heinz has built an image as a quality manufacturer of food products, an image it can extend to all types of foods. But when a client attempts to move from the mirror business to computer keyboards, as we once saw in a client, a red flag is raised. IBM made the transition from computers to office products and Yves St. Laurent from women's fashions to men's toiletries, all by establishing a quality reputation within a broadened concept of enhancing personal attractiveness.

7. *The Salesperson as a Professional Problem.* Probably the most overlooked and badly handled marketing issue among clients is the development of a competent and professional sales force. Too many

companies treat their sales personnel as "out of sight and out of mind." Yet for many clients, this is where the final and most important transaction takes place in the marketing chain of events. A poorly trained and unmotivated salesperson will talk the customer out of a product.

It is essential for many clients to revise their thinking in ways that treat the salesperson as a professional—not as an underpaid order taker or a dispensable gypsy. The concept of "professional" means a career ladder where sales personnel can visualize a lifetime career with advances in pay, knowledge, title, and responsibility—all within the sales function and without becoming a sales manager.

Case in Point

A pharmaceutical client of ours once experienced high turnover among its sales force because advancement depended on managerial skill, which many of them lacked or did not want to develop. Hence, a new career development program was designed to permit, and even encourage, sales personnel to remain in sales to the point where outstanding producers could earn more than their managers.

FALSE MARKETING ISSUES

A decline in sales or a loss in market share does not automatically mean that the problem lies in the marketing domain. Surprises are abundant if the consultant maintains a wide and vigilant eye. Clients may think that you are crazy for looking down side roads, yet that is the forte of the generalist consultant.

Case in Point

A client in the metals distribution business saw its account base slipping and decided to begin an intensive campaign for soliciting new accounts. Goals were set for each salesperson and special incentives were offered. However, after six months into the program, results were far below expectations. An initial appraisal by the consultant indicated that nothing was wrong with the planning of the program. Then one day the consultant happened to be passing the desk of one salesperson. "How's it going?" she asked. "Fine," was the reply. The consultant inquired further, "Why are you at your desk typing all that paperwork instead of being out of the office looking for new accounts?" The employee's reply was, "Oh, I can't possibly make any more calls for a couple weeks because of the paperwork required by our accounting department. I've landed several accounts with big orders, but the accounting department needs all kinds of forms for credit checks and inventory control." The solution was fairly straightforward— new accounts administration was reassigned from the sales force to the branch clerical staff.

As a generalist consultant wearing your marketing hat, don't let yourself become boxed in by complete immersion in designing ad copy for the client. Specialists can perform that service. Your value is to be sure that marketing symptoms are not spurious issues for other problems.

Case in Point

One of the authors was asked to determine why a manufacturer's sales force wasn't doing better in its marketplace. In particular, the client asked if sales goals were set too low or if the compensation program lacked incentive? While charging after these two issues could have generated large consulting fees, it would not have solved the problem. After interviewing several salespeople and finding no particular issue, the consultant decided to interview some customers. Here the finger was pointed clearly at customer service. Ineffective customer service for repairs and parts replacement had caused a tapering off of repeat orders. Further investigation revealed that customer service reported exclusively to the manufacturing department. An immediate change was made to establish a customer service liaison between the marketing and manufacturing department.

Lack of sophistication in the marketing area can make the client overly dependent upon the knowledgeable consultant. In turn, the opportunistic consultant may see the client's marketing naiveté as a gold mine for future business. However, the consultant should resist the temptation to become the client's surrogate marketing manager. If the client's marketing needs are ongoing and if the client lacks skilled marketing personnel, the eventual solution lies with an executive search firm, not with a greedy consultant.

RECOMMENDED READINGS

BALLOU, RONALD H., *Basic Business Logistics*. Englewood Cliffs, N.J.: Prentice-Hall, Inc., 1978.

BREEN, GEORGE E., *Do-It-Yourself Market Research*. New York: McGraw Hill, 1977.

CHASE, RICHARD B., "Where Does the Customer Fit in a Service Operation?" *Harvard Business Review*, November/December 1978.

GREEN, PAUL, and DON S. TULL, *Research for Marketing Decisions*. (4th ed.). Englewood Cliffs, N.J.: Prentice-Hall, Inc., 1978.

JACKSON, BARBARA B., and BENSON P. SHAPIRO, "New Way To Make Product Line Decisions," *Harvard Business Review*, May/June 1979.

KOTLER, PHILIP, *Marketing Management, Analysis, Planning and Control* (4th ed.). Englewood Cliffs, N.J.: Prentice-Hall, Inc., 1980.

LEVITT, THEODORE, "Marketing Success Through Differentiation—of Anything," *Harvard Business Review*, January/February 1980.

MARCUS, BURTON, et. al., *Modern Marketing Management* (rev. ed.). New York: Random House, 1980.

PAUL, RONALD, "When Does Your Company Need Help from Marketing Research Consultants?" *Industrial Marketing*, vol. 63, no. 8 (September/October 1979).

Resnik, Alan J.; Peter B. B. Turney; and J. Barry Mason,   "Marketers Turn to 'Countersegmentation'," *Harvard Business Review*, September/October 1979.

Shapiro, Benson P.,   *Sales Program Management: Formulation and Implementation.* New York: McGraw Hill, 1977.

Washburn, Stewart S.,   "Salesmanship—The Time-Is-Money Game," *Sales & Marketing Management*, vol. 116, no. 4 (March 8, 1976).

Wright, John S., et. al.,   *Advertising* (4th ed.). New York: McGraw Hill, 1977.

The following marketing analysis checklists may help you to consider the key points in a marketing analysis plan. The lists are not exhaustive, to allow for your creativity and resourcefulness, but are suggestive of types of factors that you should consider.

User of the Product—Target Markets

1. What types of consumers will use the product? Why?
2. What are the important segmentation bases (demographic, geographic, benefits, etc.)?
3. How many potential customers are there (by state, region, trading area, etc.)?
4. What factors limit the size of the total market?
5. Where do the potential customers live?
6. Will the estimated price of the product meet the requirements of the logical prospects?
7. Will the price of the product compare favorably with existing products of this kind and with similar products that may be introduced shortly?
8. What is the present consumption pattern of products of this type?
9. Will the market for this product be likely to change in size during the next two, five, or ten years?
10. How often will consumers buy this product?
11. Will the product sell evenly throughout the year or will the bulk of sales be concentrated at certain seasons?
12. What features of the product appeal most to consumers?
13. What are consumer prejudices, if any?
14. On what terms are products of this kind usually bought by consumers?
15. Does the product have possibilities for industrial, consumer, governmental, export use?

Demand

1. Emerging?

   Long-term growth potential?
   Short-term, fad item?

EXHIBIT 7-1 (cont'd)

2. Established?

   Growth market?
   Staying the same, saturated, or limited?
   Declining?

3. Not determined?

   May develop in the future?
   Must be promoted?

Competition

1. Who are the major competitors that the product will face? What competing products are substitutes for the product?
2. What is the reputation of competitive firms and brands?
3. Are manufacturers likely to enter the field with products similar to this one?
4. Can any competitor bring out a seriously competitive item quickly?
5. Will the marketing of the product cause competitors to give additional or keener competition on established products?
6. How does the company stand in relation to competitors in the field to be served by the new product?
7. With regard to the company's standing or lack of reputation in the market for the new product, is it best to trade on the company name in introducing the product, or would it be easier and more satisfactory to build up a separate name for the product?
8. Can the product compete favorably with similar products already on the market? What advantages does it have?
9. To what degree does nonproduct competition exist for the item (e.g., commercial laundries versus washing machines)?
10. How do competitors operate (policies, distributors, etc.)?
11. Is the field overcrowded?
12. Do leading firms dominate the market? Do they have their share of the market locked up?
13. Do competitors have natural advantages?

    Location?
    Product line strength?
    Lower costs?
    Outstanding reputation?
    Patents?

EXHIBIT 7-1 (cont'd)

Control channels of distribution?
Technology or manufacturing advantages?

The Market Opportunity

1. Who are the potential customers for our products?

    By industry classification?
    Target markets (socioeconomic, life cycle, etc.)?

2. How many actual versus potential customers are there?

    By region?
    By state?
    By trading area?
    By type?

3. What is the potential sales volume?

    Dollar volume?
    Units?
    Break-even volume?

4. What market share can we get (potential sales volume less volume sales to substitute products less competitors' share of market)?
5. What effect does the overall level of economic activity have on demand?
6. Can total demand be stimulated (increase total market) or can business be diverted from competition?
7. What is the nature of the buying decision (individual, family, group)?

Marketing Research

1. What is the exact purpose of the research? What decisions do we need to make, and what data do we need to make these decisions?
2. Is a thorough search of secondary sources being conducted before primary research is begun?
3. Which research method is best to gather the needed data (observation, experimentation, survey)?
4. If a survey is required, which survey method is best (telephone, mail, personal)?
5. Has careful attention been given to questionnaire design?

    Types of questions (open ended, close ended, projective)?

EXHIBIT 7-1 (cont'd)

Sequencing of questions?
Guided interview?

6. What is the sampling plan?

Who?
How many?
How selected?

Product

1. Why would customers buy our products and/or services?

   What usage and performance features are important to them?
   Styling? Colors? Versions?
   How much is it needed? How will the customer use it?
   What are the customers' buying practices? Is the product a convenience, shopping, or specialty good?
   What quality should be engineered into the product? Effect on price?
   Why is the product better than competing products?

2. Are service, warranty, and application advice an integral part of the product's value?
3. Can our product be copied easily? Is patent protection available?
4. How will we manufacture the product? Make or buy? What is the expected per unit cost of manufacture or acquisition?
5. What is the expected impact of introducing this product on the remainder of our product life? Complement? Direct sales from other products?
6. Where are our other products and/or services in their life cycles?
7. How shall the product be packaged?

   Package form, shape, function?
   Protection?
   Information?
   Secondary use?

8. What brand policy should be adopted (no brand name, individual brand, family brand, brand extension, etc.)?

EXHIBIT 7-1 (cont'd)

Channels of Distribution

1. Through what channel or channels are consumers accustomed to buying products of this kind? What are our traditional channels for present products?
2. Is there any reason for using channels other than these?
3. Assuming that the product is to be distributed through retailers, what kind of retail stores will sell it? What degree of exposure is required?
4. What information has the company about the operation of this type of retailer? What are traditional discounts required?
5. What percentage of total sales volume in this field is done by independent stores, corporate chains, voluntary chains, manufacturer-owned chains, consumer cooperatives, and others?
6. On what basis do competitors usually sell products of this kind to retailers (exclusive franchise, selective distribution, or general distribution)?
7. What is the best and most economical method of selling to these retailers? Direct? Indirect?
8. How many wholesalers, jobbers, or other intermediate distributing organizations are there that can handle the product logically? What discounts or commissions are traditionally paid?
9. What is the best and easiest method of selling to them?
10. What policies are important to the selected channels?

   Discounts or commissions?
   Territory agreements (selective or exclusive distribution)?
   Channel support (cooperative advertising, point of purchase displays, etc.)?

11. Who is likely to be the controlling factor in the channel of distribution?

Physical Distribution

1. By what means will we move our products to our customers (direct, through wholesalers, through distribution centers, etc.)?
2. What transportation modes are appropriate? Costs?
3. What inventories will be required? Where stocked? By whom?

Promotional Mix

1. What is our firm's "image"?

EXHIBIT 7-1 (cont'd)

Are we known in the industry?
What do our customers think of us?
What do our customers think of our products?

2. What are our promotional strategies?

Introductory, growth, reminder, etc.?
Desired audience?
Push or pull?
Direct or indirect action?
Consistent with marketing strategy?

3. What types of promotion are likely to be required for this product?

Media advertisements?
Catalog and catalog sheets?
Trade shows?
Brochures?
Promotional and dealer aids?
Point-of-purchase displays?

4. What level of personal selling is required?

Complicated product function?
Hidden features or values?
Industry practice?
Nature of buyers?
Nature of competition?
Negotiations required?

5. Can the existing sales force handle the new item without harming the sale of other products? What additional costs will be incurred? Could manufacturing reps or agents be used instead of our own sales force?

6. Will any changes in the sales department be necessary to handle the new product? How is the department organized (product, territory, customer basis)? What types of sales representatives are needed (order takers, creative, etc.)? How will the sales force be compensated?

7. If a separate sales force is required, how many salespersons will be needed, what type must they be, will they require special training? What will the cost be for these employees? Who will supervise the sales force?

8. What are the goals of advertising?

Target markets to be reached?
Intended impact or effect on target market?

EXHIBIT 7-1 (cont'd)

9. Does the present advertising agency have experience with products similar to the new product?

10. What are the details of the advertising program (message design, method of presentation, selection of media, timing, layout of advertisements or commercials)?

11. What are the general sales promotion practices followed by distributors in this product line?

12. What are the sales promotion and advertising practices of other manufacturers in the field?

13. What type and how much sales promotional assistance will be given the company's sales force?

14. Is a publicity campaign (as distinguished from advertising) to be used to help make the new product familiar to the public?

15. How will the promotion and advertising budget be determined (objective build-up, percentage of sales, competitive parity, etc.)? How much promotion is required? How should the budget be allocated among the alternative promotional mix tools?

Pricing

1. What is the general price range for the product?

   What proportion of our selling price is our direct manufacturing cost?
   Has this percentage been changing?
   How many units must we sell to break even?
   What price will maximize profits?

2. Does our price reflect product quality? Is it consistent with our marketing mix?

3. Are prices of competing products increasing, decreasing, or remaining constant?

4. What will be the impact of the product's price on our other products?

5. Does the opportunity for selling related products or follow-on sales improve our profits?

6. In general, what will be the price policy on this product (one price, flexible, skimming, penetration, etc.)? How will this change during the product life cycle?

7. Can we differentiate price on the basis of product features? Do product costs of features match values of features to the users?

8. What will the schedule of discounts and allowances be for various classes of customers (retail, wholesale, and ultimate)?

EXHIBIT 7-1 (cont'd)

9. Considering the trade custom in the field of the new product, what is the policy to be with respect to pricing (FOB point, credit, cash, and functional discounts, returned goods, consignment, order cancellation, damaged or unsatisfactory goods, resale price maintenance, etc.)?

10. Have insurance and transportation costs as well as costs of manufacture and selling been considered in determining price? What geographical pricing policies will be used (FOB, zone, delivered, basing point, etc.)?

Legal and Related Problems

1. Is the new product patentable?

2. Is its trademark protected?

3. Are all claims to royalties or other indemnities settled?

4. Do royalties limit the market for the product?

5. Is there anything in the product, its labeling, or advertising that may cause the company to become involved in a possible violation of a federal, state, or local statute or ordinance?

6. Is the nature of the product such that regulations, trade agreements, and the like may restrict or prohibit its sales in certain areas?

7. Is there anything in the company's pricing policies, trade practices, or selling set-up that might involve a violation of federal, state, or local statutes or ordinances?

8. Have local licensing and tax problems been considered?

9. Has a determination been made as to how the product should be prepared for shipment?

10. Will it be desirable to insure the product while in transit to market?

11. Are there any special regulations that affect the product?

12. Are there any labor or union regulations that might affect the manufacture or distribution of the product?

13. Are there other problems peculiar to the product that should be considered?

EXHIBIT 7-2 Detailed Marketing Analysis

Charles, Cranston, Kato & Kent
Consultants to Management

DETAILED MARKETING ANALYSIS

City Savings has, in recent years, experienced a deterioration of
its savings market share. The purpose of this review is to identify the reasons for this decline in market share and to recommend
an approach for reversing this unfavorable trend. Our analysis
is organized under four headings:

    A. Description of this Problem

    B. Specific Reasons for Loss of Market Share

    C. General Evaluation of Marketing Activities

    D. Recommendations

A.   Description of the Problem

Market Share Decline - City's savings performance for 1976 - 1980
is summarized in the following table:

Table 7

	S. Carolina S&L Savings (millions)	CS Market Share	Fidelity Market Share
12-31-76	$ 599	28.6%	18.2%
12-31-77	659	28.9%	18.9%
12-31-78	811	28.2%	19.7%
12-31-79	1,033	27.5%	20.3%
12-31-80	1,193	26.8%	20.7%

EXHIBIT 7-2   (cont'd)

These figures show that City's market share increased from 1976
to 1977, but has declined since then. Further, it is clear that
other, small but more aggressive associations such as Fidelity,
while they do not have the extensive, state-wide branch network
held by City, have, nevertheless, expanded their market share at
City's expense.

Had the association been able to maintain its market share at
least, savings deposits at December 31, 1980 would have been
$345 million, some $25 million more than was the actual case.
Those $25 million in deposits have gone to other institutions
and it will take extraordinary efforts to get them back.

Account Growth - The following table shows savings account
growth from 1978 - 1980.

Table 8

	1978	1979	1980
Number of Accounts	8.86%	7.5%	3.9%
Average Balances	9.2 %	8.9%	6.8%

These figures reveal an interesting dimension to the savings problem, since most associations have experienced marked increases
in both number of accounts and the average balance during this
period. It appears that City not only experienced a very low
growth rate in number of accounts, but also failed to induce
depositors to add significantly to their existing accounts.

EXHIBIT 7-2 (cont'd)

B.   Specific Reasons For Loss of Market Share

The fact that City's market share was on an upward trend for
several years prior to 1977, and took a definite turn at that
time, raises the question, "What specific events took place
since 1977 that caused City to lose savings to its S&L competitors?" In this section, we will identify the specific factors
which we believe caused the recent market share reversal. In
the next section, we will evaluate a broader range of marketing
activities which generally impacted City's loss of market share.

Based on our analysis, we believe that the specific reasons for
City's loss of market share are as follows:

1.   City's Lending Policies

   It cannot be emphasized enough how much the policies of
   accepting only the very best loans have reduced City's
   market share throughout the State. Behind every realtor
   bringing a loan application in to the association is the
   realtor himself and his family, the borrower and his family,
   the contractor, builder and any number of friends and
   relatives - all of whom are potential savers. For every
   loan applicant the association has "turned off" or flatly
   rejected, some six to ten potential savers have also been
   "turned off" and this rippling effect in the past two years
   has been devastating.

EXHIBIT 7-2   (cont'd)

2.   <u>City's Diversity of Markets</u>

City is based in Tobacco City; however, as 1981 begins, more than half of its customers are outside this area. They are farmers, ranchers, servicemen and small business proprietors allied with these market segments, yet City has not developed any specific marketing campaigns to attract these kinds of customers, nor have any services been developed which address their specific needs.

3.   <u>Marketing Orientation</u>

The total marketing effort to this point has been media advertising and a few promotions. However, most current media studies show that media advertising does little more than maintain awareness. It does not, in and of itself, bring new savers to the association. The premium promotions have been sporadic, often at the wrong time and usually only because other competitors are doing it.

4.   <u>Sales Orientation</u>

City only recently implemented the "Innovative Program." This is an excellent program to improve customer sensitivity; but, by itself it is not a substitute for a marketing approach to savings solicitation training and performance oriented reward systems, both of which still need to be developed in the association.

C.   <u>General Evaluation of Marketing Activities</u>

The marketing of savings and loan services must undergo a significant change. This change would include:

EXHIBIT 7-2   (cont'd)

1. Less reliance upon media advertising;

2. Branch Manager and Loan Officer training in personal
    selling techniques;

3. Emphasis on market segmentation and targeted (or
    direct) marketing;

4. Measuring the cost effectiveness of marketing dollars;
    and,

5. Recognizing that personnel from Branch Operations,
    Training and Lending have a significant role in the
    marketing process and should participate in marketing
    planning.

It is from the viewpoint of this broadened marketing concept
that we have evaluated the marketing activities of City. Our
purpose is to clarify ways in which City can increase its
market share.

Advertising - During the next few years, City's advertising
program should undergo significant changes.

1. Media Advertising has increased both in dollars and as
    a percent of the total budget. Dollar expenditures have
    grown from $570,000 in 1979 to $614,000 in 1980. This
    represents 87.0% of total marketing expenses. This is
    contrary to current industry trends toward targeted
    marketing. Branch area promotions and product develop-
    ment must be greatly expanded.

2. The use of direct mail advertising to specific market
    segments must be developed, and test mailings conducted.

EXHIBIT 7-2 **(cont'd)**

3. Local media must be utilized to a greater extent in an effort to promote different services and appeals according to the specific market area.

4. Emphasis must be shifted from promoting premiums to promoting products and services.

5. Assuming the problems connected with overly conservative lending policies can be resolved, the association, to regain lost share of market, especially in the Tobacco City area, should consider devoting as much as 3% of its total operating revenue toward marketing, sales promotion and services development as opposed to the present 2.46% allocated.

We believe that each of these shifts in advertising strategy is desirable. However, as new approaches are tested, it is essential that some means of tracking their effectiveness be developed. This requires an on-going process of establishing objectives for each program, and developing a feedback mechanism for this information. This will facilitate the task of allocating advertising dollars to those kinds of programs which are most effective in acquiring and retaining savings dollars. (This process should be applied to all marketing activities as we shall discuss later on.)

Promotion - The major promotional programs to be considered by City in its marketing planning are discussed below.

1. Premiums
    The association has, in the past, spent large sums of money on premiums. In 1980, for example, the total

EXHIBIT 7-2 (cont'd)

premium expense was $100,000. Management should monitor
results of this effort closely to observe the effects
upon savings flows. Many associations believe that it is
the same group of customers who continually take advantage
of premium offers. When premiums are discontinued, this
group may be lost to competitors, but City may find that
the overall effect is to increase profitability and these
dollars could be used to develop other new customers.

2. Branch Promotions

The association has not developed a comprehensive branch
promotion package. We believe that such a package could
be consistently effective if it were tailored to the
character of the specific branch. This requires a more
detailed analysis of the branch area demographics than
has been previously undertaken.

3. Ranchers and Farmers

A significant promotional program should be undertaken to
attract ranchers and farmers. Additionally, as many families
are geographically distant from branches, a strong save-by-
mail campaign should be developed and maintained.

4. VIP Club Planning

A VIP Club represents a most significant promotional
activity. Such clubs are much more important in retaining
present customers than in attracting new ones. However,
Fidelity Savings has had good success in the Tobacco City
area with its club. Farmers or Ranchers Clubs on a smaller
scale might be viable in other areas of the State. A
serious attempt should be made to estimate the impact on

EXHIBIT 7-2   (cont'd)

profitability of (a) developing a club and its facilities,
or (b) allocating the dollars to other marketing activities.
If a club is to be developed, it should be promoted
aggressively as an attraction for new customers.

Business Development - In view of the growing industry trend
toward personal selling, business development takes on added
importance for City. In late 1980, City formed a Savings Division
and launched a formal effort centered around the "Innovative
Program." We believe that this was a wise and timely move.
However, the business development effort can be improved in the
following ways:

1.   More Realistic Objectives for Branch Managers
      Most associations are experiencing deposits of about $3.5
      million per full time Branch Manager per year (based on
      10 calls per week). Branch Managers have objectives of
      only a few calls per week and no specific volume objective
      by type and mix of savings. If objectives are revised upwards
      and outstanding performance recognized and rewarded, results
      should improve accordingly.

2.   Branch Managers Should Be Encouraged to Make Calls
      In the past, Branch Managers' call schedules have not been
      frequently discussed with the managers. As a result, some
      managers are not developing their sales skills. There are
      indications that selling may become increasingly important
      in the coming years. Branch Managers should be made to take
      advantage of this transition period to develop and upgrade
      their sales capability.

EXHIBIT 7-2 (cont'd)

3. Develop Improved Promotional Materials

   Sales personnel are currently using a small brochure
   (designed to fit into literature racks) as a selling tool.
   There is a need for a brochure specifically designed to
   be used in explaining savings programs step-by-step to
   prospective customers. In addition, other associations
   have found that a customer kit, containing a transaction
   record and all necessary envelopes, instructions, etc., is
   a useful sales aid as well as a helpful organizer/record-
   keeper for the customer.

4. Test the Use of Advertising in Specialized Media to
   Support the Business Development Effort

   We believe that the Tobacco City area can easily accommodate two to three full time savings solicitors. Additional
   solicitors should be considered for rural branches. Also,
   the association should develop a telephone program to
   increase retention of maturing certificates. This was
   found to be very effective in other large associations.

5. Develop an Improved Reporting System

   It would be most helpful to have a reporting system
   which clearly shows:

EXHIBIT 7-2 (cont'd)

a. Accounts/Volume attributable to savings solicitors.

b. Accounts/Volume attributable to Branch Managers'
outside calls.

c. Accounts/Volume attributable to inside branch efforts.

d. Transfers from other accounts.

e. Gross savings by new accounts vs. additional deposits.

f. Withdrawals as partial vs. closed accounts.

New Product Development - With the proliferation of new products
and services which savings and loan associations are permitted
to offer, it is important to allocate available time and money
to those with the most potential. The development of the
"Pay-BY-Phone" program and NOW accounts in 1980 were excellent
moves, in our opinion.

In 1981, it should be planned to place additional special emphasis
on the following products and services:

1. HR-10

2. IRA

3. Transmatic

4. Direct Deposit of Government Checks

5. "Between Investment" Programs

6. Save-By-Mail

7. Mortgage Life Insurance

8. TFT Services

9. Mortgage Re-financing Programs

10. Consumer Loans

11. Debit Cards

EXHIBIT 7-2   (cont'd)

The key question, we believe, is the degree of emphasis to be placed on each of these programs. This should be determined by an analysis of market potential and the setting of realistic objectives for each. For example, there is much excitement in the industry about the potential of Direct Deposit of Social Security checks. Yet, no objectives have been established and there is no clear indication as to what, if any, new savings deposits might be generated. This objective setting should be an integral part of the annual marketing planning process.

Market Research - In the past year, City has become aware of how critical market research is in its decision making process. Yet, no sophisticated market research has been performed. City does not know who its customers are, or more important, who are not its customers. There have been no customer or branch market customer profile studies, nor any loan customer profile studies. One of the major failings of many research projects is that they are not translated into action and once decisions are reached on an extensive list of data requirements, the information must be developed and a plan constructed as to its dissemination and use.

Branching - The performance of new branches has been mixed. Several points have already been made regarding branching. They are repeated here for emphasis.

1. There is no long range merger plan based on the association's long range expansion objectives. Such a plan should be developed, and general areas for future mergers or additional limited facility branches should be identified and prioritized in areas such as Tobacco City, Winston-Salem and Wilmington.

EXHIBIT 7-2   (cont'd)

2. The site selection process for new limited facility
    branches must be a logical decision based upon demo-
    graphics, traffic flows, etc. A site location metho-
    dology should be developed.

3. Branch opening programs and promotions for existing
    branches should be more personalized, tailored to
    the demographic and attitudinal characteristics of
    the specific branch areas.

Marketing Plan - City has no annual Marketing Plan which describes the major marketing activities for the year. The plan
should be fairly comprehensive. First, it must be specific as
to the results to be expected from each activity. (For example,
Save-By-Mail expenses budgeted, say, at $150,000, should have
a specific statement of the results expected for this expenditure. This should be true of all other promotional activities,
direct mail programs, new products, etc.) Second, there must
be product development plans outlining the products to be
developed, expected savings/lending volume from each and estimated inauguration dates. Third, if the style of presentation
were concise, the plan would be an excellent communication
device. Fourth, there is a need for inputs by others in the
association. Specifically, a Business Development Section and
Training Section should be incorporated into an overall marketing
plan. Finally, there is a need for emphasis on loan marketing
in addition to savings.

EXHIBIT 7-2 (cont'd)

D.   Recommendations

As a result of our analysis, we suggest that City Savings consider
the following steps:

1.   Undertake a research project to identify the characteristics
     of all S&L savers in North Carolina. Compare them with the
     profile of City savers to determine whether or not the
     association is attracting a more sophisticated saver, or
     savers from all market segments.

2.   If the association is not appealing to the less sophisticated
     investor, develop a strategy to do so (without weakening
     the position with the current savers). This might include
     local promotional efforts.

3.   Design a public relations strategy to overcome any residual
     negative publicity from the conservative mortgage loan
     policies prevalent in prior years.

4.   Develop an on-going program of measuring results of all
     marketing programs and activities. To do this, it is
     necessary to:

     a.   Establish objectives for each program;
     b.   Develop means of tracking results; and,
     c.   Prepare cost/benefit analysis for each program.

5.   Start to test targeted marketing, including local media,
     direct mail, outdoor, etc. Measure and compare results
     of test programs.

EXHIBIT 7-2 (cont'd)

6. Tailor future branch promotional programs to meet the needs
    and characteristics of the community. Set higher objectives
    for new business and develop action plans to ensure objec-
    tives are met. Do not be constrained by traditional
    budgeting limits if additional expenditures can be cost
    beneficial. Develop branch teams to increase market pene-
    tration and provide better training for savings solicitation.

7. In the future, before undertaking promotional programs,
    analyze the audience to be reached and evaluate its appro-
    priateness versus the budgeted costs.

8. Upgrade the Business Development Program by undertaking the
    steps described in detail earlier and summarized below:
    a. Establish higher objectives.
    b. Encourage Branch Managers to make calls.
    c. Develop improved promotional material.
    d. Test specialized media advertising.
    e. Add additional savings solicitors.
    f. Develop a CD retention program.
    g. Improve the reporting systems.

9. Prepare a new product development plan including:
    a. Products/programs to be developed.
    b. Objectives of each.
    c. Scheduled completion date.
    We believe that priority should be given to a refinancing
    program, telephone bill payment service, consumer lending,
    and save-by-mail.

EXHIBIT 7-2   (cont'd)

10. Develop a long range merger plan.

11. Develop an improved branch site location methodology for additional limited facility sites in Tobacco City, Winston-Salem and Charlotte.

12. Improve the marketing planning process in the following ways:
     a. Organize the Annual Marketing Plan into the following sections:
         1. Product Development Plan
         2. Advertising Plan
         3. Promotional Plan
         4. Business Development Plan
         5. Branching Plan
         6. Training Plan
         7. Market Research Plan
         8. Budgeted Expenses
     b. In each section, include plans for marketing consumer and refinancing loans as well as savings.
     c. Establish an objective for each planned program or activity.
     d. Estimate the cost of each program or activity and compare it to the expected benefits.
     e. Include an estimated completion date for research projects, products to be developed, etc.
     f. Invite participation in the planning process by savings, lending and training personnel. Have the Training and Business Development Sections prepared by those responsible.

EXHIBIT 7-2   (cont'd)

g. Be sure that each element of the plan is included in
    someone's objectives. This will, in turn, assure
    implementation of the overall plan.

8

Financial Analyses
and Studies

Financial skills are an essential tool in the briefcase of any generalist consultant. Key signs of a client's economic health are measured by how efficiently the client uses its monetary resources to produce a product or service at a reasonable profit.

It is tempting for clients (and even consultants) to measure success in terms of absolute increases in sales or profits over the preceding years. Nevertheless, the financial strengths or weaknesses of a client are determined more by hidden factors that require a deeper analysis. The client can, in fact, be going bankrupt despite apparent signs of sales and profit growth.

There are two conditions under which a generalist consultant should undertake a financial analysis of a client's operations. One is obviously when the client directly perceives an immediate financial problem. Most often this request occurs in the event of capital insufficiency or cash flow inadequacy where, in essence, the client is lacking investment funds to build additional plant and equipment or is unable to generate money fast enough to pay its bills. Such problems are the principal cause of bankruptcy in fast-growing companies, even when the future looks promising.

The second condition, which is usually the case faced by generalist consultants, occurs when there is no directly perceived financial problem but when a careful financial analysis may shed light on other problems. It may arise as a routine part of a "management audit" where the consultant is assessing all facets of a client's operations. Or it may arise around a specific problem, such as a sales decline or ineffective strategic planning.

The authors, for example, once investigated a serious decline in a client's sales volume, a problem posed originally by the client as a "sales force motivation" issue. However, the real problem lay in a cash flow shortage that was preventing the purchase of raw materials to manufacture and deliver the product on time to demanding customers. In strategic planning studies, we often find financial analysis to be useful in measuring how well a client's top management is meeting its previously stated goals as well as in setting realistic targets for the future.

KEY ISSUES
FOR ANALYSIS

Before getting buried in which financial figures to analyze, where to find them, and how to analyze their meaning, we should review some of the overriding financial questions to be asked of any client's fiscal condition. There are certain fundamental questions that, though basic in their simplicity, are profound for their added insight.

1. *How does the client make money?*   Is it due to one key product, despite several losers? Is it through high sales volume on low-margin products? Is it via high-quality products with a high markup? Or is it through advanced product features that lead the competition? Has the way in which the client makes money changed substantially in the past few years?

2. *What does the Company do with the money it makes?*   Does it pay out high dividends to the owners or large bonuses to employees and managers? Or does it reinvest earnings in R&D or reserves for future plant and equipment expansion?

3. *How efficiently does the company use its resources?*   Does it collect its receivables on time? Is excess cash carried in the bank at no interest? Does it scrutinize each capital investment carefully for its expected return? Does it have too much short-term debt when it should have long-term debt at a lower cost?

4. *What risks does the company face as a result of its financial*

management and strategies? Is cash flow and capital adequate to meet future demands? If sales dropped 20%, could its current liabilities be paid? Does it have reserve sources of credit?

5. *How effectively does the company use and maintain its sources of financial information?* Are key indicators of performance reaching the appropriate managers on a timely basis? Do they understand them? Is the financial staff and the techniques it uses sufficiently competent and sophisticated?

Wherever a financial analysis might lead in its specific details, the consultant should periodically come back to these five basic issues to ensure a critical perspective. Financial analysis is not a mathematical game, because endless hours can be spent buried in numbers without ever clarifying the real problems facing a client.

PROFIT SOURCES

Without a clear understanding of how a company generates its profits, there is little opportunity to plan for increased earnings. Some of the varied ways that companies make money include

- Development of a unique product without any serious competition. Xerox, in its early years, built its success on the patents it held.
- Long-term repeat sales due to the loyalty of customers attracted through extraordinarily high levels of customer service. The Boeing Company gained its premier position in the aircraft industry through placing the customer first.
- High sales volume on low-margin products derived from a marketing "push" complemented by tight cost controls. Procter & Gamble and General Mills have both succeeded on this basis.
- The cost-efficient design of products to meet specific customer specifications. Fluor and Bechtel, the largest engineering companies in the world, became highly profitable giants through the effective management of huge construction projects.
- Unique locations in high traffic areas to maximize impulse buying. Many successful boutiques, such as Gucci, and fast-food chains, such as McDonalds, pursue this methodology.
- Extremely effective and unique manufacturing capabilities that lead either to extraordinarily high-quality goods or to extraordinarily low-cost production. Japanese auto firms have utilized advanced robotics to gain a competitive edge, and their watch companies have used microelectronics to undercut the jewel watch.

The perceptive consultant will discover that the answer to a client's source of profitability is often different from the beliefs of top management. If the CEO has a financial background, don't be surprised if he or she attributes profitability to shrewd debt management, when in reality the true genius is a mad scientist in R&D with an aptitude for new product discoveries.

ALLOCATION OF RESOURCES

No financial analysis is complete without making a determination of how the client allocates its economic resources. This requires a careful review of the client's opportunities for capital deployment and asset leveraging versus the payback anticipated, the efficiencies of current asset and liability usage, and a comparison of these results with the stated objectives of the company.

In the banking industry, for instance, Asset/Liability Management is a central concern. Banks make their money almost entirely from the narrow differential between the cost of their deposits and borrowings and the rates that they negotiate on loans. Bankers learned a long time ago that to be profitable, the bank must match 10% deposits with 12% loans, 14% borrowings with 16% loans, and so on.

Yet, in industrial and manufacturing enterprises, the consultant will often find the concept of Asset/Liability Management, here called the allocation of resources, to be lacking. A client may recognize that cash flow can be increased through a lengthening of accounts payable but it fails to reinvest the additional cash at an interest rate in excess of the finance charges on its delayed payments.

Other companies compare their historic returns on equity to peers in the industry and proudly accept a 4 or 5% return as "outperforming" the competition, even when the cost of money may be as high as 18%. Numerous manufacturers have faded over the years because their capital was eroded by inflation and poor returns from outmoded product lines. They could have earned more by placing their net assets in a money market instrument.

RISK ISSUES

Risk taking is present in all aspects of business management. No business can grow without making investments to secure a better future return. Yet, if the business borrows to make these investments and if future sales turn sour, the company is in deep trouble.

The responsible consultant must assess not only the degree of risk in the client's present financial condition, but avoid proposing solutions that overextend the client's limited resources. Critical questions for the consultant to ask are the following: What is the client's actual risk position versus management's philosophy toward risk? Is the company highly leveraged or does it pride itself in never having to borrow? What are the attitudes of the board, the CEO, and management toward risk?

Many of today's largest conglomerates have grown by leveraging one subsidiary's assets to obtain funds to buy another company, whose assets, in turn, are leveraged to buy yet another enterprise. Unfortunately, several conglomerates, when attempting this strategy, have ended up in bankruptcy because of their inability to service a cascading debt.

Frequently, in small- and medium-sized companies managed by a founder-owner, the consultant finds a management that is adverse to risk of any kind. Ironically, the founder took a great deal of risk in setting out as an entrepreneur but later does not want to risk losing what has been built and is owned personally. This overly safe posture becomes a constraint to future growth, preventing the company from expanding into new markets or enlarging facilities.

Other key issues to explore in the area of risk include the following: What is the purpose of leverage being used in the client's present debt structure? Is the money being drained off to cover short-term expenses without creating added value through long-term investments? Would it be cheaper to arrange bank loans or to seek equity financing for future growth? For companies currently leveraged aggressively, what would be the effect on net earnings if the cost of debt service were lowered? Would debt interest servicing be matched or exceeded by new revenues? Would equity financing be more economical or would it endanger control of the firm?

FINANCIAL COMPETENCE

Any financial analysis leads the consultant into close contact with the client's finance and accounting staff. It would be unprofessional for the consultant not to form some objective opinion of the staff's effectiveness in serving management. A marginal business can be saved by bright, state-of-the-art financial direction, while the strongest of organizations can be brought to the brink of nonexistence through fiscal mismanagement.

Many clients confuse finance with accounting, believing that capable accountants can also render shrewd financial judgment. In reality, the two fields are quite different; rarely is the accountant who deals with standard reporting procedures the same person who can negotiate a long-term loan with bankers.

Both parties and skills are essential to the successful financial management of a client. The credentials of the chief financial officer can be particularly revealing. A capable CFO cannot be a glorified bookkeeper who was promoted on the basis of tenure and loyalty. Does he or she have prior experience in banking or investment analysis? Was his or her education in finance and economics? Does he or she attend financial management seminars to keep up with the profession?

What about the accounting function? Is the controller a CPA? Is anyone else in the accounting department a CPA or CMA? Does the controller maintain close ties with the accounting profession? Are the books audited by a reputable CPA firm? Does the firm employ a full-time tax specialist?

Case in Point

One author's client saves over $100,000 a year in audit fees and has been doing so ever since it hired a CPA tax specialist away from a local accounting firm. This individual and his staff now perform 80% of the work necessary prior to the annual audit and tax calculations, thus reducing the outside audit fees by $50,000 a year over and above their own salary costs to the company.

How does the company manage its relationships with its banks? Does the CFO shop around to get the most dollars for the lowest rates or does the company deal only with one bank "because we've been using them for the last 25 years and they know us"?

Does the company have a platoon of bookkeepers employed solely to reconcile its dozens of bank accounts, or has the CFO arranged for the placement of a CRT in the accounting department, which is on line to all its major accounts at the bank, thus allowing instant, electronic account reconciliation at one-tenth the personnel cost?

To each of these questions the client and even the consultant may ask, "What's so important about fancy financial footwork?" After all, as one client told us, "We could hire two good salespersons for the price of one CPA from a Big-8 firm." And another stated, "The use of a budget officer may be appropriate for an ITT or an IBM, but not for our $200 million company."

To these questions we respond bluntly that any client company cannot afford to be without strong financial and accounting personnel. Regardless of its plans, regardless of record sales volume or the development of a new widget to outperform all previous widgets, the company will not reach its earnings potential if its finances are not managed to the last penny in the smartest possible way.

NUMBERS GENERATE
USEFUL QUESTIONS

The secret to good financial analysis is to let the numbers "talk" to you. While this may raise the vision of Harry Frobush, Harvard MBA, class of 1975, staring at an annual report while moving his lips, that is exactly what a consultant should do when performing a financial analysis. The numbers can and will expose a great deal about a company if you learn how to hold an intelligent conversation with them.

For example, let us assume that International Widgets achieved a net profit of $5.0 million in 1981, up from $4.5 million in 1980. The president of International Widgets states in the annual report that these improved results were due to an overwhelming acceptance of a new left-handed widget by its customers. But you also know from other interviews that the senior vice president of sales attributes the increase to "the best damned sales force west of Albuquerque." Each key manager in the company no doubt has his or her self-serving explanation for why profits rose 11%.

So let the numbers tell the story; it may be that both the president and vice president are correct, or it may be that both are up in the clouds. The consultant performing a financial analysis will peruse the last five years of balance sheets, P&L statements, sales reports, and budgets— always asking the question, "Why?" The conversation might develop as follows:

Consultant:	Why were profits up 11% this year, and how does that compare with those of previous years?
Annual Reports:	Profits were up 11% after a sales growth of 15%, while the cost of goods sold and administrative expenses were held to only a 10% increase. That is much better than the performance of the last three years when profits grew only 3% per year.
Consultant:	How does the 10% increase in cost of goods sold compare with figures in previous years? And what about the 15% jump in administrative expenses?
Annual Reports:	Cost of goods sold increased an average of 15% in each of the previous four years. And administrative expenses increased an average of 20% in each of the previous four years.
Consultant:	Why was 1981 different?
Budget Reports:	Under administrative expenses, while utility costs increased 35% in 1981, the largest segment of administrative expense, officer and employee compensation, did not rise at all in 1981 and, in fact, the total number of personnel declined 3%. Also, the cost of raw materials declined 17% in 1981.
Annual Reports:	That's because inventories, which had been high until 1980, declined significantly in 1981.

Consultant: Was there a change in inventory policy and what will happen next year if inventories continue to be reduced at a similar rate? Was the decline in personnel planned? How did it occur? What are the limits of productivity and capacity of the current work force? Can it handle another 15% sales growth this year? And next year?

Such a conversation lasts for several hours and covers a broad range of issues. It provides a few definitive answers, but it arms the consultant with a list of questions about financial, nonfinancial, strategic, and marketing issues to be discussed in subsequent interviews with the client's management and employees.

Admittedly, it sounds weird holding a Socratic conversation with an annual report, but the eventual outcome may be the solution to the client's problem.

Case in Point

One author performed a financial analysis for a client and found that, while sales had been declining by about 5% for each of the last three years, advertising expenses had grown 200% over the same period. When quizzed about this seeming contradiction, the client professed that product demand was the result of advertising and that sales were off due to an incompetent advertising agency that was about to be replaced. But the consultant also noticed that sales commissions to the wholesale reps had also declined exactly in proportion to sales, in spite of local inflation running at 10% a year. The author then surveyed the wholesale reps and discovered that they were neglecting the client's products because the client's commission structure had not kept pace with the competition. Once this was uncovered, commissions were increased and advertising budgets cut back—and the problem was solved.

WHERE TO FIND
THE "NUMBERS"

The most obvious sources of financial information are the *balance sheet* and the *profit and loss statement*. Each statement yields different insights into how effectively the client is managing itself. Both can be found in annual reports for previous years and in unaudited reports prepared for the current year. Old and out-of-print annual and quarterly reports can usually be located in the files of the company secretary or the secretary to the chairman.

The balance sheet provides a beginning basis for assessing three key issues: Where is the client deploying its assets over the short and long term? How efficiently are these assets being managed? And what is the degree of risk facing the client at present and in the future?

More specific questions to ask within these three areas of inquiry are: Is the client investing in new plant and equipment to handle future growth? Is there excess cash that is not earning interest? How fast does the client collect from its customers? How long does it take to pay its bills? Is too much money tied up in inventory? Is the client living too close to the edge in meeting its short-term obligations? Has the client financed its growth through debt, or retained earnings, or stock? How much long-term debt does the client have, what is it costing, and can future interest payments be met?

The profit and loss statement provides not only additional information to answer questions raised on the balance sheet but takes the analysis a step farther into measuring the client's success in the marketplace. It depicts the amount of revenues gained from customers and the costs expended in their achievement.

Immediately, one can tell from the *P&L statement* if the client relies on high-volume–low-margin products or on low-volume–high-margin products. This conclusion, in turn, provides insight into the client's marketing strategy—is it spending large amounts on advertising (which it should for a high-volume–low-margin product) or is it relying on an expensive sales force (which it should for a low-volume–high-margin product)? Are sales increasing as a result of this strategy or are they declining? How well are overhead costs being managed; for example, are administrative expenses increasing faster than sales growth? What is the relative cost of labor to materials in the final product? Is the client depending more on the manual and mental efforts of its work force or is it capital intensive with large amounts of plant and equipment?

No definitive answers emerge from examining the balance sheet or the P&L statement or in comparing notes across them. They give an overall picture of the client's business and its results so that the consultant has a "feel" for the entity with which he or she is working. In addition, they raise questions that the consultant can pursue in follow-up interviews as well as focus attention on certain "nonpublic" numbers still to be provided by the client.

Less public sources of data are financial budgets, sales forecasts, and operating results prepared on a monthly or quarterly basis by the client's management. Here you can deepen your understanding of the business, especially in terms of how well the management plans for and stays on top of its operations. Expense categories are more detailed, so you can determine what subcomponent of a general cost category, such as "computer leasing" within administrative expenses, is increasing faster than other components. Are sales targets being met or does the client consistently fall short? Is the client a victim of the business cycle with high sales revenues in one quarter and high manufacturing costs in another quarter? Do financial budgets seem to agree with subsequent results, or are actual expenses grossly out of line with budgeted expenditures?

Clients with more sophisticated information systems can provide useful breakdowns of quarterly reports by different product lines or functional departments. Are certain products earning more profit than other products? Does one market area, such as the East Coast, provide the bulk of sales? How well is the manufacturing department controlling its costs, especially waste and overtime? Is the marketing department gaining the most sales from its senior sales personnel to whom it pays the highest salaries or are they surpassed by younger more ambitious salespersons?

Additional data can be found in the *10-K report* for public companies. It is an SEC-required report that documents such issues as repair and maintenance costs, capital investments, in-depth reviews of accounts payable and receivable, compensation to top officers, contingent liabilities, lease commitments, and the like.

Should consultants feel that the time and fees are justified, they can write the SEC to ask for a corporation's *10-Q report*, which is its original filing statement with even more detail than the annual 10-K. If the corporation is five years old or less, the 10-Q often makes an enlightening cornerstone of information against which to measure the client's financial progress. Even if the corporation is not registered with the SEC, each state has a similar information filing requirement.

For smaller clients, such as closely held corporations, proprietorships, or partnerships, the organization's *annual tax return* may be the only source of data. Many small clients do not have sophisticated or even monthly or quarterly reports, but they all have to file tax returns.

Finally, the consultant should seek out data on the client's industry and its key competitors. Such data may already have been collected by the client's marketing or finance groups. If not, it can usually be found in industry trade journals or with stockbrokers and investment analysts.

DISPLAYING NUMBERS

Simply wading through a pile of financial reports seldom yields a depth of analysis that gives both an overall perspective and helps to pinpoint troublesome issues. It is too easy to become lost in trivia, to say nothing of wasted time.

What is needed is a "format" to display the numbers so that useful comparisons can be readily made. Here a research assistant can be invaluable for assembling the numbers within a format provided by the consultant.

The first step is to display all the numbers from the balance sheet and profit and loss statement on two separate sheets that cover at least a five- to ten-year time span. Next, all the numbers should be put on a common basis, for example, through the use of percentages or indexing. In this manner, we can tell, for instance, if advertising expenditures have been increasing or declining as a percentage of total sales.

Another common step is to display certain key numbers in terms of ratios. For example, the ratio of current liabilities to current assets gives an indication of the client's ability to pay its bills over the short term. It can also be a measure of liquidity, indicating that the client has excess funds that can be put to better use. What follows is a list of 15 key financial ratios derived from balance sheet and income statement items. These 15 ratios, while not the only ones that can be developed, are commonly used by independent analysts and creditors.

Key Financial Ratios

1. Current ratio (current assets to current liabilities)

   - provides a general view of the company's ability to meet current debt payments and is used to evaluate the quality of the company's major current assets: receivables and inventory.

2. Current liability to net worth

   - measures the impact of creditors to the business and the extent of short-term leveraging.

3. Total liabilities to net worth

   - measures the impact of creditors to the business and is a measure of collateral already pledged.

4. Inventory to working capital

   - measures the dependency of working capital (excess current assets) on the stated value of inventory.

5. Trade receivables to working capital

   - measures the dependency of working capital on trade receivables; this, together with the previous ratio, serves as an indication of the company's fragility.

6. Long-term liabilities to working capital

   - indicates the effectiveness of long-term borrowing;
   - measures the ability of the company to make additional borrowings;
   - together with the previous ratios, measures the company's overall financial soundness.

7. Net profit to net worth

   - measures the return on investment.

8. Net sales to fixed assets

    • measures the efficiency with which plant, equipment, land, and so on are utilized.

9. Net sales to working capital

    • measures the demand on working capital to support sales.

10. Fixed assets to net worth

    • measures the extent to which net worth is tied up in low-earning or nonearning assets as opposed to productive assets;
    • measures the extent to which capital is still available for investment into earning assets and operations.

11. The collection period

    • measures and analyzes the company's trade receivables and the maximization of cash management strategies.

12. Net sales to inventory

    • measures the extent of inventory movement and sales efficiency.

13. Net sales to net worth

    • measures the extent to which the company's sales are supported by capital; often referred to as the trading ratio.

14. Net profit to net sales

    • measures the amount of profit on each dollar of sales; a measure of success in meeting key objectives.

15. Miscellaneous assets to net worth

    • a secondary but key evaluation of the efficiency of capital deployment.

All the techniques cited depend upon comparative analysis. The comparison used most frequently is an historical assessment of the client's current situation with its past record. This gives a quick indication of what seems to be improving and what seems to be getting worse. A second useful comparison is to match the client's past and present results with its competition. Even though the client may be improving over its past record, it still can be trailing its industry. Next, the client's actual results can be compared with its planned targets (known as "variance" analysis). Here we have a test of management's ability to set realistic goals and meet them. Throughout these comparisons, you can use percentages or ratios displayed across a number of years. The patterns emerge as you observe the trends and talk to the numbers.

More sophisticated methods to display numbers are geared to particular problems facing the client. One key problem is cash flow inadequacy and the need for a cash flow forecast. Table 8-1 shows a cash flow forecast for a lingerie manufacturer, Frilly Fashions, which was a recent client of one author. The forecast was prepared by the consultant based on future sales estimates and an extrapolation of past cash flow patterns as bills were paid and revenues collected. It clearly reveals a cash deficit from May to August as goods are manufactured in preparation for the Christmas market. However, the deficit turns around in September as sales receipts begin to arrive. The consultant helped the client to locate a temporary line of credit to support the summer cash deficit as well as to improve collections from customers in the fall. Previously, Frilly Fashions has been living month to month in a state of crisis as it neglected careful planning for its cash flow.

Another useful technique is "break-even" analysis to show at what level of sales the client begins to leverage its profits. Figure 8-1 portrays the break-even point for Frilly Fashions, indicating that sales must reach $540,000 monthly and $6,480,000 annually before fixed and variable costs are covered fully. At this point, profits will increase substantially because only variable costs are left to be covered. Interestingly, Frilly Fashions had never made this type of analysis and as a result had failed to set its sales targets high enough. At the same time, its management was perplexed as to why the company was losing money even though sales were increasing. The answer was simple—the firm had failed to cross the break-even point in its sales achievements.

WHAT TO DO
WITH THE DATA

The first thing that consultants should do with significant findings arising from their dialogue and other analyses is to return to the source of the numbers, usually the controller or the chief financial officer, to determine if the numbers used are accurate and if the conclusions reached are appropriate.

Regardless of what the numbers may show superficially, the consultant cannot write a report critical of financial strategy until he or she has talked with the treasurer to learn what, exactly, was the financial strategy and on what assumptions it was based. Only then is the consultant in a position to deliver credible critiques and recommendations for future action. An example of such a financial analysis appears as Exhibit 8-1.

It is too simple to assume that a financial problem is solved exclu-

TABLE 8-1 Frilly Fashions, Inc., Cash Flow Projection, Fiscal 1982

		MAY	JUNE	JULY	AUG.	SEPT.	OCT.	NOV.	DEC.	JAN.	FEB.
Beginning balance											
Checks due and written	($290,000)										
Additional due	(50,000)										
Available from factor	200,000										
Net	($140,000)										
Sources											
Sales		$503,103	$494,108	$571,005	$728,298	$876,414	$972,749	$1,011,017	$667,807	$675,702	$643,863
Noncash		7,300	7,300	7,300	7,300	7,300	8,000	8,000	8,000	8,000	8,000
Total available		$510,403	$501,408	$578,305	$735,598	$883,714	$980,749	$1,019,017	$675,807	$683,702	$651,863
Uses of cash:											
Operating expenses		192,122	192,122	192,122	192,122	229,515	229,515	229,515	229,515	229,515	229,515
Direct labor		124,600	124,600	133,000	145,600	159,600	159,600	159,600	159,600	159,600	159,600
Indirect labor, factory overhead, design		105,000	105,000	105,000	105,000	109,000	109,000	109,000	109,000	109,000	109,000
Materials		206,440	231,930	257,876	257,856	123,500	151,000	151,000	173,000	173,000	173,000
Total direct		$628,162	$653,652	$687,998	$700,598	$621,615	$655,115	$655,115	$671,115	$671,115	$671,115
Bank Loan		12,000	12,000	12,000	12,000	12,000	12,000	12,000	12,000	12,000	12,000
Designer royalty			24,000								
Loan repayment							150,000	50,000			
Capital expenditures			5,000	20,000	25,000	20,000					
Total uses		$640,162	$694,652	$719,998	$737,598	$653,615	$817,115	$717,115	$683,115	$683,115	$683,115
Net available	($140,000)	($129,759)	($193,244)	($141,693)	($2,000)	$230,099	$163,634	$301,902	($7,308)	$587	($25,252)
Cumulative before bonus	($140,000)	($269,759)	($463,003)	($604,696)	($606,696)	($376,597)	($212,963)	$88,939	$81,631	$82,218	$56,966

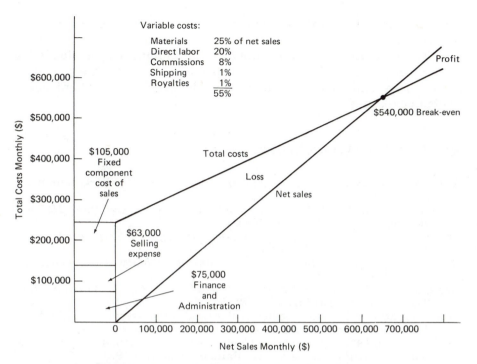

Variable costs:

Materials	25% of net sales
Direct labor	20%
Commissions	8%
Shipping	1%
Royalties	1%
	55%

Profit

$600,000

$540,000 Break-even

$500,000

$105,000
Fixed
component
cost of
sales

Total costs

$400,000

Loss

Net sales

$300,000

$63,000
Selling
expense

$200,000

$75,000
Finance
and
Administration

$100,000

0 100,000 200,000 300,000 400,000 500,000 600,000 700,000

Net Sales Monthly ($)

Total Costs Monthly ($)

FIGURE 8–1   Frilly Fashions, Inc.—Break-Even Analysis

sively by a financial solution. The break-even problem at Frilly Fashions required a new marketing strategy designed to attract more Christmas customers and thereby raise the level of sales. And the cash flow problem necessitated a new product line, swimwear, to increase revenues earlier in the year.

THE GENERALIST IS NOT A SPECIALIST

This chapter has addressed only a few of the financial issues and techniques that a generalist consultant will face on a client assignment. We, therefore, caution the reader that a great deal more study and practice is required for any consultant to present himself or herself as a financial specialist.

Financial management in the 1980s is one of the most rapidly growing and sophisticated areas of management practice. For every generalist consultant who thinks that he or she knows something about financial management, there are a dozen specialists with proven approaches to taxation, cash management, capital budgeting, and inventory control.

The generalist consultant should retain a financial specialist in his or her firm or, if working as an independent consultant, a part-time financial specialist can be employed in the event that a client needs in-depth expertise.

RECOMMENDED READINGS

ALTMAN, MARY ANN, ed.,   *Financial Handbook* (5th ed.). New York: John Wiley & Sons, 1981.

ANTHONY, ROBERT N.,   "Making Sense of Non-Business Accounting," *Harvard Business Review*, May/June 1980.

BREALEY, RICHARD A., and STEWART MYERS,   *Principles of Corporate Finance.* New York: McGraw Hill, 1981.

DONALDSON, GORDON,   *Strategy for Financial Mobility.* Homewood, Ill.: Richard D. Irwin, 1971.

GALE, BRADLEY T., and BEN BRANCH,   "Cash Flow Analysis: More Important Than Ever," *Harvard Business Review*, July/August 1981.

GOLDMAN, ROBERT I.,   "Look to Receivables and Other Assets To Obtain Working Capital," *Harvard Business Review*, November/December 1979.

RAPPAPORT, ALFRED,   "Measuring Company Growth Capacity During Inflation," *Harvard Business Review*, January/February 1979.

SPIRO, HERBERT T.,   *Finance for the Non-Financial Manager*, New York: John Wiley & Sons, 1977.

EXHIBIT 8-1   Sample Financial Analysis

CHARLES, CRANSTON, KATO & KENT

CONSULTANTS TO MANAGEMENT

123 PROGRESS AVENUE

GOTHAM CITY, U.S.A.

The financial activity charts which have been prepared for City Savings are designed for use in planning and monitoring performance against planned Association objectives. They have also been designed for diagnosing problems and for determining the type and amount of corrective action required to achieve or increase profitability.

The financial highlights of City's performance are summarized below. They are based on our analyses of the financial data depicted on the charts and other data supplied to us through December 31, 1980.

PROFITABILITY

A useful context for analyzing City's profitability is to compare after tax Return on Net Worth to comparable institutions. The Association has operated profitably for many years. In 1977, City's return was 13.3% compared to an FHLB 2nd district average of 9.0% and an overall industry average of 7.0%. In 1978, the Association realized a Return on Net Worth of 16.3% compared to its district average of 7.87% and an overall industry average of 6.2%.

However, the Association's Return on Net Worth shows a declining trend. In 1978, the Return on Net Worth was 16.3%, but in 1979 it slipped to 16.1% and the 1980 Profit Plan calls for a return of only 9.6%.

The cause for this decline is predominantly a slower growth in Gross Operating Revenue than the growth in the Association's Cost of Money, thus leading to reduced margins as a percentage of Gross Operating Revenue. (Refer to Table 1 for a summary of these changes from 1977 through 1980.)

EXHIBIT 8-1   (cont'd)

TABLE 1

GROSS REVENUE, COST OF MONEY AND MARGIN

	1977	1978	1979	1980 (Planned)
Gross Revenue ($000)	20,262	21,537	28,896	30,462
Increase Over Prior Year		6.24%	34.2%	5.42%
Cost of Money ($000)	13,945	17,439	20,140	22,458
Increase Over Prior Year		25.1%	15.5%	11.5%
Margin ($000)	6,317	7,528	8,756	8,004
As a % of Gross Revenue		35.0%	30.3%	26.3%

EXHIBIT 8-1 (cont'd)

This trend is typical of institutions unable to plan and manage their profits and control their revenue growth through the con-tinual planning and development of new customers and markets and the improvement of their existing sources of revenue.

The net effect of these shrinking margins is further compounded through the enormous increases in Operating Expenses experienced by the industry in the past 5 years. City, too, has been unable to escape this trend. Note the declining growth in operating margin and increasing growth in operating expense in Table 2 below.

TABLE 2

	1977	1978	1979	1980 (Planned)
Margin ($000)	6,317	7,528	8,756	8,004
Increase Over Prior Year		19.2%	16.3%	(8.59%)
Net Operating Expense ($000)	4,031	4,290	5,455	5,764
Increase Over Prior Year		6.4%	17.2%	5.67%

The end result of these trends shows that, while Pre-Tax Net Income (after deductions for profit sharing) has increased each year in absolute dollars, as a percent of Gross Revenue, it is steadily declining. This trend is clearly depicted in Table 3 below.

TABLE 3

	1977	1978	1979	1980 (Planned)
Pre-Tax Net Income	2,281	3,053	3,301	2,240
As a % of Gross Revenue		14.2%	11.4%	7.35%

The methodology most successful in reversing such trends is to concentrate on the analysis of the Association's current sources of revenue and its improvement. There are some strategies which can be used to reduce Cost of Money in a limited way; however, as associations grow and increase their customer base, absolute deposits increase also. Unless the assets are more effectively invested each year, this margin will decline regardless of savings mix or CD rate strategy moves.

EXHIBIT 8-1 (cont'd)

Gross Operating Revenue has increased over prior years in each of the previous three years. Total revenue as a percent of prior year's total revenue was 233% in 1977, 123% in 1978 and 115% in 1979. Though seemingly excellent, this growth rate is inadequate in light of the revolutionary changes in industry operating expenses in the past few years. The trend in yields has been 8.25% on Net Assets in 1977, 8.54% in 1978 and 8.73% in 1979. These asset yields are excellent, but they are the result of artificially high yields due to restrictive, conservative and non-competitive loan policies.

A brief review of the elements of total revenue will provide more insight into a number of missed opportunities. Essentially, the dramatic recent trend toward higher interest rates has resulted in longer term portfolio elements yielding a below average share of total revenues.

A principal theme of this review is that the contraction in real earnings is the result of the growth in the Cost of Money exceeding the growth in recurring sources of revenues. The cause of that situation is slow loan revenue growth based on a decline in the growth of new loan volume and a lack of effective planning leading to too great a reliance on only "solid gold" loans and trading profits in recent months.

TABLE 4

COMPARISON OF SOURCES OF REVENUE BY % OF REVENUE

AND % OF NET ASSETS

	1977	1978	1979	1980 (Planned)
Net Loans as a % of Net Assets	86.4%	87.8%	83.8%	84.3%
R.E. Loan Interest as a % of Revenues	74.2%	71.6%	73.5%	78.2%
Trading Profits as a % of Revenues			5.4%	
Consumer Loans as a % of Net Assets	8.8%	7.7%	6.8%	7.0%
Consumer Loan Rev. as a % of Revenues	10.3%	11.4%	7.8%	7.7%
Cash and Securities as a % of Net Assets	9.4%	8.1%	9.9%	8.8%
Securities Revenue as a % of Revenues	8.9%	7.7%	8.8%	6.0%

EXHIBIT 8-1 (cont'd)

As can be seen from Table 4, there has been a continual shifting back and forth between real estate loan investments and securities investments. The height of these cyclical swings appeared last year when more than 12% of the Association's assets were placed in securities and cash during most of 1979 even though the yield on this particular portfolio, including trading profits, was some 130 basis points below the average 9.02% loan yield.

At the same time, consumer loans have been allowed to decline steadily from 8.8% to 6.8% of total assets even though, as an asset category, they provide the highest yields to the Association.

In the past two years, in spite of record savings inflows, the Association's real estate loan activity has declined from a peak gross new lending rate of 31.5% in 1978 to approximately 25% in 1979. This decline in origination rate, combined with GNMA and loan sale trading activities in 1979, increased the R.E. loan portfolio runoff rate from 13% in 1978 to more than 17% in 1979 so that the overall R.E. loan portfolio growth rate declined from 18.5% in 1978 to less than 9% in 1979.

These trends all signify reactive lending activities and a lack of planning and coordination between lending, cash management and savings which resulted in a failure to maximize loan revenue opportunities in 1979.

This trend is projected to continue in 1980 with liquidity ratios far in excess of the statutory 7% and no planned growth in the consumer loan portfolio. Further, real estate loan yield is forecast to decline from the present 9.02% to less than 8.95% in 1980.

The task of increasing revenues in order to improve both Return on Net Worth and Return on Average Assets requires success in three areas, the first two being: asset portfolios must be increased and yields in the portfolios must be preserved. Because yields are already good, asset growth through more flexible and far greater loan origination will be one of the most important elements in increasing revenues, but there still is considerable opportunity available for revenue improvement.

Revenue improvement, in turn, can be supported only by the third challenge to City: improved investment planning and coordination in all portfolio areas. By being aware of and oriented toward the yield opportunities in each portfolio area, annual and monthly plans can be developed to reallocate resources to higher yielding portfolio elements and by concentration on the improvement of each portfolio element.

Current trends show that City could eliminate its real estate loan portfolio in slightly more than 5 years and its consumer loan portfolio in slightly more than 4 years.

While the flexibility of assets provided by these high runoff rates allows maximization of earnings, it is a valid strength only to the extent of the validity of loan origination under-writing philosophy and capacity and cash flow planning.

EXHIBIT 8-1   (cont'd)

The implications of the high runoff rate in the real estate portfolio are manifold. Maintaining or increasing the runoff rate
through planned loan sales and mortgage banking activities,
expanding and improving the mix of construction and commercial
financing, and aggressively encouraging refinancing of existing
lower rate loans will all serve to raise yields if the portfolio level is maintained. All imply more new loans and more
origination points and the latter also implies extra interest
income.

The consumer loan runoff rate implies an ability to move resources
into and out of high yielding installment loans limited only by
the Association's marketing and origination capabilities, and
the risk/reward policy of the Board.

In any event, the Association's trend in recent years to allocate loan resources away from the highest yielding categories
must be turned around and both real estate and consumer loan
origination capabilities must be planned, coordinated and greatly
expanded merely to maintain portfolio levels - let alone increase
them substantially.

SECURITIES REVENUE

The disproportionate relationship between securities revenue as
a percent of revenue and securities as a percent of assets has
already been demonstrated. However, these yields would be even
lower if there had not been significant profits from the sale
of some securities in 1979. Less the trading profits, the pure
interest yield was only 5.8%.

While securities trading profits are always welcome, they cannot
be relied on to achieve annual profit plans and with the present
decline in securities and bond yields, it is difficult to understand the historically high liquidity position at City. This
excess liquidity and the loss of revenue as a result is demonstrated in Table 5:

EXHIBIT 8-1   **(cont'd)**

TABLE 5

ANALYSIS OF LOST REVENUE THROUGH EXCESS LIQUIDITY

	1977	1978	1979	1980 (Planned)
Savings (Avg) ($000)	221,000	272,000	307,000	340,000
Liquidity Requirements (Avg) ($000)	14,365	16,320	21,385	23,800
Actual Liquidity ($000)	22,212	36,277	33,000	35,000
Excess Liquidity ($000)	7,847	19,957	12,625	11,200
Difference in RE Loan Yields/ Securities Yield	0.24%	3.22%	1.30%	3.73%

					4 Year Total
"Opportunity Lost" Revenue ($000s)	18.8	642.6	164.0	417.8	1,243.2

In summary, the Association should review its overall liquidity policy and its securities and cash portfolio with a view to reallocating more resources into loans on a regular basis.

COST OF MONEY

The average improvement of Revenue over prior years has been 15.2% including 1980's Profit Plan. Cost of Money during the same period has averaged an annual increase of 17.4%.

The margin over the past four years has shrunk from 2.04% in 1977 to 1.7% forecasted for 1980. These points are demonstrated in Table 6 on the following page.

EXHIBIT 8-1   (cont'd)

TABLE 6

REVENUE AND COST OF MONEY COMPARISONS

	1978	1979	1980 (Planned)
Revenue as a % of Prior Year	123%	115%	105%
Cost of Money as a % of Prior Year	125%	115%	113%

	1977	1978	1979	1980 (Planned)
Revenue as a % of Assets (Yield)	8.25%	8.54%	8.73%	8.14%
Cost of Money as a % of Assets	5.96%	5.96%	6.09%	6.44%

The essential problem is that the deposit base is more liquid than the asset portfolio (the classic problem of borrowing short to lend long). The trend in interest rates has impacted liabilities more than assets, cutting deeply into the margin.

Ten or fifteen years ago it was typical in the S&L industry that personnel was the largest expense category. Today, at City, Cost of Money is roughly four times as great as total operating expense and more than eight times as great as any single expense category, including personnel.

This trend has been accelerated since the beginning of this decade, through the issuance of higher and higher rate CD's. And, although City has refused to enter any "rate wars" in its market area, it is currently experiencing in excess of 73% of its deposits in higher cost CD's compared to passbook deposits. This trend is accentuated when the number of accounts is reviewed. The number of passbook rate accounts has increased only 1.0% since January, 1978, while the growth rate in the number of CD accounts has increased 11.5%, or more than ten times the growth rate over the same period.

Simultaneously, the retention rate (net new deposit gain compared to gross deposits) is declining at City. In 1978, it was 34.0% while in 1979 it declined to 30%. The true impact of this can be realized when it is understood that this calculation infers that for every new dollar deposited in 1978, 70¢ immediately left the Association in the same month, leaving only 30¢ available for investment in one or another asset category.

EXHIBIT 8-1 (cont'd)

OPERATING EXPENSES/FINANCIAL REPORTING

The indices of operating expenses are somewhat high in the administration area, averaging in excess of 17%. While Personnel
expense is somewhat low, categories such as Office Building,
Depreciation, and General Administration are slighly higher than
is our general experience. Much of this can be attributable to
City's well developed branch network and the costs related to
supporting that organization over great distances.

An area that requires greater immediate concern is financial
reporting. Much of the data required to perform our analysis
was provided only after special research and data collecting
activities on the part of City's personnel. Yet, all of this
data is critical to the effective planning of revenues and
related activities on an annual and monthly basis. We recommend
that City greatly expand its data collection and reporting
systems to provide senior management with this extraordinary
information on a routine basis.

SUMMARY

City has performed well compared to most of its peer institutions
in its FHLB district and in comparison to other associations of
similar size throughout the nation.

However, this performance is being eroded dramatically in the
areas of margin and asset allocation. The greatest challenge
appears to be in the area of profit and cash flow planning, the
flexibility of lending policies, the planning and control of
deposits and the ability of the Association to develop and market
new, lower cost, higher yield products and services. Finally,
the Association presently lacks an up-to-date financial and
activity reporting capability which would allow senior management
to delegate more responsibility and accountability to lower
levels of management and then effectively monitor and measure
performance against plans.

9

Organization and Systems Studies

A client's organization structure and its accompanying systems represent its anatomy and circulatory system, respectively. Even though the client possesses a brain with a vision and a strategy of which direction to take, it will not make much progress without both a structural skeleton pointed in the same direction and a set of systems to monitor and regulate its progress.

Consultants are commonly employed to perform organization and system studies because the client is neurotically attached to past practices. Senior executives derive power and reward from their formal positions, which understandably makes them hesitant to recommend changes in organization. They often want to retain their present positions and structure regardless of any planned changes in the goals of the company. But that is wishful thinking, which will eventually undermine the company's progress.

Organization structure becomes the concrete means through which people are assigned to tasks, the designation of authority for making decisions, and the placement of accountability for results. Numerous mistakes are made in these decisions by clients as they form the wrong groups to accomplish tasks that are beyond their control or they assign authority to the wrong levels for making key decisions.

Many new structures exist for helping managers and employees cope with growing variations in technological and market characteristics. No longer is the classical pyramid the only alternative for directing an employee's work effort. It is the consultant's job to design an appropriate organization structure and recommend systems that enhance rather than block employee performance.

The effective organization and systems consultant needs to be aware of various structural alternatives and then to assist the client in choosing one that fits the firm's particular capabilities and needs. To do so requires a careful diagnosis of the work flow for turning out a product, a thorough knowledge of the marketplace, an understanding of the client's strategic goals, and a keen sensitivity to power relationships among managers. All these forces must be considered and woven together into a new organization fabric that is more effective and workable for the client.

COMMON ISSUES

Organization and systems studies often arise out of strategic planning or marketing engagements. A new strategic plan, if it is to be implemented, may require a new organization structure that is "flatter" or "taller," depending upon where authority is to be assigned. Or a new marketing plan may necessitate the addition of a new sales and manufacturing organization to introduce a new product line. Sometimes, however, the client will propose an organization or systems problem directly with the following characteristics:

1. *Decentralization.* How can the organization be made more responsive at lower levels? Clients will sometimes recognize that so many levels have been added that the company is "top heavy," suffering from an excess of decision makers and bureaucratic red tape. The problem is to push decision making down to lower levels, to remove the needless levels, and to streamline the systems for faster decision making.

2. *Centralization.* Just the opposite problem arises when an organization has become too diffuse at its lower levels and senior management has lost control over key decisions. The objective here is to place lower-level units under tighter control so that resources and capital can be deployed more effectively.

3. *Regrouping.* Frequently an organization structure has experienced ad hoc growth, with new departments added to supply additional expertise. However, at some point, these appendages need to be reevaluated and combined with other units to achieve a more efficient use of

personnel as well as to improve coordination. For example, we once recommended to a client that the new product development department should be removed from the manufacturing division and assigned to the marketing division to increase contact with consumer needs.

4. *Coordination.*   All too often organizations consist of several fiefdoms that do not speak to each other. Yet changes in the marketplace may require greater coordination across functional departments. Changes can be made here, for example, by installing a coordination department or by establishing lower-level liaison positions to maintain direct contact with other departments.

5. *Job analysis.*   A proliferation of redundant jobs or too many people performing minute tasks is not uncommon to many clients. The job here is to make a careful analysis of the work flow and then to draw boundaries around where each job should begin and end. Such a systematic analysis can eliminate redundancy and may even make work more interesting for employees who are given greater responsibility.

6. *Information, measurement, and control.*   Who should receive what information, in what format, and by what date? Managers cannot act if they lack sufficient information prepared on a timely basis and in a form that they can understand. Such a standard for efficient information systems sounds logical, but organizations rarely follow that precept. Instead, trivial data are accumulated in piles of computer printouts sent to the wrong people. Each level and function in an organization needs certain kinds of information to stay on top of its performance. Consultants are frequently used to improve and rationalize the information system, whether through computerized data banks, new report formats, or the simple rerouting of memoranda.

7. *Planning, goal setting, and budgeting.*   We have already discussed strategic planning in Chapter 6, but there is also tactical planning for short-term goals. Many clients believe that tactical goals can be determined at the top and handed down to lower levels. However, they forget that lower levels probably know their specific situations better than top management does. Also, one department may have to set its goals first, such as marketing, before other departments know what they have to produce. Consultants can be helpful in designing goal-setting systems that cause employees to pull together rather than in separate directions.

SCHOOLS OF ORGANIZATION THEORY

Clients frequently get into trouble when a CEO is biased toward one philosophy of management and tries to impose it on the organization, even when that philosophy is inappropriate for managing the business.

It is one thing for a CEO to make this mistake, but a consultant cannot afford to take his or her organizational bias out on client after client.

Most of us have grown up conditioned to a *classical* approach that depicts organizations as pyramids with a strong authority figure on top issuing directives downward to subordinates. The classical school specifies such principles as a clear chain of command, limited span of control, specialization of labor, and making authority commensurate with responsibility. The top of the pyramid is manned by a few chiefs who do the planning and deciding for the hordes of worker "ants" out on the assembly line.

Competing with the classical school is the *human relations* approach. Its credo is participative management through decentralization and team decision making. Organization charts are frowned upon; when drawn, they resemble a flat structure of overlapping teams or a series of concentric circles flowing out from a management core. Authority is delegated downward to teams while top management devotes its attention to strategic decisions.

Both schools have their advocates and detractors. Proponents of the classical school argue for its clarity and ease of control while criticizing the vagueness of a participative organization. Conversely, the human relations advocates subscribe to its motivating power and fast decision-making philosophy while decrying the rigidity and depersonalization of pyramid structures.

How does the practicing consultant resolve this dilemma of organizational choice, which lies at the basis of most organizational studies? Is one approach, indeed, better than the other? Consultants will encounter clients who are wedded to classical management, only to meet up with still others who are enamored with participative management.

Fortunately, an "answer" does exist that does not force an either/or choice. A third school, *contingency* theory, provides a rationale for accepting both the classical and human relations schools, although limiting their use to certain conditions.

Numerous research studies have shown that a client's technology and external environment make a serious difference in choice of organization structure. Those clients with a complex technology and a rapidly changing environment require a human relations structure built around teams, delegation, and participation. On the other hand, clients with a relatively simple technology and stable marketplace can be managed better through a hierarchical structure. Thus, a computer company is more likely to require a decentralized and free-flowing organization design, whereas a manufacturer of railroad cars can use a pyramid.

Consultants applying contingency theory must be adept at diagnosing the technology and environment of each client. Such a skill should also be carried downward within the client organization to recognize inherent differences in departments, such as between production

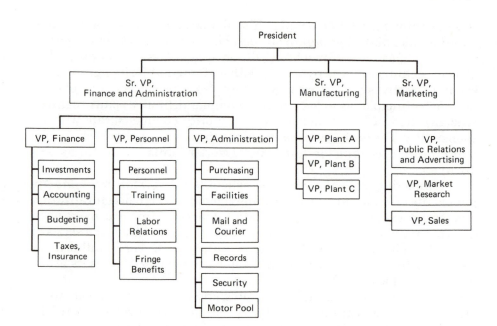

FIGURE 9-1   The Flat-Out Tire Co., Shredding, Pennsylvania

and R&D. In client companies with a standard manufacturing technology the production function can be organized more formally to schedule work and personnel. Yet the R&D function, which is working on the forefront of knowledge, must be kept looser and more sensitive to the creative process.

ALTERNATIVE STRUCTURES

There are five basic structural forms with which any organization consultant must be intimately familiar: *functional, product, geographic, project,* and *matrix.* These five forms spread themselves out across a continuum from the classical school to the human relations school, with the functional structure being the most pyramidal and the matrix being the most free flowing.

Functional Structure

Here the organization is divided into separate departments, with each unit performing a specialist discipline, such as production, market-

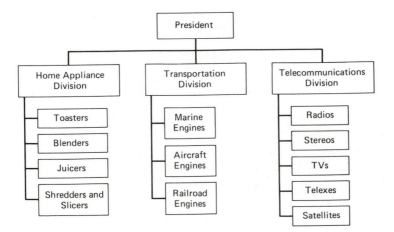

FIGURE 9-2   Shazam Electronics, Inc., Marvel, Minnesota

ing, administration, and research. Each department is headed by a vice president reporting to a CEO (see Figure 9-1).

Functional structures are most appropriate for producing a single product that is manufactured with a simple and proven technology and sold through a common sales force. These organizations can be, and usually are, run in a directive manner. The only major innovations may be a new wheat puffer that can puff more wheat faster at a lower cost per ton, or there may be a superficial name change from the "SR-70" radial tire to "XG-95," or yesterday's "sugar goobers" become tomorrow's "smack snacks." The basic product, however, remains the same. These companies are straight-line, no-nonsense organizations.

Product Structure

When a company is market driven and when it has a variety of products directed at different customers, it tends to adopt a product structure. Thus, we find IBM with a separate division to design, produce, and sell its large computers as opposed to its office equipment division with typewriters and dictating equipment.

Figure 9-2 portrays a product structure for Shazam Electronics. Each division is headed by a general manager who has considerable autonomy for managing a profit center with bottom-line responsibility. These divisions operate like self-contained businesses, each conducted independently from the other. Top management is expected to devote its attention to broader issues, such as acquisitions, capital allocations, and reviewing the performance of decentralized units.

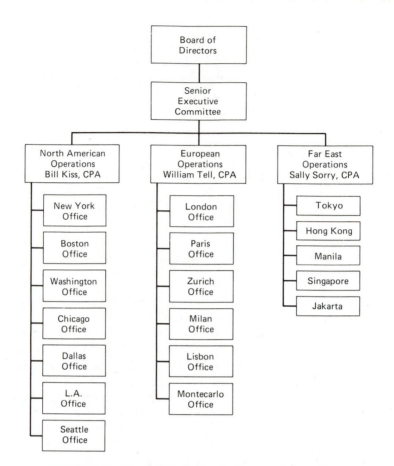

FIGURE 9-3   Kiss & Tell, CPAs—Auditors to Aristocrats

Geographic Structure

This form of organization is similar in concept to a product structure except that geographic boundaries determine the scope of each decentralized unit, such as the East and West regions. Geographic structures are necessary when close proximity and frequent contact is required between seller and buyer, such as in public accounting firms or the fast-food businesses (see Figure 9-3). Each district office of such organizations is located in a rich market where the customer base is large. The executive in charge of each office is responsible for penetrating the market as much as possible within its geographic limits.

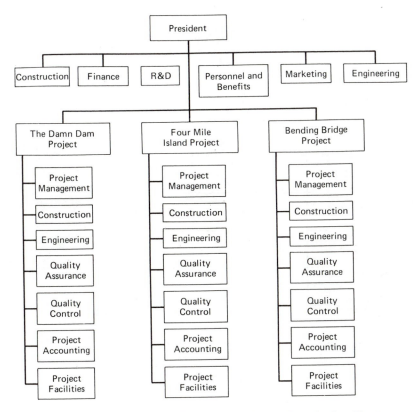

FIGURE 9-4   Calamity Construction Corp.—Organization Chart

Project Structure

Our fourth model, the project organization, deals primarily with engineering firms, special technology businesses, or construction companies. These organizations are relevant to businesses with a few one-of-a-kind projects, usually of massive size that move from a development stage to production and phase-out. It may involve the building of an oil refinery in Kuwait or the launch of the space shuttle. The economics of each project are sufficient to hire a full complement of employees, although at some point they will be transferred or laid off when a project is completed (see Figure 9-4).

Matrix Structure

A recent innovation is matrix organization, which represents a combination of functions and projects, and even sometimes a third

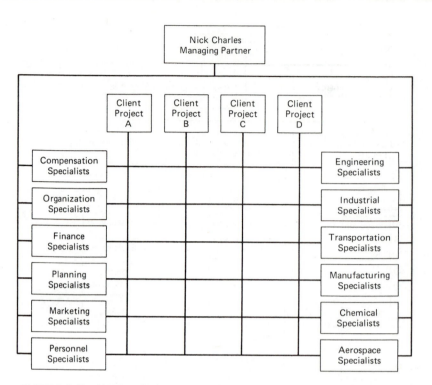

FIGURE 9-5   Charles, Cranston, Kato & Kent—Consultants to Management

dimension of geography. Such a structure can be found in R&D-oriented companies, consulting firms, entertainment businesses, educational institutions, and advertising agencies. Their projects are usually too small or short lived to support all their own staff. Thus, a matrix structure is formed with pools of employees in functional disciplines who are continuously assigned out to project managers (see Figure 9-5).

Matrix structures defy classical rules; since employees often work for at least two bosses at the same time, project managers are given more responsibility than authority, and decisions are made more by group consensus than by fiat. They are basically "flat" organizations that operate in a free-flowing "organic" mode.

THE DESIGN PROCESS

None of the five model structures can be applied in an arbitrary fashion. Each client's situation varies in its particular technology, strategic goals, customer expectations, and employee capabilities. Sometimes a hybrid structure is necessary; for example, the manufacturing operation may be set up as a functional entity while establishing product units within marketing to market a variety of products. In addition, the organization structure of various subunits may vary from one division to the next, such as the use of a geographic structure for one product group and a matrix structure for another product group.

All this argues for the consultant to "tailor make" each structure to "fit" the client's needs. Three major aims for any design process are to determine (1) how the organization should be grouped on a *horizontal* basis, (2) how many levels the organization should have on a *vertical* basis, and (3) which groups should report to what level to achieve *integration.*

Decisions about these three issues will be made after a careful analysis of the technology and work flow, coupled with an intensive look at the marketplace. The number of horizontal groups to be formed will depend on the variety of different disciplines required to produce and sell a product. The number of levels will depend on how much authority is needed at lower levels to make decisions. Integration in reporting relationships is dictated by determining which groups should be brought into close contact with other groups.

Case in Point

One client of ours was perplexed over why its decentralized plants, each producing a different product, were always complaining about delays in receiving parts from suppliers. We found that the purchasing department was buried two levels down in the accounting department and was separated organizationally from the manufacturing division. A change was made to decentralize purchasing to each of the manufacturing plants and to increase its importance by having it report directly to each plant manager.

In drawing up an organizational blueprint, emphasis should also be placed on what structure will be needed in the future. For example, if growth through new products is anticipated, consideration should be given to the gradual introduction of a product structure.

Case in Point

A consumer goods client had maintained a functional structure over many years while deriving large profits from a patented invention. As the established product began to lose appeal in the marketplace, two new products were designed and turned over to the sales force. However, neither was given much attention because of long dependence on a single product. The consultant's recommendation was to break up the functional structure and establish three separate product groups. The result was an immediate take-off for the new products.

A cardinal rule is never to design organizations to fit the preferences of senior executives. These individuals, as capable as they may be, will come and go. Besides, much of their training is conditioned by the past. Structures should be aimed toward getting the future job done, not satisfying the whims of a few people presently in power.

This is not to say that compromise between structure and people is ill advised. After designing the ideal structure, it will always be necessary to make a few judicious compromises to ease the present power structure through the transition. However, the ideal blueprint will serve as a constant guideline and reminder as executives retire and new ones are appointed.

SYSTEMS PLANNING

No organization structure can run effectively without a "package" of systems to monitor and regulate its effectiveness. Two basic types of systems are required by an organization: one is an *information and control system* to facilitate decision making; the other is a *human resource system* to motivate, reward, and develop employees. In this chapter, we will discuss the information system, leaving to Chapter 10 an examination of the human resource system.

The term "system" is often misused and abused by consultants and executives alike. It can be regarded as being "machinelike," as if the computer is the answer to controlling an organization. Many consultants sell their services on this mechanistic basis, seeking to rectify problems of the client through ever-larger computers that spew out vast amounts of information on every subject imaginable. Figure 9-6 shows a planning chart used by one such systems consultant.

While we have no quarrel with the important contribution of computers to managing discrete problems, such as inventory, purchasing, scheduling, and billing, there is much room to question the notion of letting a piece of hardware (the computer) determine a solution where virtually everything is thought to be programmable.

Our advice is to place the term "system" within the context of the client's particular organization structure. In essence, functional structures require systems different from product or matrix organizations. The consultant's focus should be on the specific needs of the client's organization, not on technological hardware.

Case in Point

We were recently called into a high-technology firm with a matrix organization. The symptom was cost overruns, but the real problem turned out to be the corporate controller who had failed to provide an information system

Arthur Andersen & Co.
Preliminary Systems Design
Planning Chart — Information Systems

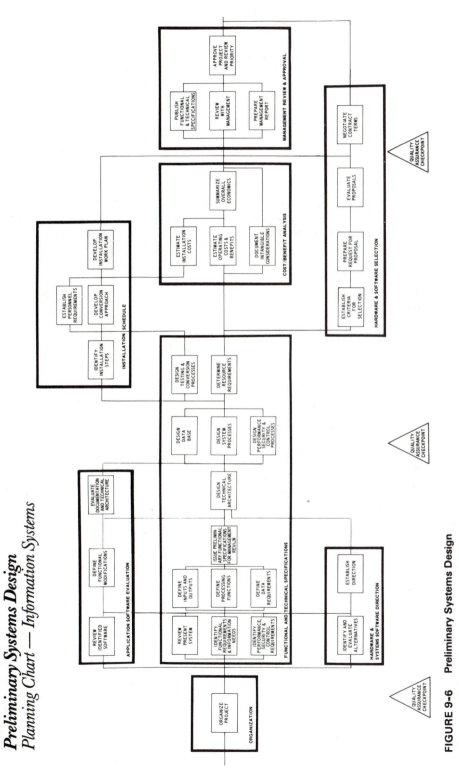

FIGURE 9-6 Preliminary Systems Design

Source: *Guide to Information Systems Planning Charts.* Copyright 1981. Arthur Andersen & Co., 18, quai Général-Guisan; 1211 Geneva 3, Switzerland.

that supplied up-to-date information to project managers on each project's costs. The controller had, instead, developed an information system for serving only top management with overall results on a quarterly basis—all compiled by an expensive computer programmed by a "systems" consultant. The controller was replaced.

INFORMATION AND
CONTROL SYSTEMS

Managers cannot operate in the dark; they rely on information to guide their decisions. Formal reporting methods should be dictated by the client's strategy and structure. If the goal of the organization is new accounts, then these results should be reported to the relevant managers. If the organization is based on a geographic structure, then each district and regional office becomes a control center with information reported regularly on its accomplishments.

The client's budgeting and goal-setting system becomes the focus of information systems design. It requires close attention to the following areas:

1. *What is the purpose of the system?*   Unless the purpose is clear to all concerned, numerous misunderstandings can arise. Is it to evaluate, or communicate, or reward, or some combination of all? Knowing the purpose will also help to make other systems consistent with the measurements, such as compensation.

2. *What goals should be set and measured?*   Here there is a wide variety of possible objectives to be set, ranging from cost reduction to employee development. Whatever the case, the goals should be controllable by those setting them. In addition, the goals should be important, meaningful, and few in number, as contrasted to a laundry list of housekeeping items.

3. *Who should participate in the system?*   One choice is for top management exclusively to set the goals and budgets. But most companies are too dynamic to presume complete knowledge on the part of senior executives. Should goals be set first based on the sales forecast? How participative should the system be? How important is it to set goals in team meetings?

4. *What should be the time frame for goals and budgets?*   It is common to set goals and budgets on an annual or semiannual basis. But this may be unrealistic when much longer-term objectives are at stake or when a short-term crisis is at hand. No system should be limited to a rigid fiscal calendar.

5. *Who should receive progress reports and in what format?*   Too often interim reports are made to the wrong managers and in a format that is difficult to decipher. Our advice is that all people involved

in goal-setting should receive timely reports on their efforts. Moreover, the data should be presented in a format that does not require a statistician or calculator to unravel.

6. *How should the goal-setting and budgeting system be linked to other systems?* Care should be taken to determine if operating goals and budgets are consistent with long-term objectives contained in the strategic plan. Another critical linkage is with the compensation system to make sure that rewards are consistent with goal attainment.

7. *Do managers and employees have the skill to implement the system?* It is easy to design a highly sophisticated system, but for what purpose if employees don't know how to use it? The old football adage of concentrating on blocking and tackling before running fancy pass patterns also applies to the design and management of systems. Often it will be necessary to conduct an intensive training program to assure understanding and skill with a new system and then to follow up periodically for making improvements.

Beyond the design of a formal goal-setting and budgeting system, which is accompanied by a complementary information system, the systems consultant should also address other means through which managers obtain and use information to solve problems and make decisions. Too often we, as consultants, are tempted to think that all relevant information is contained in numerical reports submitted by corporate accountants on a periodic basis. While this quantitative and routine source is highly useful, managers also rely heavily on informal means, such as spontaneous phone calls and impromptu meetings.

Day-to-day decision making requires facilities and arrangements that permit employees to share information readily. We give a lot of attention to the physical location of offices so that executives can contact each other easily. An effective committee structure is necessary; the committee should have a clear charter, and its members should meet regularly. Long-distance telephone communications should be readily available. Periodic conferences should be planned for larger groups, such as the sales force, on a quarterly or semiannual basis to obtain information from field managers and to brief them on what is happening.

Case in Point

A client was experiencing production delays in a two-shift factory operating on a job shop basis. One shift was continually blaming the other for mistakes, despite the keeping of careful records. Arrangements were made for the supervisor from one shift to arrive 45 minutes early so he could be briefed on prior events. Rapport increased and arguments ceased.

Another Case in Point

The executive committee of a large corporation met every Friday morning to discuss operating results and management development. The problem was that the discussion of performance crowded out time to discuss key executive appointments and to review middle-management personnel. A simple change was made to devote the Friday meetings exclusively to performance results and to set up a biweekly meeting on Thursdays for the sole purpose of addressing executive development.

FINAL CAVEAT

While there is much for the consultant to know about the intricacies of organization and systems design, we cannot emphasize enough the requirement to remain sensitive to each client's unique situation. It may be tempting to overwhelm the client with the latest organizational fad or systems hardware, but such zeal will only result in an embittered client.

In addition to the need to "tailor make" a structure and a set of systems, there is the crucial principle of "fit" to be applied to each recommendation. How well does the recommended structure fit with the client's strategy, technology, and marketplace? How well do the proposed systems fit with the organization structure? How well does the information system fit with the compensation system? And so forth.

Such recommendations cannot be made piecemeal; otherwise, there will be serious contradictions that will drive the client's employees to the asylum.

RECOMMENDED READINGS

DAVIS, STANLEY M., and PAUL R. LAWRENCE, *Matrix*. Reading, Mass.: Addison-Wesley, 1979.

FIEDLER-WINTER, ROSEMARIE, "Divisionalisation as an Aid—With or Without Consultants, Unrest Is Unavoidable," *Management International Review*, vol. 14, no. 6 (1974).

GALBRAITH, JAY R., *Designing Complex Organizations*. Reading, Mass.: Addison-Wesley, 1973.

HAYES, ROBERT H., and ROGER W. SCHMENNER, "How Should You Organize Manufacturing?" *Harvard Business Review*, January/February 1978.

MASON, RICHARD O., and E. BURTON SWANSON, *Measurement for Management Decisions*. Reading, Mass.: Addison-Wesley, 1981.

MINTZBERG, HENRY, "Organization Design: Fashion or Fit?" *Harvard Business Review*, January/February 1981.

MINTZBERG, HENRY, *The Structuring of Organizations*. Englewood Cliffs, N.J.: Prentice-Hall, Inc., 1979.

NOLAN, RICHARD L., "Managing the Crises in Data Processing," *Harvard Business Review*, March/April 1979.

ROCKART, JOHN F., "Chief Executives Define Their Own Data Needs," *Harvard Business Review*, March/April 1979.

SYNNOTT, WILLIAM R., and WILLIAM H. GRUBER, *Information Resource Management*. New York: John Wiley & Sons, 1981.

WEICK, K., *The Social Psychology of Organizing*, Reading, Mass.: Addison-Wesley, 1969.

10

Human Resource and Compensation Studies

Human resource studies deal with the psyche of the enterprise. Consulting in this field is the most subjective of all types of studies, yet it is apt to be the most important. Nothing happens in an organization until people take action. The art of administration is to accomplish goals *through* people, not around them or behind them, or without them.

The human resource consultant focuses on how people within client organizations relate to the organization and its objectives, to each other and mutual objectives, and to themselves in their work. Emphasis is placed on improving how the organization mobilizes itself to recruit, motivate, evaluate, reward, and develop its employees.

Many organizations today are using human resource consultants because of three major forces that are new to executives: (1) intense competition and declining productivity, (2) a proliferation of laws to assure equal opportunity and safety for employees, and (3) changing values among the work force with regard to the ways in which various employees want to be treated and involved in their jobs.

These new issues are causing companies to reevaluate their standard practices toward compensation, management training, career development, and performance appraisal. Fortunately, a great deal of research has been done on these subjects so that consultants do not have to propagate old myths. Moreover, many new and innovative techniques are available for replacing traditional practices.

THE COMPENSATION SYSTEM

About 50% of all human resource consulting is concerned with pay problems, and for good reason! The cost of compensation to clients constitutes from 25% to 40% of their total costs, and it is even higher in professional service firms. Moreover, national surveys of employees show about 50% of them to be dissatisfied with their pay.

All too often, the compensation plan is not evaluated carefully for its real effects on meeting both organization and individual goals. Instead, the pay system is tinkered with over the years to the point where it represents a mysterious catchall for the whims of yesterday's executives. Even the most up-to-date systems need to be reviewed continuously because of changes in the marketplace, employee social values, government legislation, and new techniques for awarding compensation.

Furthermore, research studies on pay and motivation reveal that employees have more complex needs than simply putting more bread on their tables. Beyond economic meaning, pay conveys to employees the values of their top management and identifies their "worth" within the company. How employees relate their pay to their peers is usually more important to them than the absolute amount of a paycheck.

DESIGNING BASE PAY

Pay is made up of three components: base salary or hourly wages, fringe benefits, and incentive compensation. Each element is determined in different ways and then put together as a total compensation system. Base pay is usually determined in a *job-based* manner; that is, what is the amount of pay that should go with the responsibility of a particular job? Fringe benefits are increasingly being designed for *person-based* reasons, thereby permitting individuals to select those benefits that best fit their life situation. Incentive pay tends to be *performance based*; that is, what additional rewards should be paid for exceptional performance. Easier said than done.

Most compensation consultants concentrate their base-pay analysis on determining what each job is worth, both within the company and in the labor marketplace. Hay Associates, the largest compensation specialists with annual billing of over $40 million, evaluates each job on the following basis:

- *Know-How.* Rating the technical, procedural, experience, education, O.J.T., managerial, and activity skills required to have sufficient knowledge to perform the job in question.
- *Problem Solving.* Rating the environment of thinking about the business, the restrictions the job places on thinking, and the degree of problem solving demanded by the job.
- *Accountability.* Rating the answerability of the job for the actions and consequences of the decisions made, the degree of supervisorial scope, the technical level of supervisory skill required, the degree of control to be exercised, the freedom to act, and the overall effect of the job on the bottom line.
- *Working Conditions.* Rating the job's environment, including working conditions, physical effort, degree of hazards, concentration and speed required, and so on.

Once each job has been evaluated on its own merit, all jobs are ranked relative to each other. They are then placed in a grade structure, similar to the one shown in Table 10-1 where grades range from E-1 to E-7. This determines their "internal worth."

Specific salary amounts and ranges for each grade are determined based on "external worth" after a careful market survey of pay scales used by the competition. It may be that the "competition" is not so much the industry but the surrounding geographic area. Employees are likely to leave if they learn that their jobs are valued more highly outside the client's firm.

Salary surveys are an art unto themselves and care must be taken to assure that those jobs being compared across companies are indeed similar in responsibility. Consulting firms with a compensation expertise routinely prepare surveys, as do industry trade associations. Sometimes, the consultant can ask the client to sponsor a survey on its own, while volunteering to share the data among the responding companies. Exhibit 10-1 represents such a survey request. The survey questionnaire typically contains a number of job descriptions and asks for the amount of compensation attached to each job. The motivation to respond is the promise of shared results, which are then communicated without identifying the companies involved.

Typically, salary ranges within a grade are set according to a "maturity curve" concept. Simply stated, this concept assumes that employees within a given salary grade will progress more rapidly in the early stages; then as they become more familiar with their responsibilities, they will reach a peak of maturity. Using this concept, an employee should only be hired or promoted into a new position at or below the

TABLE 10-1 Tar and Tobacco Industries Recommended Management Salary Ranges

GRADE	OFFICE OF PRESIDENT	PRODUCTION	FINANCE	ADMINISTRATION	MARKETING	SALES	RANGE
E-7	President and CEO						$150,000 125,000 100,000
E-6	Executive vice president	General manager, high-technology plant					112,500 94,000 75,400
E-5	Corporate CFO	General manager, retail goods plant; assistant general manager, high-technology unit	CFO, high-technology plant		Director of marketing, high-technology unit	Director of sales, high-technology unit	85,000 70,000 56,000
E-4	Corporate directors of administration, marketing, and legal	General manager, tobacco plant; assistant general manager, retail unit; plant supervisor, high-technology unit	CFO, retail unit	Administrative director, high-technology	Direct marketing, retail unit; assistant director of marketing, high-technology unit	Director of sales, retail unit assistant director of sales high-technology unit	63,000 52,500 42,000
E-3		Assistant general manager, tobacco unit; plant supervisor, retail unit; production engineer, high-technology unit	CFO, tobacco unit; controller, high-technology unit	Administrative director, retail unit	Assistant director of marketing, retail unit	Senior sales representative, high-technology unit	47,000 40,000 33,000
E-2				Administrative director, tobacco unit			35,500 30,000 24,000
E-1							27,000 22,500 18,000

midpoint of that position. The following are some common guidelines for handling points along the maturity curve:

1. *Minimum Value.* This level represents the amount the client would expect to pay for the minimum required performance of the job as it relates to a person new to that job and experiencing a high, fast learning curve.
2. *Midpoint.* This level represents what the client would pay for average performance of an adequately experienced employee in any particular rate range. Generally, most employees would be performing at or near the midpoint of their position's rate range.
3. *Maximum.* This level represents the maximum amount the client is willing to pay for an employee performing a particular job. The maximum value of a rate range is set so that the value, and hence the salary, of an employee in that range is never worth more to the company than the maximum figure.
4. *Control Point.* The control point is set at 80% of the range in any salary grade. The control point shown for each salary level is a "flag" that signals that only one or two more increases can be given to an employee before reaching the maximum in that level. When the control point is reached, the employee must be evaluated very carefully for promotion. If it appears that the employee has reached maximum effectiveness and should not be promoted, the next increase will bring that employee to the maximum for the range. Further increases will then be made only when the level itself is changed with new established minimums and maximums. When an employee reaches the control point, performance should be discussed at length on a personal level with the immediate supervisor.

The issue of base pay at lower levels in the organization is currently the subject of much debate and experimentation. Hourly wages has been the most common method of payment. However, an increasing number of companies, such as IBM have adopted a salary system for all employees, believing that it will reduce worker alienation and promote loyalty. Other companies, such as General Foods, have experimented with pay for "learned jobs," which encourages employees to learn as many jobs as possible in a plant. Employees are then paid for the number of jobs mastered, regardless of their current jobs.

Managerial levels are also being exposed to new compensation plans. At Donnelly Mirrors, a leading auto supply company in Michigan, managers are permitted to set their own salaries within a team framework. Each team is given a salary pool and is expected to set individual salaries around the average midpoint of a grade structure similar to the one described previously. However, any group may set salaries above the average midpoint, which is indexed at 100, provided that they regard their performance as outstanding. All indices are published and other teams may challenge the index of another team if they feel that it is too high.

FRINGE BENEFITS

There are many different kinds of fringe benefits and incentives. Financial fringes include cash bonuses; group health, life, disability, and dental insurance; company cars; and continuing education programs. Nonfinancial fringes include vacation periods, extra days off, shorter workweeks, company-sponsored social and sports events, trips to industry conventions, and so on. Delayed fringe benefits, most of which are financial, include retirement programs, stock options, and extended bonus awards. Perquisites or "perks" are variations of fringes for senior executives, such as a Cadillac in place of a Chevrolet, free annual physical exams, free legal and tax counsel, use of the corporate jet, and first-class air travel.

The compensation consultant should approach fringe benefit analysis based on a client's industry practices, its management's philosophy, and its employee preferences. One of the best sources of information is to ask employees themselves. Fringe benefits can be very costly yet not appreciated. A questionnaire to employees asking them to rank their present fringes and to list new ones they want can reveal a lot.

A growing practice is the "cafeteria" approach, in which employees are allowed to choose from a shopping list of benefits. Younger employees may want more benefits in the form of cash or greater vacation time; older employees may want more life and health insurance. TRW Systems has pioneered in this flexible method of fringe allocations.

INCENTIVES

The most uncertain and experimental area is the awarding of performance-based incentives, now called "gain-sharing" plans. Traditional practices built around cash bonuses and engineered production standards are giving way to delayed bonus plans and group incentives. Senior executives are receiving incentives that have multiple payoffs over several years, the rationale being that consistent performance is more important than short-term profitability. At the worker level, group incentives, such as the Scanlon plan, are being used to encourage cost reduction and innovation. Teams of workers are allowed to share in the fruits of their labor when they exceed goals set jointly between management and themselves.

All performance-based plans vary from company to company. It is easier to attach incentive pay to work that can be measured more objectively than to subjective jobs. Technologies that require interdependent effort are more conducive to group incentives than is individualized production work. Most important is the willingness of employees to accept whatever incentive plan is presented to them. If they do not understand the plan or if they feel that it is unfair, then motivation to perform is diminished.

PERFORMANCE APPRAISAL

Probably the most frustrating human resource issue for clients is the design and management of an effective performance appraisal system. Subordinates typically complain that their appraisals are unfair, whereas bosses hate to "play God." As a result, the vast majority of employees end up with "average" to "favorable" performance ratings; high performers are rated downward and low performers upward.

Three types of ratings are available: *individual traits, job behavior,* and *goal achievement.* The trait method, which assesses individual characteristics such as intelligence and drive, has never proven out in research studies to predict performance, although it is still used in many companies. The job behavior method identifies those actions required by a specific job, such as cooperation or punctuality, and research evidence reveals some positive relationship with performance. By far the soundest and most supportable method, both from a research and employee acceptance standpoint, is an appraisal system based on goals set by the employee.

Management by objectives (MBO) has been the principal goal-setting method used with success in performance appraisals. The installation of MBO in many companies has fallen largely on human resource consultants who are knowledgeable in its details. Basically, MBO involves setting goals in a participative manner between subordinates and supervisors. In this way, both parties share a common expectation for what is to be accomplished. Performance appraisals are conducted around the extent to which a subordinate meets or exceeds preset goals. A self-appraisal written by the subordinate is helpful in leading to a constructive dialogue when conducting a review session with an anxious boss.

Underlying any appraisal method, however, there are three phases that should be given close attention in its design and implementation. One step is to make sure that the boss and subordinate reach an understanding beforehand of the job itself—what are its requirements as seen through the eyes of both parties? Next, there should be agreement on what elements of performance are to be measured. Last, there should be a constructive follow-up session in which both parties have sufficient opportunity to discuss and assess the results.

Questions often arise as to how salary and career development should be handled in terms of performance appraisal. Our advice is to separate the three issues into three separate discussions. Trying to tackle all three issues at once can result in a lot of defensive behavior with disastrous outcomes. A performance appraisal session held a few weeks before a salary session can add valuable information that may not be known to the boss, and it may also help the subordinate to understand better any future salary decisions. Personal development sessions should follow later on as the subordinate has had time to think about what he or she needs to do to make longer-term improvements.

CAREER DEVELOPMENT

Human resource consultants are frequently used to help clients in developing long-range systems for assuring a capable work force five to ten years off. Organizations must know how many new people will have to be recruited to fill turnover and handle growth requirements. They must also know the kinds of job skills that will be required from either new employees or those who are promoted.

Personnel planning systems are based on projections made about the future size of the client, and these numbers are in turn matched against calculations about how many people will leave through retirement, resignation, and termination. A recruitment plan can then be drawn up to calculate how many people to hire each year. The computer is useful in making these projections, as it is in storing valuable background data on each employee. When a job opening arises, the computer bank can be tapped for likely candidates to fill the vacant position.

Another developmental activity centers around technical training and management education. The present work force cannot stand still if future challenges are to be met. Consultants should perform a "needs assessment" by examining the capabilities of present employees and then designing, and even conducting, training sessions. Considerable monies are spent needlessly on training without tailoring each training program to the particular needs of employees and the future organization.

Equal employment laws have given rise to the need for affirmative action programs. Consultants who are expert in the implications of the EEO laws are working closely with clients to avoid hiring and promotion practices that discriminate and prevent costly lawsuits. These practices must assure objectivity and receive complete documentation. More important, the goal is to open up all positions to the best talent.

Effective career development programs will include counseling services to assist employees with alcohol and drug problems. Career-path planning can be used to increase alternative routes for promotion, rotation, cross-training, and on-the-job training. Medical services can be used to promote a healthy work force through company-sponsored physical exams and stress reduction programs.

EXECUTIVE SEARCH

A specialist activity performed by a number of consulting firms lies in the domain of executive search. The term "head-hunting" has been used unfairly to characterize this important service to clients. While its negative image applies to those few firms that deal only in want ads, most professional firms develop an extensive consulting relationship with the client before searching for prospective candidates.

Executive search consultants need to spend a great deal of time "up front" with the client to understand fully what the vacant job requires, what are its future expectations, what was good or bad about the previous employee, and to whom will the prospective employee be reporting. Behind this analysis, the consultant needs to determine if the job itself is structured properly and given sufficient support to assure the right conditions for success.

Case in Point

A previous client was searching for a new director of engineering services, after terminating one executive who was deemed "too nice" and one who was seen as "too authoritarian." The client was looking for the "perfect" personality. However, a deeper analysis revealed that the job itself was given so little authority that just about anyone was doomed to fail. New job specifications were written, and a successful candidate was hired.

After studying the job requirements, it is useful to develop an employment advertisement to attract the right people. The job should be described briefly but accurately without creating unrealistic expectations. The required background experience and education should have sufficient detail to appeal only to the most likely candidates (but be careful to watch your EEO laws). Then place the ad in *The Wall Street Journal*, local major newspapers, and trade publications—the choice of which depends on whether or not the search is nationwide. Also, don't forget about alumni placement offices of the key business and technical schools. Another good source is letters or phone calls to executive friends who may just know of someone (including themselves!).

In the job advertisement, don't run a return address or ask for a resumé. Any nincompoop can spend $50 to hire a professional to prepare and write a fancy resumé. It's a waste of a recruiter's time to plow through 500 to 1,000 resumés sent to a post office box. Instead, print only a toll-free number or a number the respondent can call collect. The deadbeats and nonself-starters won't even bother to call. Based on responses to telephone questions such as "Why are you looking for a new job?," "Why do you want to leave your present employer?," and "What are your career aims?," the best and the brightest will separate themselves from the thundering herd. Then, from these key people, ask for a resumé. Upon reviewing all the submitted resumés, start the interview process with the ten best and narrow the field down to the top three.

At the final interviews, which should be conducted with the client, be present to help ask the right questions, to be a calming influence on the candidates, and to make sure that each gets a fair shot at the job. After the interviews, you should act as a negotiator for the client with respect to salary amount and fringe benefits. Never offer more money without checking with the client, and remember that, once the client has decided who it wants, you are the salesperson for the client.

Finally, never, ever say anything to any of the final three candidates until the first choice has accepted the client's offer in writing. If either party changes his or her mind or an agreement can't be worked out on salary, title, or whatever, you want to be able to go back to the other candidates in terms of *their* belief that they were "number 1" in the selection process. Always send a letter to those interviewed who didn't get the job, thanking them for their time, and, of course, offering to keep their resumés on file.

Search fees are somewhat unique and standardized in the industry. Most executive search consultants charge 25–30% of the employee's first year's salary for jobs paying $25,000 a year or less and 30–35% for jobs over $25,000 per year. This is the professional fee only, and related expenses for advertisements, travel, telephone, and so on should be billed separately.

ORGANIZATION DEVELOPMENT

Even when a client organization has a well-designed human resource system in place, numerous human problems still arise out of daily interaction between employees. Consultants can be especially helpful in identifying these important human problems that are escaping the attention of senior executives and in bringing organization development skills to the resolution of these problems.

One such approach is to perform a "culture analysis" of the organization. All organizations have an informal structure composed of norms for how "good" employees should behave. The consultant can identify these norms and indicate their consequences for productivity and morale. We prefer a data-gathering method that uses a combination of confidential interviews and an anonymous questionnaire, both of which seek to answer the question: "How should an employee behave if they want to get ahead in the company?" A careful investigation will clearly identify the "do's" and "don'ts" for employee behavior.

Case in Point

A *Fortune* 100 corporation sought our assistance in determining why it had been unsuccessful in its diversification program. Our analysis found the answer in its corporate culture. Some significant "do's" of the culture were "Be careful" and "Pay your dues by working for years in the company's traditional line of business." Some "don'ts" were "don't be different" and "don't take risks." The consequence was that newly hired entrepreneurial executives in the diversified divisions felt isolated and unwanted; as a result, they were leaving in droves.

A second useful organization development activity is process consultation and team building. Many executive teams do not function effectively as a problem-solving group. The skilled process consultant will sit in on meetings and make observations about such issues as how the group handles conflict and trust. Experiential exercises can be used to heighten the group's awareness of their destructive behavior patterns. An even deeper analysis can be made privately through interviews to understand why certain individuals are withholding cooperation from others; then the warring parties can be brought together by the consultant for an open and constructive confrontation of the issues.

Action research is a technique employed often by organization development consultants to flush out critical problems that affect a large segment of the employee population. Questionnaires are used to inquire about a broad range of subjects from job satisfaction to the leadership effectiveness of supervisors. Results are then analyzed and reported back to management in an open discussion forum. Instead of the consultant's drawing definitive conclusions and proposing solutions, the management group is asked to reach its own conclusions and to decide for itself on a plan of action. The following list includes organizational and attitudinal issues for action research analysis.

Survey Categories

1. *Immediate Supervision.* Effectiveness of relationship between employees and their immediate supervisor.
2. *Top Management.* Trust, confidence, and respect for top-level management.
3. *Meaningful Work.* Satisfaction with the job, its worth, and contribution to the organization.
4. *Innovation.* Flexibility and creativity in organization.

5.   *Personal Growth and Advancement.* Opportunity to develop within the organization and the likelihood of being promoted.

6.   *Recognition.* Extent to which employees feel that they are rewarded for good work and are appreciated.

7.   *Compensation and Benefits.* Adequacy of the present salary structure and the benefit program(s) available.

8.   *Teamwork.* Cohesiveness and intradepartment loyalty and cooperation.

9.   *Organizational Clarity.* Understanding of the organization's goals and expectations of employees.

10. *Responsibility.* Extent to which employees feel that they are delegated the appropriate amount of responsibility and authority.

11. *Identification with Company.* Long- and short-term commitment to the organization.

12. *Decision Making.* Employees' active voice in organization and/or departmental decisions.

13. *Interpersonal Relations.* Supportiveness of the work environment within the organization.

14. *Performance Standards.* Employee and organization concern for high performance standards.

15. *Organizational Vitality.* Extent to which the organization is dynamic, venturesome, innovative, and responsive.

16. *Communications.* Effectiveness of dissemination of information about operations and activities within the organization.

17. *Responsiveness to Employees.* Responsiveness of the organization to input by employees.

18. *Conflict Resolution.* Present way of resolving conflicts in the organization.

19. *Affirmative Action.* Present hiring and promotion practices relative to women and racial minorities.

20. *Causes of Turnover.* Reasons why people leave the organization for another.

21. *Reactions to New Policies and Programs.* Understanding, acceptance, and implementation of recently established policies and/or programs.

22. *Organization Structure.* Organization structure's relation to organizational goals and operating efficiency.

23. *Employee Development.* Training and development available; its contribution to performance and promotions people receive to improve their present performance and promotion potential.

24. *Technical and Administrative Competence.* The organization's use of competent, knowledgeable people.

Another way in which to identify important problems is through the use of retreats attended by 15 to 25 key employees. The consultant acts as a moderator in helping the attendees to focus on major problem issues. Our approach is to ask each participant to bring along a list of four to six issues that, in his or her opinion, need attention by the larger group. We then divide the total group into three to five subgroups that meet for a few hours to merge their individual issues into a group consensus. The various subgroups then report to the total group, from which a composite list of issues is created. New subgroups are formed to work on solutions to each of the issues. While decisions are rarely taken in these meetings, each subgroup can be asked to make a final report within a few weeks after studying the issues more carefully.

All these organization development approaches, as well as many of those mentioned earlier, are presently being used by consultants in quality of work life (QWL) programs for clients. Such programs involve the redesign of work to increase employee autonomy and give a sense of whole task accomplishment, introduce the payment of group rewards for increased production, and promote the use of participative supervision. These broad-based efforts are intended to develop a total human resource philosophy that simultaneously enriches life at work and enhances productivity.

TECHNIQUES ARE NOT SYSTEMS SOLUTIONS

We have continually warned against the indiscriminate use of techniques, as if swallowing a bottle of green pills will cure the disease. Human resource consultants are frequently guilty of this superficial practice.

The effective human resource consultant will seek *systemic* solutions. For example, clients with a matrix structure will require a human resource system completely different from clients with a pyramidal structure. Professional employees in the matrix will hold completely different career and reward expectations from workers on the assembly line. Clients with complex technologies will require a great deal of attention in promoting team creativity, whereas simpler technologies will require new motivational techniques to relieve worker boredom and alienation.

To improve the human resources system of a client, it is likely that a number of interrelated solutions will be required. The current fad around "quality circles" is a good example. Simply involving employees in brainstorming sessions may provide an initial emotional lift, but when the wider system does not reward suggestions or when senior managers do not endorse participative methods for other activities, employees will "turn off" to these hypocritical solutions.

RECOMMENDED READINGS

BECKER, STEVEN, "How To Work With - And Manage - Outside Training Consultants," *Training*, vol. 13, no. 7 (July 1976).

DYER, WILLIAM G., *Team Building: Issues and Alternatives*. Reading, Mass.: Addison-Wesley, 1977.

ENTHOVEN, ALAIN C., "Consumer-Centered vs. Job-Centered Health Insurance," *Harvard Business Review*, January/February 1979.

FOULKES, FRED K., "How Top Nonunion Companies Manage Employees," *Harvard Business Review*, September/October 1981.

HACKMAN, J. RICHARD, and GREG R. OLDHAM, *Work Redesign*. Reading, Mass.: Addison-Wesley, 1977.

HUMBLE, JOHN W., *Management by Objectives in Action*. New York: McGraw-Hill, 1970.

JAQUES, ELLIOTT, "Taking Time Seriously in Evaluating Jobs," *Harvard Business Review*, September/October 1979.

KRAUS, DAVID, "Executive Pay: Ripe for Reform," *Harvard Business Review*, September/October 1980.

LAWLER, EDWARD E., III, *Pay and Organization Development*. Reading, Mass.: Addison-Wesley, 1981.

LIPPITT, GORDON L., and LEONARD NADLER, "Emerging Roles of the Training Director," *Training & Development Journal*, vol. 33, no. 6 (June 1979).

NOLLEN, STANLEY D., "Does Flexitime Improve Productivity?" *Harvard Business Review*, September/October 1979.

RAPPAPORT, ALFRED, "Executive Incentives vs. Corporate Growth," *Harvard Business Review*, July/August 1978.

SKINNER, WICKHAM, "Big Hat, No Cattle: Managing Human Resources," *Harvard Business Review*, September/October 1981.

STATE, RAY, and MODESTO A. MAIDIQUE, "Bonus System for Balanced Strategy," *Harvard Business Review*, November/December 1980.

STEINBRINK, JOHN P., "How To Pay Your Sales Force," *Harvard Business Review*, July/August 1978.

EXHIBIT 10-1   Sample Covering Letter for an Industry Compensation Survey

CHARLES. CRANSTON. KATO & KENT
CONSULTANTS TO MANAGEMENT
123 PROGRESS AVENUE
GOTHAM CITY. U.S.A.

Mr. I. M. Obese
President
Skinny Foods, Inc.
Infarct Plaza
Cholesterol, Colorado 77322

Dear Mr. Obese,

We need your help. As national management consultants to the
health food industry, we have been engaged by one of your peer
organizations to determine recent and present compensation
trends in your industry. If you are willing to participate in
this survey, we will send you at no cost a copy of the overall
industry results we compile. These results will show how your
firm ranks in the industry with respect to executive compensation, both salary and fringe benefits. To sponsor such a study
on your own would cost thousands of dollars. By participating
in this survey, the cost to you will be no more than a few hours
time of your Director of Personnel.

We would appreciate your giving him or her the enclosed Questionnaire to fill in and return to us no later than September 15,
1981. Should Personnel have any questions, they should contact
Mr. Lamont Cranston of our firm. We thank you sincerely for
your assistance and cooperation.

Respectfully yours,

Nick Charles

Nick Charles
Managing Principal

NC/jec
Enc.

II

Data-Gathering Methods
The Art of Inquiry

Each client's situation is sufficiently different from textbook models to require an in-depth study of the client's problem. Chapters 6 through 10 have provided you with some "deductive" tools that suggest what to look for when the client problem resembles the model type. But models can be elegant traps if used to provide ideal answers without carefully examining the realities and uniqueness of each client.

Medical doctors (and, it is hoped, consultants) are trained not only in models but in data-gathering skills. That is why doctors move out of the classroom to become interns. Models suggest typical symptoms of a particular disease, but the doctor learns quickly that each patient is unique—that symptoms can be misleading unless understood within the context of a careful diagnosis of each patient's medical history.

This chapter highlights the principal data-gathering methods available to the consultant. These include interviews, questionnaires, observations, and other sources of data routinely available in- and outside the client organization.

Consultants must become proficient in utilizing all four approaches as each has advantages and disadvantages that enlighten or limit one's view of the client's problem. For example, interviews can yield a richness of opinion that far exceeds sterile numbers from a questionnaire, but interviews can also be costly and time consuming. Moreover, how does one know if interviewees have told the "truth"?

We will discuss each of these four data-gathering methods in some detail; however, the experienced consultant will also realize that reading about them is not the same as being able to practice them skillfully. Each technique takes a great deal of skill acquired through years of both study *and* practice.

DATA AND THEIR MULTIPURPOSES

Consultants gather data for a variety of reasons, the most obvious being to shed light on the client's problem. The problem, as outlined in the written proposal, is often a statement of symptoms but not the deeper problem itself. Continuous probing by the consultant will turn up data from lower-level employees that are not available to senior executives. These data frequently suggest a new set of underlying causes and perhaps even a completely different definition of the problem.

Case in Point

At a recent executive conference in a large insurance company, one of the authors conducted a series of "informal" interviews at the evening cocktail party. The first evening found executives complaining about the "lack of decentralization" in the company. The next night, when the author asked "why the lack of decentralization?," it was explained by several executives that there was a "lack of corporate strategy," which made it impossible to decentralize unless there was a clear direction for the company. Finally, the third evening yielded an entirely different version of the situation: when probed for explanations about the lack of corporate strategy, numerous comments were made that strategic planning was impossible because the chief executive was going to retire and his successor had not been found. The author pondered later what would have happened had he accepted and acted upon the original problem definition given at the first cocktail party?

Another important purpose for data gathering is to discover "solutions" based on the emerging preferences, abilities, and weaknesses of the client. Quite frequently, the client's employees will possess among themselves some very creative solutions that are hidden three levels down and that the consultant might never have dreamed up alone.

Even if a brilliant solution doesn't appear in the data, the consultant can often sense from various data-gathering contacts those types of solutions that might be well received or rejected. We have discovered on numerous occasions that a client's problem cannot be solved, as it theoretically should be, by hiring a new executive from outside the company because "promotion from within" is too cherished by the client's management and employees.

Data can also be used to persuade the client—"objective" evidence is usually needed beyond the consultant's word. Physically ill patients may defer easily to their esteemed doctors, but consulting clients are rarely so trusting in their consultants. Therefore, the consultant's final report will usually contain tables of questionnaire results or typical quotes from interviews, displayed as a means of convincing the client of the consultant's conclusions.

Some consultants, in fact, concentrate on presenting data without conclusions, leaving it to the client to engage in its own analysis and interpretation of the findings. This approach, called *action research*, assumes that the client will become more motivated to change if involved directly in the problem analysis. More sophisticated clients often prefer to see the actual data, since they view their analytical powers as comparable with the consultant's.

Finally, data gathering serves as a check and restraint on the consultant's biases. All consultants, no matter how experienced or educated, bring a set of "pet" theories and solutions to each client. Consultants should welcome data gathered objectively as a source of control on their own impulses. Otherwise, they might prescribe chemotherapy when the patient only needs aspirin.

THE INTERVIEW

Interviews are a primary source of a consultant's findings and are usually the sole basis of information prior to preparing a proposal for work. Interviews are relevant to all types of consulting projects, from installing new accounting systems to performing an executive search. They provide a richness of facts, perceptions, feelings, and opinions that cannot be obtained through any other method. And they also allow the consultant to become "acquainted" with the client; otherwise, the consultant remains a faceless firm that may be seen as too impersonal to trust.

There are disadvantages and limits to the interview approach; it has all the frailties of any human, one-on-one encounter. The effective consultant realizes that interview data are purely one individual's perceptions. Truth is in the "eye of the beholder," and it may be distorted for personal or unconscious reasons. No matter how convincing an executive's opinion may sound, the careful consultant will double-check it further through additional interviews and with other data-gathering methods.

Ideally, every employee should be interviewed, but that is obviously impractical. Interviews are costly in terms of time consumed, so you must choose and schedule them wisely. A representative sample should be picked; its size and breadth will vary with the problem and the size of company. Broad problems in large companies will often take 50–100 interviews to develop a reliable base. In medium-sized companies 30–50 interviews will do, and in small firms most managers and supervisors can be interviewed.

We never limit our interviews exclusively to senior management. The larger the organization, the less likely is bad news to reach the top—the hierarchy has too many filters. So schedule your interviews to include not only the top five or six senior officers, but twice as many midlevel managers, and at least an equal number of first-line supervisors.

If the scope of the consulting job is purely marketing, one would naturally want to interview everyone in marketing. But watch out for group bias! All you may get is marketing's self-serving perceptions of itself ("great but unappreciated"), its unique view of the budget ("we never get enough and are the first to be cut"), and its denigration of the client's ad agency ("if they would only follow our plans, we wouldn't have so many conflicts").

So always look for opinions from "outsiders" to the problem; you may get a very different picture. For example, if the problem is defined as the design of a new control and information system, don't confine your discussions to the EDP experts and accountants. Your best clues for a practical design will probably come from the user managers who are not so impressed with numbers and the computer.

Another way in which to control for bias is to use group interviews. One employee cannot distort information so easily in a group because others are there to evaluate a comment's validity. The major disadvantage of group interviews is that individuals may not speak up with their true feelings because their peers are listening.

Interviewing is an exercise in active listening. It is not a time for the learned consultant to educate the client or to tell war stories from past engagements. You must stay tuned to the idea or feeling being expressed by the interviewee. Your own comments should be brief, confined more to questions, restatements, or a simple "umm."

Each interview should begin with a brief introduction of yourself and the project. State the purpose of the interview, which basically is to learn how employees see the problem under study. During the initial moments, you should concentrate on putting the interviewee at ease. If you are tense, so will be the interviewee.

Most important, before turning the talking segment over to the interviewee, is to give strong reassurance of confidentiality. A cardinal rule is to never reveal the source of specific comments to senior executives or your client sponsor, and this should be made clear to the interviewee. It is a basic policy for obtaining trust; don't violate it, even when grilled later by a senior executive. Violation will not only ruin the trust level but may cost you and others their jobs.

There are two distinct types of data that one gathers from interviews: facts and personal opinions. To gather facts, you should ask direct questions such as, "How many people report directly to you?" "What is the average day's production capacity for the widget welder?" Be certain that you also discover the source of these facts through the use of testing questions: "Is that what is shown on the organization chart?" "Does that number come off a company report?"

Gathering personal opinions, which in turn unveils other kinds of facts, is often more complicated. The authors have a preference toward exploratory and open-ended questions: "What do you think is working well for the company and you in your job; what is not going well, what's getting in the way; and what is not being done that ought to be done?"

These are broad questions that, unfortunately, can lead to broad answers. The perceptive consultant must narrow the scope of responses with such probing questions as, "Why do you say that? What makes you feel this way? Is the production manager that angry with everyone, all the time? What specifically do you think ought to be done? Why hasn't it happened?" Each question is designed to bring out a more concrete and complete picture of the problem.

Invariably, the consultant will run into one manager who is "Mr. Untroubled." For reasons of hostility, self-preservation, company loyalty, or whatever, no matter what the consultant asks, the response will be, "Everything is fine. . . . We're a great company and I'm proud to be on the team."

The authors have found only one way (aside from walking out) in which to deal effectively with Mr. Untroubled, who is stonewalling the consultant; it is the confrontation approach. The consultant should confront Mr. U with some of the findings to date (but never the sources). For example, "I understand your concern to protect old Farnsworth, but we already know a great deal about him and his relationship with Miss Peaches . . . all I want to know is how Farnsworth affects your work." Another counter to Mr. Untroubled is, "I respect your concern for confidentiality, but everyone here has been very candid about things and the end result may be helpful to you and your job. This is your chance to really say what you think." And, if all else fails, you can always try the "you are alone" approach: "I realize your discomfort in talking about these sensitive issues, but everyone else has been very candid with us, and if you aren't, you'll be the only one who thinks everything is just wonderful."

QUESTIONNAIRES

The questionnaire survey is the consultant's most powerful tool for yielding maximum information in the most efficient manner. Next in importance would come the client's financial data for the last three years, but information gained from questionnaires is powerful brew.

Questionnaires are used most commonly in management audits, market research, organization and compensation studies, attitude surveys, and the development of training programs.

Questionnaires serve a different purpose from interviews. A questionnaire can cover many more people, especially at lower levels of the corporation. It elicits numerical values that can be analyzed with statistical techniques to sort out complex relationships. Numbers are also useful in documenting findings in presentations to senior management. A great many questions can be asked in a questionnaire because of its structured format. It is also a good follow-up to interviews because the consultant can substantiate more precisely the subjective opinions and feelings gained from earlier discussions.

Disadvantages of the questionnaire approach center around its overall cost and potential superficiality. While the cost is low per respondent and even lower per bit of information obtained, the total cost can easily run over $30,000 for designing, printing, and analyzing returns from 1,000 employees on a very basic survey.

Superficiality is a risk because questionnaire design and its accompanying statistical analyses require skills not usually possessed by consultants. Entire books have been written on how to design a questionnaire that measures more than the momentary whims of the respondent. Complex statistical techniques and computer programs are necessary to show how one factor is related to another, such as how morale is related to pay in explaining employee turnover. Questionnaires, therefore, are not to be dreamed up on the spur of the moment, nor are the results to be analyzed casually.

Three critical elements exist in the development of a questionnaire: its design and content, the method by which it is introduced, and the use of follow-up interviews to test and clarify the findings.

We suggest the following guidelines, along with lots of practice and reading from scholarly books, in preparing the design of a questionnaire:

- Start the questionnaire with a brief statement of its purpose, and stress the confidentiality of responses. Make signing the questionnaire voluntary or anonymous.
- Include a self-addressed, stamped envelope with which the respondent can return the questionnaire directly to your firm; no one else in the client organization should see these responses.
- Set aside a section to obtain as much data as possible on each respondent's

background and position in the company (without, of course, being able to identify that person by name). These data, such as department, level, age and seniority, will provide the basic categories for analyzing the results. For example, do long-term employees feel more commitment to company goals than do newcomers?

- Structure 90% of the questions to be answered quantitatively. Open-ended questions are extremely difficult to tabulate and should be limited to a "write-in" section, or "comments," or "other suggestions."
- Utilize questions that can be rated on a five- or seven-point scale. Avoid the use of simple "yes or no" or three-point scale questions, which are too insensitive to show a realistic spread of opinion.
- Occasionally work in a question twice with different phrasing to test the consistency of the participants' responses.
- Phrase the questions simply in a short, terse, and concrete style; avoid using complex words to impress the respondent.
- Divide the questionnaire into sections on different subjects, so that respondents will not feel bored or overwhelmed by an endless list of questions from 1 to 300.
- Pretest the questionnaire with a few of the client's employees. This will eliminate the inevitable bugs due to an outsider's not fully understanding the language and practices of the client.
- Use a continuous ring binder to put the questionnaire together so that pages will not get lost, as well as to give the questionnaire a professional, important appearance.

See Exhibit 11-1 for a sample of style and technique in a typical questionnaire.

Equally important to the design and content of the questionnaire is the atmosphere and method by which it is introduced. Here are a few suggestions:

- Allow the client to review the questionnaire to make one or two editorial changes so as to give a feeling of participation and ownership. But do not allow the client to rewrite the questionnaire, as some will try to do.
- Work with the client to identify which groups of people in the organization should receive the questionnaire; try to go as deep in the organization as possible, since first-line supervisors often know more about the root problems of companies than do senior managers. Also, try to cover as many employees as possible who are affected by the problem, or if the number of employees is too large, use random numbers; don't allow the client to selectively pick respondents by name.
- Ask the CEO, or a respected senior executive, to write a cover letter to all employees asking for their cooperation and candid responses, while reassuring them on confidentiality.
- Four weeks after sending out the questionnaire, investigate if the response rate is below 70%. A lower rate suggests that something is wrong; interview some employees; send out a follow-up letter to relieve any concerns. Make additional copies available if any have become lost.

The follow-up phase will help to clarify ambiguous questionnaire results. You will develop as many questions as answers from questionnaire results. For example, we recently did a survey where the findings caused us to ask in subsequent interviews, "Why do the questionnaire results show dissatisfaction with performance reviews but high satisfaction with pay levels?" "Why are shop supervisors reported as highly authoritarian?" "Why is morale lower in one section of R&D than in another?"

Such issues can only be clarified through follow-up interviews with a sample of questionnaire respondents. Often the consultant will discover the questionnaire results to be valid but the reasons behind them to be something unexpected.

OBSERVATIONS

So far we have discussed methods whereby the consultant "intrudes" on the situation, either by asking questions in an interview or by sending out a questionnaire. Both methods are "unnatural" in that they are not a normal occurrence in everyday organization life. Both methods ask for perceptions of what is happening, but are not measures of the actual event. As a result, one must always remain suspect as to the validity of what is said or reported.

Observations by the consultant are more natural and "unobtrusive." Moreover, the cost is zero—only a pair of well-trained eyes to look at how people actually behave in the organization. Are people so informal as interviews have proclaimed? Are people so busy and under so much pressure as reported on a questionnaire?

Skills at acute observation are difficult to learn and perform. The consultant is usually so busy keeping on a tight schedule or is absorbed in what someone else is saying that it is difficult to be sensitive toward the wider environment. Significant events happening right before the consultant will go overlooked.

One place in which the consultant can start is to distinguish between "content" and "process" when observing interactions between employees. Content refers to the subject matter being discussed; process is the underlying behavior. For example, we always make a point of sitting in on executive meetings to observe both content and process. At the content level, we look for the explicit agenda—are they mainly communicating everyday information or are they trying to solve important problems? At the process level, we observe if they are sufficiently open to examine a great deal of information or if they are dominated by one or two individuals? Such data gives us a "feel" for how the key executives work together, information that can prove useful when it comes time for making a final presentation to the same group.

The distinction between content and process can also be helpful as you move informally throughout the organization. Once we observed a CEO who claimed that his door was always open and that subordinates never hesitated to argue with him. So we just kept our eyes open whenever we were near his office. The facts were quite different from what he said: rarely did anyone enter his office, and when someone did it was with a lot of deference. This observation came in handy later when we held a frank discussion with the CEO over the results of our assignment from him—to find out why "decentralization" was not working in his firm. He was the problem!

Another related way in which to make observations is to think in terms of nonverbal behavior; it yields a great deal of information about the organization's culture. Are people friendly and smiling? Do they warmly greet you or volunteer to help you? Are people in the office talking with each other, or do they sit quietly at their desks? Do people dress formally in white shirts and three-piece suits, or is the dress more casual? How do they address one another, especially subordinates to bosses—by first or last name? How do they sit in meetings—are the senior people bunched together at one end of the table with the big boss in the center, or are people of different rank and seniority scattered around the table?

A third observational guideline is to stay tuned to the physical characteristics of the client setting. How are offices laid out—are they formal with desks in the center or more informal with tables and couches? Are office areas well lit and bright, or are they dim and shabby? Do employees have a way of meeting informally and talking with each other, such as in a coffee room, or are they kept separate? Who gets the best parking spaces? Is there one cafeteria or are there separate facilities for senior executives? Is there variety in office decor, such as the color of walls, plants, and picture displays or is there a regimented sameness? Are departments that require a great deal of cooperation with each other located in ways to facilitate their interaction?

Case in Point

One consultant we know was hired to design a new organization structure for coordinating two departments that had been in continuous conflict. Before getting to work on the specifics of a new structure, the consultant decided to look into the roots of the conflict. She examined the leadership styles of the two bosses and found no serious problems; then she studied the existing coordination procedures, which also seemed adequate. So what was behind the difficulty in coordination? Her explanation came from observing that the two departments were located four floors apart in a skyscraper where the elevator banks required a trip to the lobby before reaching the other department. The two departments were moved to the same floor, and the conflicts virtually disappeared.

Your own eyes and ears can tell you a great deal about the environment or "climate" where you are working. Ask yourself what feels and looks good about the work locale? What seems out of place? How do your observations "fit" with what you've learned already from interviews or questionnaires? No single item or observation will enlighten you, but a look for patterns across many bits of data may reveal an explanation. For instance, do a majority of employees continually look grim and downtrodden, or is it just on Thursdays when dear ole' Fred Smedley, the plant manager, makes his dreaded inspection tour?

ROUTINE DATA

A neglected yet valuable source of data is information already available before the consultant arrives on the scene. Too often consultants feel that they must generate their own data; apparently they don't trust information created by other hands, even if the cost is practically zero.

One source of routine data is public information available outside the company. All consultants, whatever their expertise or whatever the problem being researched, should do fundamental homework on the client before entering the organization. You should know the financial condition of the company, as reported in the annual report and 10-K statement. You should understand their basic lines of business—which products they make and who are their major competitors. You should read any articles written about the company in such publications as *Fortune, Barrons, Business Week,* or *Forbes.*

This information provides a background understanding for the context in which you'll be working. If you ask for this information later, you may be seen as ill prepared and even unprofessional. Knowledge of public information can help you to understand the causes behind the problem you are researching.

Case in Point

One client came to us asking for help in reducing the high turnover of plant managers in its largest division. As part of our background reading, we learned from studying articles on the industry that it was a "dog eat dog" business where long manufacturing experience was necessary in knowing how to keep down costs, and well-developed personal contacts in the local community were essential in maintaining sales customers. When we arrived at the company, we found the plant manager position in several plants being filled by young Wharton MBAs who were being hired by a slightly older Wharton MBA. It did not take long to conclude that the wrong people were being hired by the wrong person. These new "hot-shot" general managers didn't have the manufacturing experience or the established market contacts needed to succeed in the job.

Another type of routine data, which we call "private" information, comes from within the company in terms of organization charts, planning summaries, performance reports, and turnover and absenteeism figures. Gather this information wherever you go in an organization. Even data seemingly unrelated to your project may surprise you. For example, while working on a planning study, one author never understood the delays and hesitation by his client sponsor in obtaining requested information, until he asked for and examined the company's organization chart. He then found that his "vice president" sponsor was buried two levels down from other vice presidents.

A trend analysis of private information over a three- to five-year period can reveal historical forces that may help you to understand the source of today's situation. The same client sponsor mentioned was a vice president assigned two levels up on a chart three years previously, so he obviously had fallen out of favor. We therefore had the problem of redefining our client.

Finally, there is "loose" information that the consultant can dig out from files and closets because it is not collected systematically by the organization. A little ingenuity is sometimes needed to acquire this information, but the payoff can be sizable. Here are some examples:

- An analysis of memos circulated in the top management revealed the power structure of the organization through the listing of names at the bottom.
- A client claimed that his plant was promoting good young managers out of the plant to other parts of the company. An analysis of the personnel records showed this not to be the case; in fact, managers with high appraisal ratings were being kept back, and those with low ratings were rotated out.
- A CEO who was well read in management theory lectured the consultants on how participative he was in running the company—until the consultants examined his calendar pad to find that he remained in his office 95% of the time and seldom held a meeting.
- A consultant hired to design an alcoholism program for a company found the participants for the program by analyzing time clock records to see who was chronically late on Mondays.

With these various tools in hand, we are now ready to encounter the reality of gathering data in a client engagement. It will dictate not only the choice of methods but the unique phrasing of each question you ask. You cannot make the situation "fit" the tools; quite the contrary, tools are to be kept in your briefcase until the situation suggests their relevance.

As we shall see, each stage in the consulting process requires different types of data that are gathered in a tailor-made fashion.

RECOMMENDED READINGS

COLLUM, T.J., "Use of Consultants for Installing Cost-Effectiveness Programs Within the Insurance Agency," *Bests Review Life/Health*, vol. 73, no. 5 (September 1972).

DELLON, ROBERT E., "The Management Audit Process: Room for Improvement," *Public Utilities Fortnightly*, vol. 103, no. 3 (February 1, 1979).

LEVINSON, HARRY, *Organizational Diagnosis*. Cambridge, Mass.: University Press, 1972.

LOPEZ, FELIX M., *Personnel Interviewing Theory and Practice* (2nd ed.). New York: McGraw Hill, 1975.

MITROFF, IAN I., *The Subjective Side of Science*. Amsterdam: Elsevier Scientific Publishing Co., 1974.

NADLER, DAVID A., *Feedback and Organization Development: Using Data-Based Methods*. Reading, Mass.: Addison-Wesley, 1977.

O'LEARY, LAWRENCE R., *Interviewing for the Decisionmaker*. Chicago: Nelson-Hall, 1976.

OPPENHEIM, A.N., *Questionnaire Design and Attitude Measurement*. New York: Basic Books, Inc., 1966.

PETERSON, ROBERT A., and ROGER A. KERIN, "The Effective Use of Marketing Research Consultants," *Industrial Marketing Management*, vol. 9, no. 1 (February 1980).

SCHOENFIELD, GERRY, "How To Stroke That New Breed of Cat," *Marketing Times*, vol. 25, no. 4 (July/August 1978).

WEBB, EUGENE J.; DONALD T. CAMPBELL; RICHARD D. SCHWARTZ; and LEE SECHREST, *Unobtrusive Measures*. Chicago: Rand McNally-College Publishing Co., 1966.

EXHIBIT 11-1   Random Sampling from Typical Questionnaire

To: Survey Participants
               Planning & Resources Department
               Puerto Rico Power

<u>INTRODUCTION</u>

This is a long and complex questionnaire. We suggest that you briefly read through the questionnaire before filling it in.

Please answer <u>all</u> of the questions to the best of your knowledge. Do not leave any questions blank unless it is not relevant to your role in the organization. In such cases, please so indicate by N/A (Not Applicable).

Your candor in responding and commenting on the questions are particularly important to us to provide a clear understanding of the organization. It is our practice in all such surveys to examine the detailed responses in order to understand and report on major issues of import to the future of your activities and their impact to your organization. Therefore, we want to assure the confidentiality of your responses by retaining all questionnaires for our eyes only and by making our report in terms of grouped rather than individual responses.

If at any time you have any questions, please feel free to call Mr. Kato at (201) 123-4567.

When you have completed the questionnaire, please return it to us as quickly as possible in the enclosed envelope. All questionnaires must be mailed back no later than Monday, December 3, 1980, for us to begin compilations. Finally, we want to reaffirm that all personal statements and opinions, expressed or implied, will be treated confidentially. Your openness and directness in your answers will ultimately benefit Puerto Rico Power, your fellow employees, and you.

Thank you.

EXHIBIT 11-1 (cont'd)

PUERTO RICO POWER

CONFIDENTIAL SURVEY

This questionnaire will be treated with the highest confidentiality. No personal opinions or comments will be
divulged by CCK&K.

NAME: _____ DATE: _____

POSITION TITLE: _____

MY IMMEDIATE SUPERVISOR(S) IS: _____

EMPLOYMENT HISTORY PRIOR TO JOINING PUERTO RICO POWER, OR PRIOR
TO YOUR EXISTING POSITION:

Employer (if PRP, write same) _____

Last Position _____

Dates of Employment: From _____ To _____
                          Mo. - Year   Mo. - Year

Duties and Responsibilities _____

_____

_____

Starting Salary (Annual) $ _____ Bonus _____

Ending Salary (Annual) $ _____ Bonus _____

Other Benefits (Insurance, car, pension, etc.)

Describe your motivations and reasons for joining PRP.

_____

_____

_____

_____

Have your expectations been satisfied? Explain.

_____

_____

_____

EXHIBIT 11-1 (cont'd)

SECTION I - ORGANIZATION

FUNCTIONS AND RESPONSIBILITIES

1. Briefly describe the purpose of your position. Why does it
   exist? _____

   _____

   _____

   _____

   _____

2. Please think about your present position. List in detail
   the typical functions and responsibilities involved in
   doing your work, i.e., what do you do, how do you do it,
   how does it contribute to the planning function? Number
   each statement and indicate the approximate number of
   hours you spend weekly on each.

Duties	Hours Per Week
TOTAL:	

3. What is the <u>minimum</u> formal education that you believe is
   necessary to perform your functions and responsibilities?

   _____

   _____

   _____

   _____

EXHIBIT 11-1 **(cont'd)**

4. What is the <u>minimum</u> amount and type of past experience you believe is necessary in order for a new person to perform your functions and responsibilities properly?

    _____

    _____

    _____

    _____

5. What do you feel is the most important quality of attribute that you would seek if you were hiring a person to perform a job similar to yours?

    _____

    _____

    _____

6. If you were promoted to a higher position, do you know of a specific person at PRP who could assume your job as a promotional move?

    _____

    _____

7. What functions are you not now performing which you believe you should be performing and why?

    _____

    _____

    _____

8. What functions are you now performing which you believe should be or could be performed by someone else in the organization and why?

    _____

    _____

9. Are there any functions or tasks that you feel are duplicated within your division?

    _____

    _____

    _____

    _____

    _____

EXHIBIT 11-1 (cont'd)

10. Are any functions or tasks within your division being omitted which should be accomplished?

_____

_____

_____

_____

11. Do you feel you are getting adequate support from the other departments within PRP? Please explain.

_____

_____

_____

_____

	Very True	True	Partly True	Not True
12. I have sufficient decision making authority to control and carry out my work.				

	Very True	True	Partly True	Not True
13. I get enough feedback from others in my department to know how well they like my work.				

	Very True	True	Partly True	Not True
14. I have a good understanding of what is expected of me in my work and the level of performance that will earn me recognition and advancement.				

	Very True	True	Partly True	Not True
15. My work offers me new learning opportunities on a frequent basis.				

EXHIBIT 11-1 (cont'd)

	Very True	True	Partly True	Not True
16. I understand the current objectives of my position and the relationship of my work objectives to overall departmental objectives.				

	Very True	True	Partly True	Not True
17. My participation in (or communication with) the management committee provides me with the opportunity to express my views on matters of policy.				

ORGANIZATIONAL RELATIONSHIPS

18. To whom do you report in carrying out the responsibilities of your position?

Name: _____

Position: _____

19. Do you normally receive supervision from more than one individual? (If the answer is yes, please list the persons from whom you receive supervision.)

_____

_____

_____

20. Please provide the information requested below on contacts you have with other employees at PRP? (Do not include contacts with employees who work directly for you or contacts with your immediate supervisor.)

Name of Contact	Method (Phone, Memo, in person)	Reason for Contact	Times Per Week
_____	_____	_____	_____
_____	_____	_____	_____
_____	_____	_____	_____
_____	_____	_____	_____
_____	_____	_____	_____
_____	_____	_____	_____
_____	_____	_____	_____

EXHIBIT 11-1 (cont'd)

21. What meetings do you attend? Briefly identify how these
    meetings (if any) assist you in performing your tasks.
    How much time do they take? How would you rate their
    effectiveness as meetings on a scale of 1-10?

MEETING	HRS./WK.	RATING

EXHIBIT 11-1 **(cont'd)**

ORGANIZATIONAL ANALYSIS

22. The responsibilities I am expected to assume in performing my job are:

    _____ very clearly defined

    _____ reasonably well defined

    _____ poorly defined

    Comments: _____

    _____

    _____

23. The authority delegated to me is:

    _____ sufficient to carry out my responsibilities

    _____ Insufficient to carry out my responsibilities

    _____ not clear to me

    Comments: _____

    _____

    _____

24. The work I am required to do uses my experience, professional training and personal skills:

    _____ to a very high degree

    _____ to a significant degree, but less than it should

    _____ to a much lesser degree than it should

    Comments: _____

    _____

    _____

25. The amount of routine, non-professional work required of me in my job is:

    _____ minimal

    _____ significant, but not unreasonable

    _____ unreasonably high

    Comments: _____

    _____

    _____

EXHIBIT 11-1   (cont'd)

26. I am given adequate time to organize and plan my work:

_____ almost always

_____ usually, but not as often as I should

_____ rarely

Comments: _____

_____

_____

27. The amount of work expected of me is:

_____ so great that I am under constant strain to
        keep up

_____ considerable, and often puts me under strain
        to keep up

_____ reasonable

_____ less than it should be

_____ much less than it should be

Comments: _____

_____

_____

	Very True	True	Partly True	Not True
28. The MBO process is too time consuming and there is too much paperwork involved.				

SECTION II - OPERATIONS

	Very True	True	Partly True	Not True
29. My work provides opportunities and encouragement for me to follow my individual desires in a program of self-development.				

EXHIBIT 11-1 (cont'd)

30. PRP commits enough re-
    sources to adequately
    develop its employees.
    Consider the following:

	Very True	True	Partly True	Not True
a. On-the-job training				
b. Training seminars				
c. Intra-divisional meetings				
d. Inter-divisional meetings				
e. Supervision and guidance from supervisors				

31. Is there a feeling of "task orientation" within your
    organizational group (i.e., do people agree to a common
    set of objectives and actively cooperate to achieve
    them?) If no, please explain why not.

    _____

    _____

    _____

    _____

32. Please discuss your own level of job satisfaction by
    any measures you deem important, such as: job content,
    relationships, achievements, etc.

    _____

    _____

    _____

    _____

    _____

    _____

    _____

    _____

    _____

    _____

    _____

EXHIBIT 11-1 (cont'd)

33. Describe your role in the PRP planning process. (What instructions do you receive? How is the information prepared, what is the timing for completion?)

_____

_____

_____

_____

_____

34. Do you have any responsibility for budgets or budget variances? (Do you receive comparisons of actual performance versus budget?)

_____

_____

_____

_____

_____

35. In your opinion, is the planning and budgeting process satisfactory?

Yes _____ No _____ (If no, explain) _____

_____

_____

_____

_____

_____

_____

_____

_____

_____

EXHIBIT 11-1   (cont'd)

SECTION III - PLANNING ANALYSIS

Overall Managerial Perceived Value

36. The General Manager believes the system helps him to discharge better his responsibilities.

Very True	True	Partly True	Not True

37. Other major line managers think the system is useful to them.

Very True	True	Partly True	Not True

38. Overall, the benefits of strategic planning are perceived to be greater than the costs by most managers.

Very True	True	Partly True	Not True

39. Are major changes needed in our strategic planning system?

Very True	True	Partly True	Not True

Does our strategic planning system produce the "Right" substantive answers and results with respect to:

40. Developing basic company missions and lines of business.

Very True	True	Partly True	Not True

40a. Foreseeing future major opportunities.

Very True	True	Partly True	Not True

41. Foreseeing future major threats.

Very True	True	Partly True	Not True

41a. Properly appraising company strengths.

Very True	True	Partly True	Not True

42. Properly appraising company weaknesses.

Very True	True	Partly True	Not True

43. Developing realistic current information about competitors.

Very True	True	Partly True	Not True

EXHIBIT 11-1   (cont'd)

SECTION IV - COMPENSATION

SALARY & FRINGE BENEFITS

44. My present salary and most recent increase are closely
     related to: (Select One)

       _____ The position or level I occupy.

       _____ My performance in the last year.

       _____ The cumulative effect of my performance over
               the years.

45. My compensation is satisfactory in relation to:

       _____ The compensation of others at SRP.

       _____ What I could be earning outside SRP.

       _____ How hard I work.

46. Superior performance is
     adequately recognized in
     salary increases which
     are made.

Very True	True	Partly True	Not True

47. I am satisfied with the
     division of my total comp-
     ensation between base
     salary and fringe benefits.

Very True	True	Partly True	Not True

48. The timing of my compen-
     sation payments meets
     my living needs.

Very True	True	Partly True	Not True

EXHIBIT 11-1 (cont'd)

49. Of the various parts of your compensation, please rank (1 as the <u>least</u> <u>important</u>, 10 the <u>most</u> <u>important</u>) each individual item below: (Please use a number <u>once</u> only).

    _____ Bonus

    _____ PRP Club

    _____ Educational Reimbursement

    _____ Holidays

    _____ Long Term Disability

    _____ Life Insurance

    _____ Medical/Dental Insurance

    _____ Retirement Plan

    _____ Salary

    _____ Vacation

50. What employee benefits do you like the most? Why?

    _____

    _____

51. What employee benefits do you like the least? Why?

    _____

    _____

52. What benefits would you like to have which you do not have now?

    _____

    _____

    _____

<u>PROMOTIONAL CRITERIA</u>

	Very True	True	Partly True	Not True
53. Promotions are too much dependent on whom you work for.				

EXHIBIT 11-1 (cont'd)

54. I believe that promotions below the senior executive level are based principally on merit and have very little to do with:

_____ time in grade

_____ condition of the economy

_____ change of location

_____ change of department or responsibilities

_____ performance on the job

55. I believe that doing quality work has a high priority in our organization and is recognized and rewarded.

Very True	True	Partly True	Not True

56. I am satisfied with the quality of work performed by other departments as it affects my work.

Very True	True	Partly True	Not True

57. I think that opportunities for me to advance to a higher position at PRP are:

Very Good	Good	Fair	Poor

Comments: _____

_____

_____

58. If I could press a "Good Change" button wired to the quality of staff support, the following improvements would result:

EXHIBIT 11-1 (cont'd)

SECTION V - INTERDEPARTMENTAL COORDINATION, COMMUNICATION AND
          TEAMWORK

59. The communication channels
    in PRP are upward-oriented
    i.e., views of individuals
    get to the top of the
    office and organization.

Very True	True	Partly True	Not True

60. More often than not the
    grapevine system is the
    way one learns about what
    is going on in the organ-
    ization.

Very True	True	Partly True	Not True

61. The downward communication
    is very effective and
    complete.

Very True	True	Partly True	Not True

62. Information necessary to
    perform at highest level
    of professionalism is
    quickly and thoroughly
    disseminated throughout
    the organization.

Very True	True	Partly True	Not True

EXHIBIT 11-1 (cont'd)

SECTION VIII - DEPARTMENT GOALS AND OBJECTIVES

63. Please identify below what you feel <u>should</u> be the long range
    goals and objectives of the department. Consider topics
    such as quality and quantity of planning support, research,
    levels of involvement, access to senior management, etc.
    Please incorporate your <u>own</u> opinions with no regard of
    others' opinions. Select whatever time frame you like for
    your comments. (Use additional pages if necessary.)

EXHIBIT 11-1 (cont'd)

64. For each goal/objective you identified in Question 63 of this section, identify current or potential constraints that may affect its achievement. Please be explicit. (Use additional pages if necessary.)

_____

_____

_____

_____

_____

_____

_____

_____

_____

_____

_____

_____

_____

_____

_____

_____

_____

_____

_____

_____

_____

_____

_____

_____

_____

_____

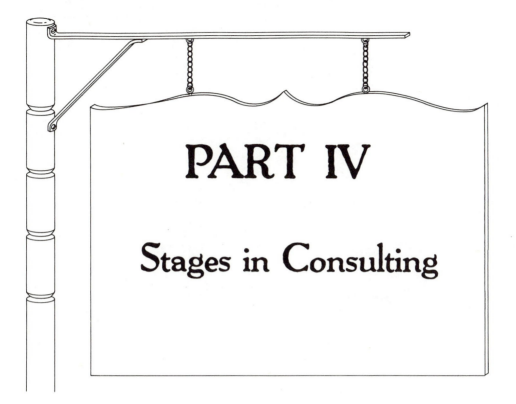

PART IV

Stages in Consulting

Having discussed what the profession is about, how to sell consulting assignments, and various model approaches to use, it is also useful to explore just what the effective consultant does to assure that the work is executed professionally and ends up benefiting the client. The effective consultant will recognize that each organization is unique in its products, employees, and technology. The skills required just to enter such a client's foreign culture are vital to the future success of any project. Then there is necessary knowledge about how to develop realistic, effective recommendations, and, finally, to persuade the client that those recommendations will indeed assure positive change. Once a project has been completed to the client's satisfaction, the decision must be made to sell more work or to leave gracefully. This, too, is a judgment requiring true professionalism.

12

Defining Client Needs
How To Enter
a Foreign Culture

The early days in a new consulting engagement are critical for determining its subsequent fate. If the consultant is perceived as a "stooge" for the hiring executive, other employees will be reluctant to talk openly. Or, if the consultant overlooks and fails to interview certain key executives, they may feel offended and become uncooperative later in supporting an implementation plan.

This chapter highlights five key areas for the consultant to consider when commencing a new engagement. One is arranging for your introduction to the client organization; the second is meeting the key executives and the power structure; the third is learning the "culture" and its acceptable ways of acting; the fourth is testing for the validity of the original problem definition; and the fifth is stepping back to determine if the initial proposal should be renegotiated with the client.

The skillful consultant deals effectively with these five steps before entering a more intense phase of problem analysis. It takes anywhere from two days to two weeks to complete this start-up period, depending on the size of the organization and the complexity of the client's problem.

NEED FOR SENSITIVITY

Once a client is obtained and a contract is signed, it is tempting for the consultant to plunge head first into an analysis of the client's problem. After all, the sale has been made and time is precious, so why fuss around with any side trips, like wooing the client further?

Task-oriented consultants can easily become the proverbial "bull in the china shop" when beginning a new engagement. They charge ahead, forgetting that a majority of the client's employees have never met or seen "the consultant." Aggressive outsiders with unknown credentials threaten the status quo, causing the organization to generate antibodies. The employee grapevine is quick to spawn paranoid rumors about the alien invader.

A tactless consultant is likely to meet with substantial resistance at a later date. Too many consultants have met their Waterloo by doing a good problem-solving job while neglecting the politics of meeting the organization.

Case in Point

The president of a diversified conglomerate hired a consultant, who was recommended by a board member, to assess whether the company should keep or sell one of its subsidiaries. The agreement was oral because of the board member's support. When the consultant told the president that it would be a "five-day job," the president was surprised because he and his staff had spent months on the same question, but he said nothing to the consultant. Two weeks later the consultant returned with a four-page report that recommended a sale, and even specified the asking price. The president and his staff were flabbergasted at the brevity of the study. When the consultant was asked if he had visited the subsidiary for interviews, he explained that a visit was "unnecessary because all the financial data for answering the question were available in published industry sources." He went on to explain that the subsidiary was too small for its industry and that the capital investment required to make it dominant was so large as to make retention unthinkable. The president and the executive committee rejected the recommendation and kept the subsidiary. Three years later, after disastrous losses in the subsidiary, the company sold it for half the price recommended by the consultant. The president later told one of the authors, "the consultant was right about the sale and the price, but he failed because of the lack of 'foreplay' in meeting and understanding the views of our key executives."

ARRANGING THE INTRODUCTION

Sit down early with your hiring client to go over the realities and sensitivities surrounding your introduction to the organization. If the client is not accustomed to consultants, you may have to take the initiative in suggesting ways of proceeding.

First, there is the question of who will be your continuing sponsor and contact within the organization. Usually, it is the client executive who hired you, but this person may be traveling a great deal or be located too far from where you are working. Our advice, in this case, is to retain the hiring client as your "general sponsor" but to arrange for other key executives to be your "daily sponsors." This will assure that you are seen as not just the president's consultant but as having local support from the head of marketing. You may need a number of daily sponsors, depending on how many organizational units are involved in the project.

Next, there is the delicate matter of announcing your presence to the organization. The hiring client no doubt has a "feel" for how outsiders are normally introduced to the organization. Most important is for all key executives affected by the study to hear officially and directly about it before the grapevine tells them.

The announcement should be in writing because oral communications can be distorted or forgotten. It should come from the client executive who hired you; if the signature of a more senior executive will carry more influence, then secure it.

As to what is said in the announcement, be candid without raising apprehension. Mention briefly the focus of the study, the credentials of the consultant, and the need for employee cooperation. Employees should know that all their comments to the consultant will be treated in confidence and that no names or sources will be revealed to senior executives. It helps for the announcement to stress that senior management is interested only in the overall results of the study, not in what any single individual has to say. Exhibit 12-1 is an announcement memo sent to one company's entire management group.

Remember, however, that your introduction will occur over and over again, especially if you're moving around a multiplant client. Inevitably you will have to reintroduce yourself, and be introduced, as you enter each new plant. Don't assume that everyone knows who you are or why you are there. Even if they've seen something in writing or heard it from others, it helps to hear it fresh from you, which also relieves the tension barrier.

A second important step is to identify a person to set up your interview schedule and to secure for you certain files when you need them. Usually this is the secretary to the senior executive who hired you. It requires a close knowledge of the client organization and its executives as well as access to confidential information. You should also arrange for a "support system," which includes office space and secretarial assistance. You may want to retreat to an office to put your thoughts together, or you may need typing performed or telephone calls answered.

Finally, before you venture forth into the organization, ask your client to give you a frank picture of the political terrain. You may be walking into a minefield, so be prepared! Who are the key executives to see? In what order? Where do they sit on the organization chart? Who belongs to which political camp? Who was in favor of bringing in a consultant? Who wasn't? Who is under what kind of pressure? Are any major organizational changes imminent that will affect these executives?

MEETING THE POWER STRUCTURE

An early goal is to meet and build a sound relationship with key senior executives. You will likely need their support later in the project. A friend made now may turn out to save your final report from another executive whom you overlooked or irritated.

The power structure contains the "shakers" and "movers" of the organization. It is seldom a monolithic group but a loose arrangement of cliques with overlapping membership. Some executives and clients will be inclined favorably toward your project, others may be waiting in ambush, and a majority probably haven't made up their minds. Get to know all of them, and don't choose sides. They will vie for your favor but will respect your neutrality greatly.

Your first task is to interview all key executives who have even the remotest relationship to your consulting assignment. It is tempting to skip the "distant" executives in your haste to get to the closest source of knowledge about the problem. But you must show courtesy according to organizational rank, or omissions may come back to haunt you. You may even learn something through this meandering, get acquainted process.

Foremost on the minds of these senior executives is "Who the hell are you?"—an appropriate question since you are the foreigner and they are the gatekeepers. Your credibility and access to their innermost opinions are at stake over your initial conduct and appearance. First impressions count in consulting, because relationships are so fleeting.

So don't launch immediately into a series of intense questions about "the problem." You just walked in the door as a guest, not as an inquisitor. Begin by explaining briefly who you are and the purpose of your project—inject a little humor and be ready for some small talk about mutual friends from the same college.

If the executive begins to volunteer information on the problem, let it go naturally from there. But more likely the conversation will center on his or her job responsibilities. Executives have egos, just like consultants. It may be that, within an hour's allotted time for an interview, you will spend only 20 minutes talking about the consulting project. But don't worry; it is time well spent. The human equation is more important than problem solving at this stage. Tell the executive you will be back for a second interview when you can discuss the problem in more depth.

Some executives will put you through the "third degree." Let them, but don't be defensive; their motives can be quite genuine. They want to know if you are independent and objective, if you've had experience in their industry, if you know anything about their business, and if you can keep information with confidence. Answer their challenges with calm and factual information—don't cower or brag at length, or you will become the interviewee.

Every second or third interview will bring you a rich lode of useful data. Some executives will be more open and willing than others to share their opinions. Exploit these interviews for all you can get, but don't push; rather, play the curious consultant who wants to learn at their pace.

LEARNING THE CULTURE

All organizations and businesses are not alike—a simple truism too often forgotten by consultants. Client organizations are unique cultures with peculiar rituals and modes of behavior, including their own language for describing and communicating what is important among themselves.

Case in Point

A consultant colleague of ours was forced to ride his motorcycle to meet a new client after his car failed to start. He hid the motorcycle in a nearby parking lot, took off his helmet and leather jacket, and replaced it with suit coat, vest, and briefcase. Upon arrival at the client's office, he found the president dressed in blue jeans and T-shirt with a motorcycle emblem. On his next visit the consultant purposely wore his motorcycle attire, only to find the president dressed in a three-piece suit. "What goes?" asked the perplexed consultant. The president laughed and explained that casual clothes were worn by himself and other employees only on Fridays, the date of the consultant's initial visit.

Why should a consultant be sensitive to organizational culture unless the project is concerned directly with human resources? All consulting assignments, be they financial or human, occur within a social and political context provided by the organization. This context dictates how any consultant must communicate and be heard if influence is to be gained.

The skillful consultant must therefore learn the nuances of the organization's culture. This includes such mundane and formal items as the organization chart and the names of people in its boxes. Also, try to gain at least a cursory knowledge of the client's product; how it is made and how it is sold. Recognize how employees tend to dress. Is their behavior formal or informal? Are decisions made in a participative manner or are they confined to a few executives? What behavior patterns seem to get rewarded in the organization, and what are the "taboos"?

Any consultant who flaunts the norms of acceptable behavior within the client organization risks being expelled as an intruder or at least discredited as a wise purveyor of useful knowledge. Consultants who show respect for the cultural context will be given respect in return.

Consultants are not anthropologists, but the latters' approach is useful. Learn the culture early; it will be too late at the recommendation stage. Talk the client's language, not the vocabulary of a professional consultant. Listen and observe more than you talk. Ask a lot of "dumb" questions!

Above all, don't inflict your personal values and behaviors on the client's culture: if they are informal and call each other by their first names, don't insist on being called Dr. Codfish. You will stand out as a consultant without even trying.

PROBING THE PROBLEM

So far, our advice has been to pay attention to everything but the reason you were hired, that is, to solve the client's problem. It is frustrating to continue eating hors d'oeuvres when the entree is waiting.

One direct step can be taken toward problem solving in this early phase, and that is to test the validity of the problem definition given in the written proposal. Are you basically on track, or were you "misled" in the proposal stage? Better to discover that you are off course at this point than several weeks and thousands of dollars later.

Interviews with five to seven executives should give you a check on problem validity. How does each executive define "the problem"? How do they react to the problem definition given in the proposal? Remember that the intent is not to explore the problem in depth but to ascertain if you are in the right ballpark.

Don't expect complete agreement across your sample, but if each executive describes the problem quite differently, or if there is a big disparity between top- and middle-level executives, then it's back to the drawing board. For example, you may have been hired to develop a new strategic plan, but several executives indicate that the problem is not the plan per se but the lack of a planning process that includes their contribution. So you will have to shift attention from the plan to the procedure, and this will likely require the client's consent.

A second step toward problem solving is to ask each executive for the degree of importance that he or she attaches to the problem relative to other issues confronting the client company. This will give you a perspective on what else is happening in the company, because the consultant is seldom at the center of the client's universe. You may find that your problem is so peripheral that it may not receive much energy in subsequent phases. If so, check back with your client before proceeding to the next stage; it may be necessary to build greater interest in your project, such as calling a special meeting to explain better the reasons for it.

Finally, as you pass through each interview, keep your eyes and ears open for any "gems" of documented materials that executives just happen to mention in passing. You will find memos and reports that, if you ask for copies, may aid you immeasurably in understanding both the company and its problem. One colleague of ours learned accidentally that another consultant had preceded him in working on the very same problem—but no one had told him until an executive casually handed him a copy of the previous consultant's report.

REEVALUATING
THE PROPOSAL

The start-up phase lays a basis for the consultant to proceed into the next stage of deeper problem diagnosis, provided that all has gone well to this point. The perceptive consultant should pause here to compare the original proposal with what has been learned to date.

One key question to ask yourself, or a colleague, is, "How much power does my client sponsor have in the organization?" You hope that sufficient power exists for the consulting project to be carried out and implemented successfully. But what if you discover that your client's power is overshadowed by several key executives who don't personally like your client?

This unhappy discovery raises the question, "Who is your client?" Many consultants define their client as the executive who negotiated the original proposal, only to find later that this is too personalized a version of the client. A personal relationship is often necessary to make the initial sale, but this relationship may eventually entrap you.

Our advice is to move toward redefining your client if there are serious problems with the original client executive. Act with sensitivity toward your original client, because he or she is the one who hired you and can still dismiss you. One solution that often finds acceptance is to form a task group to become, in essence, the new client contact point. The task group should include key people concerned not only with the problem but who will take responsibility for guiding you and reviewing your final report. The original client executive can serve as chairperson or member of the group.

A second reevaluation issue is the "problem" itself—did subsequent interviews confirm the original problem definition or must it be redefined? For example, we once agreed to study how to decentralize a client's organization structure, only to find after several interviews that a lack of capable general managers would prevent decentralization. So the problem was redefined as one of designing a program to develop managers for a more decentralized organization, which also resulted in a larger contract and an appreciative client.

If you redefine the problem, don't simply redefine it in your head. You will likely have to renegotiate with the client. If the client agrees to a redefinition, be sure that the project can still be accomplished within the original cost estimate.

A final review question concerns the "health" of your relationship with the client and the organization. How have you been received? Are people treating you as a welcomed guest or as a dangerous saboteur? Which parts of the organization seem more receptive to your presence, and which parts appear least receptive? Have you learned the organization culture? Can you spot the power brokers? How do they receive you?

Consulting relationships can go sour easily and early. Few people will tell you about a *faux pas* unless you inquire. So catch it early, because there is usually time for correction. You won't necessarily be fired for acting like an "ugly American." It's more serious and subtle than that; the client may still retain you while withholding vital data and ignoring your final report.

Self-evaluation and correction is difficult by yourself. This is why we favor having consultants working in pairs rather than alone; one consultant can critique the other. But if you work alone, try raising the question of your client relationship with someone in the organization who has acted cordially toward you and who seems to have good contacts throughout the organization. He or she may be your original client sponsor or a new friend you have met along the way.

Now that you have completed this initial honeymoon stage, and assuming that you have worked out the bugs (nothing will ever be perfect in the uncertain world of consulting), let us move on to the more intensive problem analysis phase.

RECOMMENDED READINGS

DEXTER, ALBERT S., "Making Your Call on a Consultant a Success," *The Business Quarterly*, vol. 40, no. 3 (Autumn 1975).

FUCHS, JEROME H., "Management Consulting Services Reduce Costs," *Office*, vol. 87, no. 1 (January 1978).

HALL, EDWARD T., *The Hidden Dimension*. Garden City, N.Y.: Doubleday & Co., Inc., 1966.

KAPLAN, ROBERT E., "Stages in Developing a Consulting Relation: A Case Study of a Long Beginning," *Journal of Applied Behavioral Science*, vol. 14, no. 1 (January/February/March 1978).

LIPPITT, GORDON L., "A Study of the Consultation Process," *Journal of Social Issues*, 15, no. 2, 43–50.

McCASKEY, MICHAEL B., "The Hidden Messages Managers Send," *Harvard Business Review*, November/December 1979.

RAPP, JOHN, "Cooperative Aspects of MAS Engagements or MAS-Work Smarter," *CPA*, vol. 48, no. 10 (October 1978).

EXHIBIT 12-1   Sample Memo Introducing Consultants to a Company

BOTULISM BOTTLING CO.
13 Salmonella Street
Peritonitis, Pennsylvania

MEMO FROM: U. R. Grimey, President

TO: All Employees

SUBJECT: Management Consultants

DATE: July 7, 1980

Recently, the board of directors, the FDA, the Consumer Protection Agency, and others have urged that we review our operating
procedures. This is a direct result of that very unfortunate
accident with the Momma Mia's Meatballs shipment in April and
our little slip-up with the two cases of preserved prunes we
sent to the Sacred Heart Convent in June.

As a result, I have asked the nationally renowned firm of Charles,
Cranston, Kato & Kent to review our operations. They have
suggested, among other things, that they be free to interview
a number of you and to hand out confidential questionnaires to
all of you. I wholeheartedly support these recommendations and
through this memo wish to urge you to cooperate fully with the
consulting team when they contact you. We have agreed with them
that the results of these interviews and your responses to the
questionnaire will never be shared with anyone on the management
team, including myself. Mr. Clark Kent, a partner of CCK&K,
will be using an office on the executive floor and you may call
him on extension 237 should you have any questions.

This is a unique opportunity for each of you to make a solid
contribution to the company, your fellow workers, and yourselves.
Your observations and suggestions are of greatest value to us
in our search for better ways in which to go about our business.

Sincerely yours,

U.R. Grimey

U. R. Grimey

13

Diagnosing the Issues
How To Unravel
the Problem

Completion of the start-up phase leads the consultant into an intense focus on problem analysis. Here you will dig for the roots of the client's problem. The consultant becomes a scientist searching for the underlying "causes," because no solution will be lasting unless the basic roots are found and eliminated.

Problem analysis is easier said than done. If the client could grasp the problem and its causes, there would be no reason for hiring a consultant. So don't expect a cogent explanation from the client. You cannot simply ask, "what is the problem and its causes?" and expect a tidy and valid explanation in response.

A great deal of probing, testing, and evaluating will be necessary before a clearer understanding of the problem emerges. Even then, the consultant will have to guard against human bias, either within oneself or from others, because problem analysis is essentially a subjective process. It is not a simple computer exercise in which a formula yields the correct answer.

More is at stake during this diagnostic phase than gaining an understanding of the problem. The perceptive consultant will also need to assess how ready the client is for change. Brilliant solutions will be ignored or rejected if the client's employees are devoted to the status quo. Conversely, you may be overwhelmed with suggested changes by employees. Is it wise to listen to these suggestions? Will they be of any value to you? Shouldn't you delay any discussion of specific changes until the implementation stage?

LOOKING BEFORE
LEAPING

Consultants are hired to recommend solutions, but the soundness of any solution will depend on how well the consultant understands the underlying problem. A faulty diagnosis will lead to an equally undesirable solution.

A basic precept for any consultant is that of looking before leaping—and continuing to look after leaping! The devil of all consulting is an endless temptation to make premature judgments about the causes of the problem. This "shoot from the hip" attitude is a common managerial failure that in itself creates a need for consultants. You should not fall victim to the same malady. Organizations get into trouble over myopic thinking, and so will you.

Case in Point

Three consulting firms were required to solve the mystery of "no effects" from a very costly training program for middle managers. The first firm was hired to design the program because of its expert reputation in programmed learning and multimedia techniques. Unfortunately, despite a new program that drew raves from the participants, very little was observed afterward in the way of beneficial results. So a second firm was brought in, again one that specialized in designing training programs, to rectify the faults of the first firm. It toned down the flashiness of the first program, arguing that its content had been sacrificed for entertainment value. But still no important changes were observed back on the job after revising the program. Alas, a third firm was brought in, but this time the consultants were not specialists in training methods, which was to their good fortune and a credit to the client's slowly increasing wisdom. The new consultants chose to look for the explanation of "no effects" out on the job, not in the classroom or the training design. And there they found the answer! Numerous interviews revealed that bosses of the trainees did not support the aims of the training program. Hence, no application was occurring in a hostile environment.

Why did two consulting firms fail to provide an effective training program, and why did a client buy their services? They all acted without sufficient perspective for the broader situation. The consultants had blinders that wedded them to their favorite training methods. The client was myopic for not knowing its own senior management and for continuing to hire consultants who were more technologists than problem solvers.

All of this leads to three basic principles to promote perspective and restraint in the mental discipline of problem solving:

1. *Suspend early judgment on problems and solutions.* The primary value of the consultant is to bring fresh insight and objectivity to a clouded situation. The effective consultant should strive for detachment and guard against overinvolvement. Don't be in a hurry to conclude your findings with an articulate but incorrect solution. You are a detective, not a prosecutor.

2. *Look behind every tree.* Explanations to client problems are often found in the most unlikely places. That is why the client hasn't been able to solve the issue. A handy exercise to play is the "what if" game—what if the "no effects" training problem is due to something other than the program design itself?

3. *Don't believe the client's diagnosis.* You will hear many persuasive explanations given by each employee you interview. They all have opinions—but also narrow viewpoints due to their limited vantage points. Employees rarely see themselves as part of the problem; it's always that "damn top management" or that "lazy union." In an interview, nod your head as a way of continuing the discussion, not to show your agreement.

SIMPLIFYING COMPLEXITY

As data flows in on the consultant, it is easy to feel overwhelmed by the complexity of the situation. One employee tells you this, another tells you that, and you end up thinking something else. How do you gain your bearings and begin to make sense out of all the "noise" you are receiving? What separates the wheat from the chaff?

One key step is to *distinguish between symptoms and causes.* Too often consultants stay at a level of symptoms without probing deeper. Typical symptom statements by the client are ones that make reference to "lack of communications," "high turnover," "bad morale," "low productivity," and "poor motivation." Statements such as these are rarely the cause of the problem—they are more likely the tip of an iceberg that has much hidden beneath the surface.

It helps to ask "why" each time you detect a symptom being used to explain the problem. Thus, when an employee talks about "a communication breakdown," probe further with such questions as, "What do you mean by that?" "Why do you think these breakdowns occur?" "When do they occur?" "Who is usually involved?" Seek more specific answers instead of accepting overly general and abstract statements.

A second approach is to *recognize the principle of "multicausality."* Seldom is it possible to put your finger on a single cause for the problem. Real life is far more complex than this book portrays or is reflected in the heroics of consultant war stories. Don't be satisfied with simplistic answers. For example, a problem of high turnover may be caused by low pay, as is typically assumed, but most research studies show that a combination of four or five factors contribute to turnover. Ironically, one cause of turnover is often turnover itself—rats flee a sinking ship as they see other rats leaving.

To continue to ask "what else" may explain each problem situation. Alternative explanations should be considered before crying "Eureka!" Effective solutions will address all the likely causes; otherwise, the problem will persist if only one or two causes are treated.

A third useful principle in problem solving is the *"interrelationship" between causal factors*. Rather than finding the cause of a problem to be contained within a single factor, or in several unrelated factors, it can often be traced to the relationship among three or four factors. For example, we once solved a manufacturing problem where the president was attempting to control a job shop with a standard cost system. The problem lay in the "misfit" between the job shop technology, which required unique specifications for each job, and a standard cost system that was geared more for uniform assembly-line work. In essence, the cause was neither the technology nor the control system, but the lack of fit between the two. A third related factor was the president himself who had designed and promoted the control system.

Finally, there is a *law of "interdependence,"* which suggests that there is always a "good reason for everything" that exists in organizations. The most overtly "bad" practice wouldn't be there unless something was keeping this practice in existence. You may, for instance, pin a particular problem on a bad manager and wonder why he hasn't been fired. But turn around and ask yourself why is he being kept! Many times we have found bad managers being retained because the client's promotion policy is based on seniority and promotion from within. Such companies are willing to put up with bad managers to obtain the benefits they perceive from this traditional career system. A recommendation by you to fire the bad manager would threaten the client's basic way of making career decisions for all employees. So look for the ways in which various causes to a problem may be supporting and feeding off each other.

ESTABLISHING VALIDITY

Problem solving involves numerous "checks and balances" to determine if the consultant indeed has a grasp of the problem and its causes. One cannot rely on hunches alone or a few opinions gained from three or four interviews. Moreover, all consultants are subject to bias, even after years of experience as professionals. Therefore, how does one assure that a valid interpretation is placed on the problem?

A typical check is the degree of *consistency* emerging across a broad sample of problem definitions provided by the same and different methods of inquiry. Does a similar story emerge from one interview to the next? Do questionnaire results reinforce the interview findings? If you find a consistent and complementary pattern within and between data-gathering methods, you can feel more confident of your explanation. Lack of agreement suggests that you do some further checking.

Another method is to test your hunches directly during each interview. These conversations provide a validity check if you phrase your questions carefully to avoid prejudicing the employee's answer. For example, if you sense that the head of the accounting department is blocking the design of a new information system, then explore this possibility without suggesting it directly. You can ask a series of questions, such as "What, in your opinion, seems to be preventing the introduction of a new information system?" If the interviewee mentions several factors other than the head of accounting, you can ask further if the interviewee knows the opinion of the head of accounting. A more direct approach is to state, "I've heard in other interviews that the head of accounting may be opposed to a new information system—have you heard the same thing or do you think that it's being delayed for some other reason?"

A third test of your objectivity is to collaborate with another consultant on the same assignment. Then you can check each other. We believe strongly in team consulting where each consultant gathers data independently but both compare notes in search of a joint diagnosis. In these sessions we enjoy, of course, our areas of agreement, but it is the surprises and areas of disagreement that inevitably result in a better analysis.

Case in Point

Two consultants met after several days of interviewing executives in a large manufacturing firm. For over half an hour one of them argued that decentralization of the plant manufacturing system was desirable but that it was impossible because the first-level supervisors were widely regarded by staff employees as incapable of taking on added responsibility. The second consultant, after listening patiently, replied that the other consultant's argument was circular—if no delegation took place, then the supervisors would continue to remain incapable. He went on to contribute a finding that the other consultant had overlooked—that the plant had, in fact, been decentralized several years previously until a new superintendent had taken over two years before the study. This new executive had, in turn, brought in several staff employees who were more in agreement with his philosophy of centralization. These were the same staff employees who had downgraded the supervisors in conversations with the first consultant. Both consultants were then able to agree that the problem hinged primarily on a senior management that was opposed to decentralization, not around incapable supervisors.

RECOGNIZING READINESS

In addition to gaining a valid focus on the problem and its causes, the perceptive consultant will keep an eye open for the client's desire and willingness to change. You cannot wait until all the problems have been analyzed to raise suddenly the question of change. It would be awkward and expensive to return later to each interviewee for a separate discussion of change.

So use each data-gathering interview as an opportunity to gauge both the problem and the client's readiness for change. These two issues are often linked, as the problem exists because no one within the client organization has been able to solve it. On the other hand, the decision to hire a consultant does not mean that the client will automatically accept the consultant's recommendations. Forces blocking change in the past may also rise to block the consultant as well.

One key assessment of readiness is to determine how satisfied are the client's employees with the present practices under study by the consultant. Top management, for example, may perceive a serious problem with the accounting system, but a majority of employees may feel quite comfortable with the way in which it operates currently. If so, you will face serious difficulties in implementing any changes—not with resistance from top management but from many more people who must accept and live directly with a new system.

Another barometer is the level of employee experience with change in the past. If the company has been fast growing and changing rapidly over recent years, then employees will likely be conditioned to change. But if the company has been coasting with the same practices for many years, watch out! Employees who value stability and the status quo will not have developed a positive attitude toward abandoning the past in favor of the future.

A useful question to ask each interviewee is, "Why hasn't the problem you are talking about been solved in the past?" Occasionally we find clients who understand very well the problem itself, but who do not have a grasp on the blocks to change. So probe for these underlying roadblocks.

Case in Point

We were once hired by a vice president of personnel to design a new performance appraisal system. Our subsequent interviews supported his earlier diagnosis that the old system stressed the measurement of work activities over performance accomplishment. So all that was needed was a new goal-oriented system—until we discovered that similar solutions had met with failure in the past. We learned that a major block to change was the lack of formal authority inherent in the personnel manager's job; he was the only vice president excluded from the company's executive committee. While this personnel director had proved to be quite competent on the job, his recommendations to the executive committee had always been downgraded, just as his position had. As a result, we laid the issue in front of the company president; he agreed with our diagnosis and decided to add the personnel director to the executive committee. A new appraisal system was approved when it came before the group.

Finally, you want to size up the basic strengths and weaknesses of the company. Any future change program should build off strengths and take account of weaknesses. For instance, if the client's problem is defined as a need for decentralization to bring the company closer to its diverse marketplace, then it will require a cadre of general managers who can act effectively as autonomous executives. One strength of the company would be a storehouse of such managers capable of decentralization; a weakness, as more often occurs, would be a shortage. We have seen several decentralization plans fail because this weakness of short supply in personnel was overlooked or given little weight in planning. Such a weakness could be corrected by a more gradual transition plan, or by increased training, or by hiring new managers from the outside.

COLLECTING SOLUTIONS

During this diagnostic phase of a project, you should look beyond problems, strengths, and weaknesses to detect and record numerous "solutions" that will be offered by employees. Interviews cannot be limited to problem analysis because employees will jump impulsively to their favorite solutions. They will be trying to influence you, the omnipotent consultant, to heed their admonitions and suggestions, since they assume that you have more influence than they do.

Listen carefully for these solutions; even probe for them when they are not being offered. No doubt you will hear a lot of bad ideas, but mixed in may be a few innovations that could escape you as a less knowledgeable outsider. We will often ask, after a lengthy discussion of the problem, "Well, I sense your great concern for this problem you've been discussing. Now, how would you propose to solve it, if you had the authority and leeway to do so?"

In addition to proposed solutions, you should also stay alert for new opportunities. While solutions are suggested directly by employees, opportunities will usually emerge unintentionally from seemingly unimportant information. You will suddenly see a way of solving a problem that even the employee doesn't recognize, although the genesis came from an employee comment. For example, one of the authors interviewed a client executive who was regarded by the CEO as "unmovable" to another city because of family reasons. However, the immobile executive casually informed us that he was quite ready to move, something he assumed was already known to the CEO. This bit of information led eventually to the solution of another problem in which we were trying to find a senior executive to take over a troubled plant. Our "unmovable" executive took the job with enthusiasm.

A final step is to test explicitly some of your solution hunches during interviews. You can ask, for instance, "What would be your reaction if a new MBO system, which some people have suggested, replaced the present performance appraisal method?" This inquiry can provide a good test of the water—if several people respond positively, then you know implementation may be a lot easier. Be careful not to commit yourself to a particular solution to avoid raising employee expectations. Solutions at this stage are more pipedreams than reality.

All of this brings us to the implementation stage, which provides the true test of our efforts to date. All previous work of the consultant has been confined to ideas, information, and speculation. Now we shall see if the problem can indeed be solved.

RECOMMENDED READINGS

ACKOFF, RUSSELL L.,   *The Art of Problem Solving.* New York: John Wiley & Sons, 1978.

KEPNER, CHARLES H., and BENJAMIN B. TREGOE,   *The New Rational Managers.* Princeton, N.J.: Princeton Research Press, 1981.

KRUPP, SHERMAN,   *Pattern in Organization Analysis: A Critical Examination.* New York: Holt, Rinehart and Winston, 1964.

REDDIN, BILL,   "A Consultant Confesses," *Management Today* (UK), January 1978.

SCHAFFER, ROBERT H.,   "Advice to Internal and External Consultants— Expand Your Client's Capacity To Use Your Help," *Advanced Management Journal*, vol. 41, no. 4 (Autumn 1976).

STEELE, FRED I.,   "Consultants and Detectives," *Journal of Applied Behavioral Science*, 5, no. 2 (1979), 187-202.

14

Implementing Change
How To Sell
Your Recommendations

To liken the consulting process to selling sounds crass and commercial, but unless the client's employees are "sold" to abandon past practices, no change will occur. Scholars who study the subject of change will substitute academic buzzwords such as "influence" for "selling" and "change agent" for "salesperson," but it's all the same thing! Change does not happen without a lot of persuasion, and the consultant is the prime persuader.

Even experienced consultants are often weakest in the implementation stage. It is amusing but sad to find so many consultants who assume that change occurs automatically once a lengthy and lucid report is presented that lays out a list of recommendations. This superficial approach is reminiscent of expecting a customer to buy a new car based on an impersonal letter from an unknown car dealer.

Along with naïve consultants, there are more self-aware consultants who avoid implementation like the plague because it requires a different kind of emotion, energy, and skill that is absent from their analytical makeup. The profession tends to attract analyzers versus doers, which probably explains why they are in consulting and not line management.

So it is the implementation stage that, in our opinion, distinguishes good consultants from the mediocre ones. The effective consultant brings to fruition the results of prior efforts in data gathering and problem analysis. While you may be able to develop a brilliant analysis of the problem and then write it up in an elegant report, ask yourself if that is sufficient in itself to deserve your high fees? Many consultants act as if this is the case, but we view the real value of fees being determined by the actual solution of a client's problem. Causing change is the essence of consulting. Without the accomplishment of change, consulting remains a parasitic profession.

This chapter focuses on five key areas vital to understanding and carrying out a successful change program. We begin with theories of change because a great deal is known from past research about the major pitfalls to avoid and the paths to success. Next, there is a need for developing strategies for the change program in terms of its objectives, benefits, and costs and the role of the consultant. Third, we take up the specific tactics of change, which involve phasing each action step while preserving vital strengths and sidestepping whirlpools of opposition in the organization. Fourth, we deal with the specific problem of resistance and the relevant techniques for reducing or eliminating it. Finally, we turn to the behavioral style of the consultant as he or she intervenes through various actions to persuade an anxious client.

THEORIES OF CHANGE

Theories of change are more than academic pipedreams; they are derived from years of research in organizations. From these studies we can detect some useful guidelines for planning an effective change strategy.

All theories make clear that it is actual change in the underlying behavior patterns of employees that determine whether any attempt at change is successful. You may want to introduce a new accounting system, but it will not come into reality until many employees have abandoned the previous system and accepted the new one. In other words, employees must change their behavior vis-à-vis the accounting system, or the firm will not achieve a change in the system itself.

Too many consultants believe that client acceptance is axiomatic when the marvels of a new system are explained logically to a few key executives. Unfortunately, the logic of consultants or top executives is not necessarily the logic of lower-level employees who must live daily with a new system.

Since any change tinkers with peoples' psyches, a second theory becomes clear, namely, that behavioral change is not an overnight black-to-white occurrence. Instead, numerous studies reveal that change moves through a sequence of phases as people gradually shed old behavior patterns for new ones. Various labels have been assigned by scholars to different phases of change, but the most useful version still remains that of Kurt Lewin, who in 1947 described a sequence of three stages in terms of "unfreezing," "changing," and "refreezing."[1]

The initial "unfreezing" phase refers to a period in which the client must become sufficiently anxious to want to change. Fat and happy clients seldom embrace change. So the skillful consultant needs to plan a way of arousing the client to take action. Sometimes it is the presentation of the final report where "shocking" findings are revealed to surprise and worry the client. Or it can occur in a "confrontation" meeting designed to encourage senior executives to express openly their disagreements with each other. Once these key people are motivated to act constructively and with unity of purpose, then the same process of arousal must occur again with lower-level employees. They, too, must feel the need for change.

The "changing" phase involves actual attempts at change where employees begin to master the easiest steps and then move on to the more difficult ones. Too much change in too short a time can result in indigestion. So don't overload concerned employees with unrealistic demands. They will move only as fast as their attitudes and skills can take them. Reeducation through additional training is often necessary.

The "refreezing" stage is concerned with positive reinforcement to make sure that initial changes are lasting. Unless employees gain a sense of betterment from their attempted changes, they are likely to fall back into old habits. So positive rewards, encouragement and, most of all, early signs of success are critical for maintaining momentum.

Other research studies point to the importance of *power reinforcement, leadership modeling,* and *reeducation* as key "levers" for change. The power lever refers to the need for top management support and the forces it brings to bear upon others to change. If senior management is not solidly behind the change program, then lower-level employees will see little reason to commit themselves. Steps must be taken by the consultant to assure that the power structure agrees to the program and presents a united front to the organization. We always arrange for a series of planning meetings in which top managers participate actively with us in drawing up a final plan. Failure to include senior executives in arriving at mutual commitment to change can undermine future actions.

The critical role of top management is not just a power game in determining the success of a change program. Numerous researchers have called attention to a theory of "leadership modeling" as making the difference between enthusiastic and lukewarm acceptance. Modeling

---

[1] Kurt Lewin, "Group Decision and Social Change" in *Readings in Social Psychology,* T. Newcomb and E. Hartley, eds., (New York: Holt, Rinehart and Winston, Inc., 1947).

refers to the need for top management to practice what it preaches. Lower-level employees will be watching top management, and if senior executives regard change as the responsibility of everyone but themselves, then the effort will falter. We once neglected to plan for this feature in an assignment that recommended the installation of a new MBO system. While top management accepted our recommendation for organizationwide application, they subsequently refused to practice it themselves. As a result, the change effort had to be restarted after a serious confrontation between consultants and top management.

While powerful pressure is necessary from senior levels, lower-level employees will experience difficulty in changing unless they are reeducated. They must unlearn old skills and acquire new ones. For example, a new MBO system requires added behavioral skills in holding participative discussions with subordinates. Managers accustomed to "top-down" methods of goal setting will need additional education to learn these new participative skills if MBO is to be successful. Further, they cannot be expected to become participative "smoothies" through a one-week training program or charm school; they also will need top management's patience and tolerance for initial mistakes.

Consultants not only need to put these theories into practice, but also to communicate and explain them, in simplified form, to their clients. Consultants must occasionally become teachers, acting as translators between abstract theory and the parochial world of their clients. Knowledgeable clients will act more effectively when the consultant is absent.

STRATEGIES FOR CHANGE

Before designing the details of any change program, it helps to develop an overall set of objectives. We have observed numerous attempts at change without clearly defined objectives or, worse yet, none at all. Without objectives you can easily head off in the wrong direction and perform a lot of unnecessary steps. Clear objectives will also provide criteria through which the consultant and client can measure progress along the way.

Objectives should be linked closely to your definition of the client's problems and its explanation. For instance, if you define and explain a client's problem as "lack of coordination due to an absence of supportive management systems, such as a coordination department," then the overall objective should be a literal extension of this same definition, that is, "to achieve greater coordination through new integrative management systems." If you make this direct link, you will have created a guideline for moving on to tactics, all of which is a logical and interrelated process as diagrammed:

PROBLEM→OBJECTIVES→TACTICS

"Why" → "What" → "How"

It looks obvious and simple, doesn't it? But you would be shocked at the number of consulting studies that define the problem one way and then implement a solution that fits only a pet idea of the consultant or client. The problem statement is your "ground," and all objectives and solutions must be tested against it. If you have trouble stating objectives, it is a sign that your problem definition is lacking in clarity and focus.

While most consulting assignments can be reduced to one or two major objectives, there is a danger in remaining too general in a brief summary statement of objectives. Therefore, it helps to break down overall objectives into a list of subproblems and subobjectives. Subproblems pinpoint the specific causes of the overall problem; subobjectives are aimed at remedying the specific causes. For example, in our previous statement referring to the "lack of coordination due to an absence of supportive management systems," we may define one subproblem as "the overly competitive attitude of senior managers stemming from the entrepreneurial values of the company president." A subobjective to deal with this problem would be for "the president to incorporate more cooperative behavior into his manner of handling senior management, such as through the formation of a new operating committee."

Accompanying your statement of objectives should be an analysis of benefits and costs. Benefits can be specified from objectives, whereas costs will accrue from the tactical steps described in the next section. The client is usually more interested in the benefit-cost ratio than in lofty objectives. But you are on slippery ground if you try to attach dollar figures to every benefit and each cost because you are dealing with many unknown facts. Nevertheless, you can specify certain benefits, such as "faster decision making" and "more responsive customer service," as flowing from an overall objective of "greater coordination." These benefit statements will help the client to visualize more clearly what to expect from a nebulous term such as "coordination." It will also provide measurement targets to gauge success or failure of the program.

It is essential that costs and fees be discussed because this typically involves a renegotiation of the consultant's contract. It is a natural opportunity to "sell" more work because much of the implementation stage cannot be anticipated in the original proposal. The client must know the total costs, including both consultant and employee time, so that a budget can be drawn up and funds secured. We have seen consultants and clients slide by this step casually, only to find themselves in serious conflict later when the client was surprised by the consultant's bill or by additional travel expenses required for managers to attend special meetings. A new contract should be drawn up to assure that everyone is in agreement as to the work to be performed.

In arriving at costs, the consultant should scrutinize the action steps described in the next section on tactics. Each step will provide a clue as to the amount of consultant time involved as well as the time and personnel to be provided by client employees. Cost is a negative-sounding word, so we usually refer to the "investment" that a client will have to make. This investment is expected to reap a sizable return. While it is a play on words, clients prefer a positive vocabulary to the empty hole called "expenses."

Renegotiation of the consultant contract also necessitates a discussion of the consultant versus client role during the change process. You cannot and should not expect to retain full responsibility for the change program, even though some clients would prefer that you play the "evil" role of one who upsets the apple cart. Employees who perceive the change program as "owned" by the consultant, not by their senior management, will lose interest rapidly. Moreover, the consultant will leave eventually, so gradual preparation for self-responsibility by the client is preferable to overdependence on a headstrong consultant.

Remember that you are not a line executive employed by the client, which is a tempting role as you see the client become uneasy about taking responsibility for a difficult change program. In football parlance, it is a "hand-off" that must be done skillfully but firmly. A clearer picture of this hand-off from consultant to client emerges when you consider the tactics of detailed action steps. If you are performing too many of the steps, then reassess the entire plan.

TACTICS OF CHANGE

Once you have established a program's objectives, you can work backward to specify the tactical steps necessary for the client to move successfully toward a desired end result (see Exhibit 14-1). Tactics of change require three important considerations: building off the existing strengths of the organization, formulating a series of detailed steps, and pretesting these steps for their political sensitivity and unanticipated consequences.

The data-gathering stage should have revealed a better understanding of the client's underlying strengths and weaknesses. It is important for the change program to lead from these strengths, to avoid undermining them, and to sidestep weaknesses within the client's system. In our earlier example of the client who is lacking in cooperative action among its senior management, it would be a mistake to smother competition among them in favor of a complete swing over to cooperative teamwork. Their competitive spirit brought them a long way and we know that the president favors an entrepreneurial approach. Therefore, cooperative solutions will have to be approached in a gradual manner that acknowledges the importance of retaining a certain degree of competition among senior management. The president will be persuaded more easily if you argue that entrepreneurship can be furthered through additional cooperation between overly competitive executives but not at the expense of healthy competition. That argument is consistent with the president's values.

Client weaknesses should also be considered and incorporated into your plan. If, for instance, you learn that the entrepreneurial president hates to conduct meetings, you should not force on him the responsibility for chairing a new operating committee. It may be that his executive vice president is more adept at this function, so propose him as the ongoing chairperson of the committee, with the proviso that the president be appointed as the formal chairperson who can lead the committee whenever he so desires.

A list of specific action steps serves several useful purposes. It establishes responsibility for exactly what the client must do and what assistance will be needed from the consultant. It makes clear the timing of each action so that one step sets the stage for another. And, invariably, it becomes an exercise in psyching out the politics of the organization. If you fail to include a key executive whose support you need for a certain step, this person may be offended and turn later against the entire change program.

The sequence of steps should keep in mind the phases of "unfreezing," "changing," and "refreezing." If you rush too fast and assume too much, employees will not understand the need for change. So the beginning stages require that time be spent on "feedback" of your findings in ways that arouse the client to take action. Here you will probably have to conduct several meetings, attended by key executives, where you present "the problem" backed by analysis and supporting evidence. Allow sufficient time for discussion, and be prepared to modify your recommendations when good ideas come up or when there is unanimous disagreement.

The "changing" phase moves the project from discussion into action. Often we will establish a "coordination committee" for the change program headed by a respected senior executive. This helps to transfer responsibility from the consultant to the client as well as to assure formal guidance and continuous follow-up to a foreign process that is not yet integral to the client's way of life. The consultant should work closely with this committee in reviewing specific action steps, making modifications, assigning responsibilities, and dealing with problems as they arise.

The "refreezing" stage requires close attention to the early results of change. Skeletons in the form of organizational sacred cows don't usually emerge until the door is opened. There will obviously be unforeseen problems, and those responsible for the change effort must detect them at an early stage before they fester too long.

Consultants can be helpful here by interviewing employees affected by the initial changes and by listening to their complaints and suggestions. Or an anonymous questionnaire can be administered that asks for a spectrum of employee reactions. Sometimes we will hold group discussions among affected employees to allow them an opportunity to "sound off" and compare notes with each other on "how it is going." In a small group discussion, five favorable reactions will easily outweigh one vocal naysayer whose opinions may have predominated prior to the meeting.

The focus of all these follow-up efforts should stress a "positive" attitude based on constructive criticism, without backing away from a commitment to change. Equal time and attention should be given to highlighting the positive signs of success; this can be done through performance statistics that reveal improved economic results or reduced turnover. We have also asked the coordinating committee to publish periodic reports to employees that describe, briefly, significant decisions and accomplishments flowing from the change program.

After planning the phases and steps to be taken, you must examine them critically for their "unintended" consequences. This is where you should play the "what if" game in self-critical discussions with the client. The focus of "what if" is on all the possible things that can go wrong with each proposed step. For example, if your plan is to decentralize the organization into profit centers, you should ask if there are sufficiently qualified managers to handle the job of leading each new center. We were once called by a client after a disastrous experience with massive decentralization where the previous consultants forgot to ask if the necessary personnel were available. They weren't, and the client had to retreat.

FINALIZING THE RECOMMENDATIONS

With the data analysis, information from secondary and tertiary interviews, probes and tests of possible alternatives, and frank discussions with the client playing "what if" scenarios, the consultant is ready to finalize the recommendations. A well-prepared set of recommendations will describe the current situation, the proposed changes, the rationale behind it, and the benefits anticipated from the change program.

Final recommendations can be displayed in a report in any number of ways, sequentially in list form, sequentially by type of problem to be resolved, or organizationally by functional area. Some reports may be entirely oral, others may be written, or the client may request the oral presentation of the key points from the consultant's written report.

Do all key executives, including the chairman and CEO, receive a copy of the written report?

Case in Point

When one of the authors finished a particularly challenging assignment early in his career, he wrote a very incisive, well-documented report, which he felt included sufficient logic for a radical change. It was brilliant. He ordered 25 copies of the report to be printed. His consulting boss at the time stopped the printing and asked why so many copies had been ordered. The author replied that each member of senior management and the board of directors should have a copy. He could see clearly all the follow-up business to be sold as the client was impressed by a brilliant literary work that bordered on a doctoral dissertation.

The author's boss was most understanding and agreed that the report was good. He then began to ask a few innocent questions. "Had the client been consulted as to who should get a report?" "Which members of senior management might become alienated to the consultants if they chose to read the findings as an indictment of their previous management decisions?" "How much of the sensitive data in the report might be copied by someone and used for his or her own devises?" "What if someone left the company and took a copy to a competitor—how much damage would be done to the client?"

Needless to say, the author quickly contacted the client and asked for his opinion, explaining all the possible risks. The client felt that the report should not be distributed because of "political sensitivities." The lesson was learned; always check with your client. There may be any number of reasons why the CEO or other key executives don't receive a copy, and a smart consultant won't overlook that.

REDUCING RESISTANCE TO CHANGE

There will always be resistance to change because some employees feel uncertain and even threatened by the future. However, this does not mean that resistance cannot be overcome. Instead of using force to persuade employees, the consultant and senior management must act with understanding and sensitivity in helping employees to become more comfortable with the changes ahead. Moreover, not all employees will be upset; many of them, in fact, will be looking forward to improved conditions.

Several techniques are available to the consultant to use in assisting the client with problems of resistance. Many of these techniques, if applied early in the change process, can prevent resistance from arising at a later date. Too often consultants and management wait until resistance is apparent, but then it may be so severe that the entire change program is in jeopardy. So base all your plans on the assumption that resistance is just around the corner.

One technique to prevent resistance is to "co-opt" the naysayers before they become too vocal. You will receive hints at the data-gathering stage as to who the skeptics are. Those who are powerful can be won over by including them, not avoiding them, in the planning of change. We have added them to the "coordination committee" for the change program. Or we have spent time with them informally, in going over our findings and listening to their reactions. A good catharsis of negative feelings can lead to a begrudging "let's get on with it." Also, a personal phone call from the CEO can win over a wavering executive.

A second approach is to hold widespread participation and information sessions for all employees who will be affected by the change program. Instead of keeping the program a "secret," which it never is, we believe in full disclosure. Resistance arises most frequently out of ignorance and rumor, especially if naysayers have time to invent distortions of what is actually to occur. We know of a major airline whose president, on "black Friday" (as it was later to be called), announced a major change program without consulting even his most senior executives. The change was not only a failure but the president lost his job. And, yes, a prestigious consulting firm was involved!

Third, we prefer solutions that avoid attacking sacred cows in the organization. If you eliminate somebody's pet project, you may arouse opposition to the entire change program.

Case in Point

During a recent marketing audit of one client, we felt that hundreds of thousands of dollars were being spent ineffectively. One of those items was $15,000 a year to support radio broadcasts of the local college's football games. But the team hadn't experienced a winning season in years, and the listener ratings were terrible. On the other hand, it was the chairman's alma mater, and he was adamant that the organization sponsor the games. There was not one single objective reason for continuation. Yet which is the lesser of two evils: to incur the wrath of the chairman by recommending a $300,000 shift of marketing expense or to effect a significant change and success in the relationship by recommending a $285,000 shift of expense?

Fourth, we like to present alternative solutions instead of a single program. We will then offer an analysis of the pros and cons for each alternative, and sometimes indicate our preference for a particular solution. A discussion of alternatives provides for more "ownership" by the client over the chosen solution. It is too easy to fall into the "we versus they" trap when the consultant tries to impose a single solution on the client.

Sometimes the client will pick an alternative that is not favored by the consultant, or even offer a new one of its own. But the client just may be "right"! Consultants do not have a corner on the truth. Besides, if the client selects a different alternative, at least it has decided to act. This is far better than rejecting a solution while saying a polite "thank you and goodby" to the consultant.

Another very effective technique is to propose "experimentation" in a few selected segments of the organization before spreading a change program to the entire firm. Clients may be willing to accept a radical change if the risk is reduced through experimentation. They know from past experience that bad consequences arise from massive change efforts that no one can get their hands around except the president. Mistakes made on a grand scale can be very costly. It takes only a few willing managers who, because of their added interest, will tip an experiment toward success. Also, experiments can provide a valuable opportunity to work out troublesome bugs before they extend to other departments.

Novel and unconventional solutions are a sixth technique that can be used to sidestep political sensitivities. In one situation, we drew a circular organization chart instead of a pyramid, because we wanted to avoid a conventional portrayal of who had "won" or "lost" power as measured by boxes and lines of authority. In another client, we were faced with an executive vice president who continued to control the organization, even after a very competent new president was brought in from the outside. The executive vice president had 30 years' seniority and was highly respected in the community. Our solution was to promote the executive vice president to chairman, with responsibility for external affairs. This left the president free to run the daily operations of the organization.

Finally, we believe in stressing rewards as an incentive to employees for attempting change. They are concerned about "what's in it for us," because an uncertain future can imply loss rather than gain. So be sure to translate the benefits of change, as perceived by top management, into perceived rewards for lower-level employees. This does not necessarily mean increased wages, although that can be a useful way of converting higher profits into individual motivation. Rewards can also be stressed in terms of "less bureaucracy to foul up decision making," or "more timely information from which to make better decisions," or a "less stressful and more comfortable workingplace to enhance morale." Terms such as "higher profits" and "reduced costs" are far too abstract and remote to persuade the average employee. They will be suspicious if they perceive top management and the shareholders as the sole beneficiaries.

INTERVENTION STYLES

So far we have discussed ways of introducing change through relatively impersonal means, such as by committees, reports, presentations, rewards, and meetings. However, the role of the consultant cannot be confined to such "distant" contact. Events will arise where the consultant must also intervene directly, through his or her personal and spontaneous behavior.

Interventions by the consultant can help to enhance the client's perspective and to relieve tension. Arguments will arise or managers will become bogged down in a forest of details. Without help from the consultant, they can fail to make vital decisions for moving ahead with the change program. Much will hinge on the consultant's skill in raising a pertinent question or offering a needed opinion at critical moments. Your behavior becomes, in essence, a "tool" of change.

There are many ways in which to intervene during the delicate process of change. Consultants should become aware of various intervention roles to play, as well as to know those conditions under which each role is appropriate. Rigid and obsessive behavior by the consultant, or a limited repertoire of intervention skills, will seriously limit your effectiveness. Saying the wrong thing at the right moment can easily frustrate the process.

What are some different intervention styles? We like to think in terms of three broad categories, within which there are several specific interventions. One is an *emotional* class designed to relieve tension, offer encouragement, and release undercurrents of negative feelings among participants. Such interventions involve the use of humor, listening, reflecting feelings, and lending support. Cracking a joke, so long as it is relevant, can bring others out of a morbid and overly serious debate. Listening involves asking questions that reveal hidden views or open up a silent, sulking participant. Reflecting negative feelings, such as by saying "I sense that you feel angry," can indicate your willingness to understand as well as to provide a catharsis for resentment. You can also be supportive through a variety of positive comments, ranging from "That's a good point" to "You are making lots of progress."

A second category includes *direction* interventions intended to move a wandering discussion ahead more coherently. You will often possess more perspective than the client who is tip-toeing into uncharted waters. You can assist by orienting the dialogue through such statements as, "Today our purpose is mainly to get a handle on understanding the problem, so let's hold off temporarily on a discussion of specific solutions." You can also summarize at points after a long discussion by saying, for example, "Let me see if I understand what you've been saying. . . . Several of you are beginning to define the problem as . . . ".

Another helpful behavior is probing, where you ask questions to take the discussion to a deeper level, such as by asking, "Can you say some more about what you meant by a 'communication' problem? What is behind it, in your opinion?"

The third class of interventions is *knowledge* focused, drawing off the consultant's background and rich exposure to the client. Clients will depend on you for input as a way of shedding more insight on their limited viewpoints. One input is based on theory, as you explain to the client the state of what is known about an issue they are discussing, such as "decentralization" or "management by objectives." Another useful contribution can draw from your experience with other clients as you relate to them how a company with a similar problem went about its solution phase. Another is based on data intervention stemming from your study's findings, which can be supplied when incorrect assumptions are being made without facts. For example, you might state, "You seem to be assuming that only the first-level supervisors are upset about the present goal-setting method, but let me read you some typical comments from your middle managers."

Your decision as to when and how to apply these various interventions depends on your appraisal of a combination of factors. One factor is a keen awareness for what is happening immediately in front of you. Is the situation reflecting an *emotional issue,* a *direction problem*, or a *knowledge deficiency*? The situation is not the only consideration—there is also the state of your relationship with the client. If you are trusted and feel at home, it is easier to be more authoritative. As the change process progresses, you will have to bite your tongue occasionally; the client must be weaned away gradually from an omniscient consultant. Finally, there are your own acquired skills as an interventionist—you may not be very effective at emotional interventions, which means that you should keep quiet or, better yet, work with a compatriot who has those skills.

Besides knowing about intervention skills, you will have to practice them frequently to become facile in their use. This will take a great deal of self-awareness, sensitivity, and willingness to experiment with your own behavior in client situations. Feedback will be immediate because you will see whether you have unblocked a discussion or created a "plop" that is rejected or ignored. Too many "plops" will undermine not only a brilliant analysis but client confidence in the consultant and the change program itself.

RECOMMENDED READINGS

ARGYRIS, CHRIS, and DONALD A. SCHON, *Organizational Learning: A Theory of Action Perspective.* Reading, Mass.: Addison-Wesley, 1978.

BECKHARD, RICHARD, and REUBEN T. HARRIS, *Organizational Transitions: Managing Complex Change.* Reading, Mass.: Addison-Wesley, 1977.

BENNIS, WARREN G., *Changing Organizations.* New York: McGraw Hill, 1966.

BENNIS, WARREN G.; KENNETH D. BENNE; ROBERT CHIN; and KENNETH E. COREY, eds., *The Planning of Change* (3rd ed.). New York: Holt, Rinehart and Winston, 1976.

BLAKE, ROBERT R., and JANE S. MOUTON, *Consultation.* Reading, Mass.: Addison-Wesley, 1976.

GREINER, LARRY E., "Patterns of Organization Change," *Harvard Business Review,* May/June 1967.

KOTTER, JOHN P., and LEONARD A. SCHLESINGER, "Choosing Strategies for Change," *Harvard Business Review,* March/April 1979.

MORGAN, JOHN S., *Managing Change: The Strategies of Making Change Work.* New York: McGraw Hill, 1972.

PETTIGREW, ANDREW, *The Politics of Organizational Decision making.* London: Tavistock, 1973.

ZALTMAN, GERALD, and ROBERT DUNCAN, *Strategies for Planned Change.* New York: John Wiley & Sons, 1977.

EXHIBIT 14-1   Sample Reorganization Implementation Plan

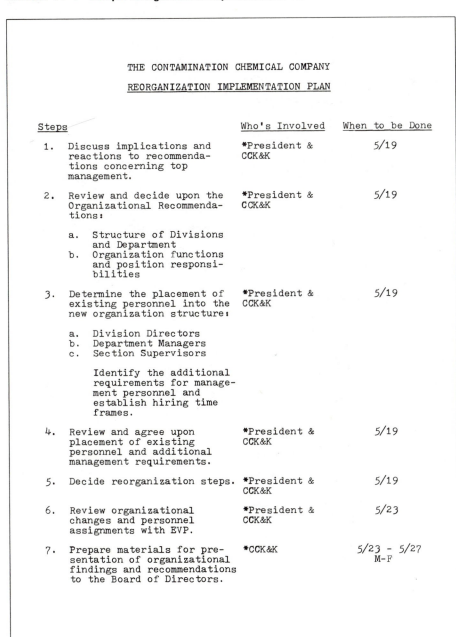

THE CONTAMINATION CHEMICAL COMPANY

REORGANIZATION IMPLEMENTATION PLAN

Steps		Who's Involved	When to be Done
1.	Discuss implications and reactions to recommendations concerning top management.	*President & CCK&K	5/19
2.	Review and decide upon the Organizational Recommendations:	*President & CCK&K	5/19
	a. Structure of Divisions and Department		
	b. Organization functions and position responsibilities		
3.	Determine the placement of existing personnel into the new organization structure:	*President & CCK&K	5/19
	a. Division Directors		
	b. Department Managers		
	c. Section Supervisors		
	Identify the additional requirements for management personnel and establish hiring time frames.		
4.	Review and agree upon placement of existing personnel and additional management requirements.	*President & CCK&K	5/19
5.	Decide reorganization steps.	*President & CCK&K	5/19
6.	Review organizational changes and personnel assignments with EVP.	*President & CCK&K	5/23
7.	Prepare materials for presentation of organizational findings and recommendations to the Board of Directors.	*CCK&K	5/23 - 5/27 M-F

*Indicates responsibility for implementing the item.

EXHIBIT 14-1 (cont'd)

Steps	Who's Involved	When to be Done
8. Prepare specific detailed schedule of meeting dates, times and personnel for this implementation plan.	*CCK&K	5/23 - 5/27 M-F
9. Prepare materials for individual meetings with Senior Managers.	*CCK&K	5/23 - 5/27 M-F

a. Position descriptions
    b. Organizational and functional charts
    c. Schedules and assignments		

10. Review reorganization recommendations with BOD.	*President, BOD	5/24 Tuesday
11. Meet with existing and new Division Directors individually, in order to:	*President, EVP & CCK&K	5/31 - 6/1 Tues. & Wed.

a. Discuss their new position's functions and responsibilities
    b. Discuss the new Divisional organization structure and functions
    c. Provide charts and new positions descriptions for their Division		

12. Conduct a meeting with all Division Directors to:	*President, EVP, Division Directors, CCK&K	6/2 Thursday

a. Formally announce and describe the new organizational structure, functions and rationale
    b. Answer questions
    c. Announce implementation plan and schedule
    d. Assign the tasks of positioning non-management personnel in their Division and identifying transition problems		

EXHIBIT 14-1 (cont'd)

Steps		Who's Involved	When to be Done
13.	Hold follow-up meeting with each Division Director individually to:	*President, EVP, Division Directors, CCK&K	6/3 - 6/4 Thurs. - Fri.
	a. Determine the placement of personnel into organization structure		
	b. Determine additional personnel needs		
	c. Determine organizational and functional charts for sections or units		
14.	Develop the program for formally announcing the organizational changes throughout the Corporation:	*CCK&K	6/6/ - 6/10
	a. Prepare announcement materials		
	b. Reproduce position descriptions and organizational charts		
15.	Conduct brief individual meetings with key managers affected by reorganization to inform them of their new roles and positions.	*President, EVP, Division Directors	6/6 - 6/10 M-F
16.	Review announcement materials with the Communications Letter	*CCK&K, President and EVP	6/14 Tuesday
17.	Mail Communications Letter to all employees informing them of the major organizational changes.	*President	6/14 Tuesday
18.	Management Retreat	Senior Management	6/15 - 6/17 W-F
19.	Obtain necessary Board of Director approvals	*President	6/21 Tuesday
20.	Each Division Director meets individually with each Department Manager to:	*Division Directors & Department Managers	6/6 - 6/10 M-F
	a. Review new position descriptions		
	b. Discuss and decide positioning of other personnel		

EXHIBIT 14-1 (cont'd)

Steps	Who's Involved	When to be Done
21. Each Division Director meets with the Department Managers and Section Supervisors in a group to review the Division organizational and personnel changes.	*Division Directors, Department Managers & Section Supervisors	6/6 - 6/10 M-F
22. Each Division Director conducts a general meeting of the Division's personnel to: a. Announce the new Division's role, organization and functions b. Answer questions c. Announce new personnel assignments	*Division Directors	6/6 - 6/10
23. Establish new management groups and committees: a. Senior Management Group b. Pollution Committee c. Dangerous Drugs Committee	*President	6/17
24. Prepare position descriptions for other supervisory personnel	*Personnel Department Manager, Division Directors	6/29 - 7/13
25. Develop new operating policies and procedures and obtain Board of Directors approval: a. Production Approval Authority b. Expenditure Approval Authority	*President, EVP & CCK&K	Assigned at Retreat
26. Develop an overall list of Company needs and priorities and assign responsibilities	*President, EVP	Week of June 29

15

How To Sell More Work—
or Leave Gracefully

It is fitting at this point to discuss what is to be done when the assignment for which the consultant was engaged is over. The answer is simple—sell more work to the client or leave gracefully. It all depends on the new opportunities before you, with the client or elsewhere, and the state of your relationship with the client. Making that choice is difficult because intimacy with the client can breed fuzzy thinking.

YOUR UNIQUE
POSITION

The groundwork for selling more work to the client is laid in the original proposal to the client. It addressed a specific need that was agreed upon by you and the client. The proposal was priced on the actual work needed to assuage the client's specific concerns at that time. This approach, as we advised earlier, is a practical step-by-step approach to the selling of consulting services. It does not overwhelm the client in the beginning stages of an uncertain relationship. Massive proposals and prices are sold occasionally by large consulting firms to *Fortune* 500 companies, but in the more mundane life of the average consultant in a local or regional consulting firm, a $30,000 proposal is a lot of money for a small client to afford. To hand a six-figure proposal to most clients is to self-destruct.

Following completion of a more modest proposal, the consultant is in a unique position to sell a second phase of work. Not only have you had an opportunity to get to know the client and become a respected professional in the firm's eyes, but also you have gained an insider's knowledge of many of the strengths and weaknesses of the client company. From this perspective, you are well equipped to help the client further—and yourself.

THE IMPLEMENTATION SALE

As we have stated several times in earlier chapters, an effective consultant is not one who generates voluminous reports that end up collecting dust on the client's credenza. On the contrary, an effective consultant is one who implements needed and positive changes to move an organization beyond the status quo. The first opportunity the consultant has to accomplish such changes is in the implementation of recommendations from the initial proposal. In many cases, the original proposal stops at a written report and presentation of recommendations. It is the implementation of these recommendations that forms the basis for a second proposal and, it is hoped, the second job with the client.

Many consultants fail at this point by leaving a report with the client and departing on the assumption that the client knows how to handle a change program. On the contrary, it is our experience that this is the time when the client needs the assistance and counsel of the consultant more than ever. It is the ideal time to sell more work.

The authors have performed a great many organizational studies over the years, most of which required extensive written reports to identify and explain the problems at hand and to emphasize the need for making specific organizational changes. At the end of these reports, the client finds several pages of recommended implementation steps. An example of such a "Recommended Implementation Schedule" was found in Exhibit 14-1.

The most successful way in which to make this additional sale is to "walk" the client through each specific recommendation in the final report. The client should be shown in great detail and with great care exactly how these recommendations should be implemented. Much can go wrong without effective management of the change process. The consultant should proceed down the list of steps, identifying which ones the client can do themselves easily versus those that require exceptional timing, special skills, added resources, and a great deal of tact.

From here it is an easy and logical step to show the client that the consultant is in the best position and has the most experience to help in the successful implementation of the more complex change steps. For example, the client might take care of announcements of the change to key personnel, either in meetings or in memos to the employees, whereas the consultant might draw up new job descriptions and prepare the graphics for formal presentations.

THE ADD-ON SYSTEMS SALE

An ideal source of additional business is the design and implementation of new systems that complement the changes made as a result of the original recommendations. For example, there is often a need for a new sales training program after a new product has been introduced or an old product repackaged. Organization studies are practically mandatory following a merger or acquisition negotiation.

The authors have frequently performed organization studies that result in a plan to decentralize the organization structure. In one case, it led to a further proposal to design three new systems to facilitate the new structure—an information system based on profit center accounting, a compensation system to provide added incentives for profit center managers, and a management development program to identify and train a larger source of general manager talent. The project could have stopped with the introduction of a new structure and the placement of managers in new positions, but it led to these additional systems as a "natural" evolution of the decentralization program.

THE NEW ISSUES SALE

Another source of follow-on business is new problems discovered in the client system during the initial assignment. It is the authors' experience that most clients, in the beginning, need more help than they recognize or are willing to admit. Therefore, by first addressing the original concerns of the client, you are in a favorable position to raise additional issues identified during the analysis stage.

For example, in a study of a client's organization structure, you may uncover a host of unrelated problems, such as high turnover and poor morale in the sales force or quality-control difficulties in the manufacturing plants. These examples provide numerous opportunities for consultants to express and explain to clients the need for additional consulting services. And, if the consultant has performed well in the first assignment, the probability of selling another project is high.

THE PROGRESS LETTER SALE

A formal method for obtaining follow-on business is the "progress letter." When a consultant has been engaged heavily for a period of several months with a major client project, progress reports in the form of letters should be sent to the client. These letters update the client as to what has transpired and serve to justify the fees paid to date.

It doesn't take a lot of imagination on the part of the consultant to expand a progress letter into three parts: *work accomplished, work-in-progress,* and *work to be performed*. The work accomplished section is a straightforward delineation of completed steps and positive results. The work-in-progress part of the letter indicates steps being taken currently by the consultant, and it forecasts remaining work to be done within limits of the original proposal. The work to be performed section is actually a proposal for additional consulting work beyond the present contract highlighting new steps needed to assure that results of current work are leveraged to the utmost. An example of such a letter appears in Exhibit 15-1.

CLOSING THE FOLLOW-ON SALE

The most propitious time for closing a sale of follow-on business is to make a verbal proposal during the presentation of results and recommendations from the first assignment. If the consultant's work has been to the client's needs, then the client should be in a receptive mood. A recommendation for additional work becomes a natural part of the change program flowing from the first phase of work. This follow-on sale merely requires the consultant to ask, "Would you like us to get these next steps started soon?" When the client says, "Yes!" the consultant has sold another job. It is an informal, casual interchange when compared with the formal courtship necessary for selling the first piece of business.

Whether follow-on work has been sold as part of the informal discussions surrounding the previous job or whether it is presented more formally in a progress letter, the consultant should develop shortly thereafter a written proposal that sets out clearly the scope of the work to be performed. Even when the consultant and the client are close friends, the consultant should not overlook the fact that fundamentally he or she still has a business relationship with the client.

You will get off to a cleaner start and prevent future misunderstandings if you restate again the six points discussed earlier in Chapter 5 on proposal writing—that is, identifying just what is the problem to be investigated; determining what the consultant will do; establishing the timing, responsibilities, and reporting relationships; and enumerating the costs and anticipated benefits. Doing this is just as important the second, third, or fourth time around, even though the proposal may be sent to the client after the follow-on work has commenced. It will likely be repetition of a previous verbal agreement, but, nevertheless, it is the professional method for handling follow-on business.

LETTING GO

Just as there are classic moments when follow-on work can and should be sold, there comes a time in every consulting relationship when it is appropriate to end the relationship.

Leaving gracefully at the right moment is an art acquired through experience and intuition. When consultants perform very narrow, limited services, such as a market survey or an executive search, it is quite clear when the job is over. However, if the relationship has been at the CEO level on one or more complex assignments, and the consultant has been deeply involved in profit improvement, strategic planning, or other extended work, the delineation between consultant and client easily becomes blurred. We know of one major consulting firm, for example, that has occupied an office in the executive suite of a client for over five years. So just how long should a client depend on outside assistance?

DEPENDENCY PROBLEMS

A certain amount of dependency naturally creeps into any long-term relationship between client and consultant. The client becomes dependent on the consultant's ready availability to offer advice and perform projects. And the consultant grows accustomed to a steady revenue stream from the client. It is not a healthy situation, however, when the consultant begins to perform tasks that should be carried out by client executives or when the consultant fears economic problems with the loss of a single client.

Client managers will eventually perceive the consultant performing work that rightfully should be theirs, and they will grow to resent the CEO's support and praise for it. The longer the engagement, regardless of the consultant-CEO relationship, the deeper in the organization this form of dependency hostility will penetrate. What might have begun as a warm welcome two or three years earlier gradually becomes a hostile and uncooperative environment for the consultant. It is time to leave.

Further, by continuing to perform major assignments for the client two and three years later, the consultant has, in fact, not done an effective job. He or she has failed to assist the client in developing its own internal capabilities to perform the assignments in question. If, for example, it has been predominantly strategic planning work, then the consultant has neglected to train and develop senior management's competence in that fundamental area. If the work has continued to be marketing research, then the consultant has failed to point out the long-term needs of the marketing division for hiring a full-time professional in that position.

There are unhealthy consequences, too, for the consulting firm in continuing a relationship too long. You begin to lose your motivation and edge for developing new business. You start to put all your eggs in one basket, while forgetting that fat dogs don't hunt. Another kind of paralysis creeps into your intellectual mentality. You cease to grow in your knowledge of new and different clients, thereby stunting your skill at solving a rich array of problems. Successful consulting firms are not built by serving only two or three clients over many years. If you see this happening to your firm, it is definitely time to leave.

ONE BAD IDEA
OUT OF FIFTY

The *one-bad-idea-out-of-fifty syndrome* eventually befalls the infallible consultant. The longer a consultant works with a client, and as he or she becomes more familiar with the company and its needs, sooner or later the consultant will develop an inappropriate or bad recommendation. The client also becomes too trusting in the consultant, thereby allowing the consultant to take risks that are not evaluated carefully.

One of the tough realities of consulting is that, regardless of the volume of positive, effective work performed for a client over time, the client will best remember the consultant for the one bad idea. A sound relationship can sour over a single bad recommendation, which can mean that most, if not all, of the consultant's positive ideas will be forgotten. If you've been with a client for two years or more and you haven't had this problem yet, then it may be time to leave—the odds are against you.

THE "RIP-OFF"
FEELING

Another danger that can lead to the deterioration of a client relationship is the cumulative effect of your fees. If you have followed some of the marketing suggestions in this book and have sold jobs for reasonable fees, one job after another, sooner or later, the board, or the chief financial officer, or even the CEO will wake up one day to say, "My God, I didn't realize how much money we've spent on these consultants over the past two years." When that happens, and it will, the consultant is put in a defensive role. You will have to justify, all over again, everything you have done, and you will have to work doubly hard to secure new, additional work. It's time to leave.

SAYING GOODBY

Never remind client executives about all the good things you've done to benefit them personally. Human nature often reacts negatively to the concept of being indebted to another person for anything. It is instant death to bid farewell to old Forbisham with, "Remember, at the start of this study, when you were only making $40,000 a year?" That is no reason for Forbisham to thank you profusely for your recommendation to promote him to executive vice president, let alone to give you more work. Most likely Forbisham feels that his new salary and title were three years late in coming anyway.

However, we do recommend, in preparing to leave a client, that you orchestrate a "goodby" meeting wherein you summarize the work performed for the client and your perception of the benefits. Attribute these positive results as much to the client's heroic efforts as to your behind-the-scenes actions. State that you are pleased with the client's success, that you have enjoyed the relationship, and that you hope to be of assistance in future years, and then get out!

MAINTAINING
CORDIAL CONTACTS

"Out of sight, out of mind," while trite, is a very real fact in the consulting business. Once the consultant leaves a client, amnesia sets in. When CEOs prepare annual reports or get together to trade war stories, you will seldom receive credit. The superb compensation job that you did last year becomes "Widget Industries is proud to be a leader in employee compensation in its industry" and the strategic planning job you did that improved client earnings 30% over two years becomes "Management's plan to provide long-term profit improvement has been realized." No CEO six months or a year later, ever thinks, "There but for the grace of Arthur D. Little go I!"

Therefore, having left at the appropriate time, aglow with warm feelings, don't let your old client forget you. Every few months send the CEO a relevant article that reflects ideas on issues you know are still unresolved in the company.

Call your old clients at least once or twice a year. Let them know that you still think of them, care about their progress, and are concerned professionally that your recommendations are working out well. Ascertain if there are any new issues or projects you could help with, learn what the newest issues are in the industry, and, of course, ask for new referrals.

Another step toward maintaining cordial relations is to refer new contacts and prospects to past clients for their advice or references. That marketing job you did two years ago will likely be presented as the client's brilliant marketing plan but, knowing that you suggested the call, they will give you some credit for the idea's success. It's good public relations, it's good client relations, and it's an indirect form of marketing.

EXHIBIT 15-1 Sample of a Work-In-Progress Letter

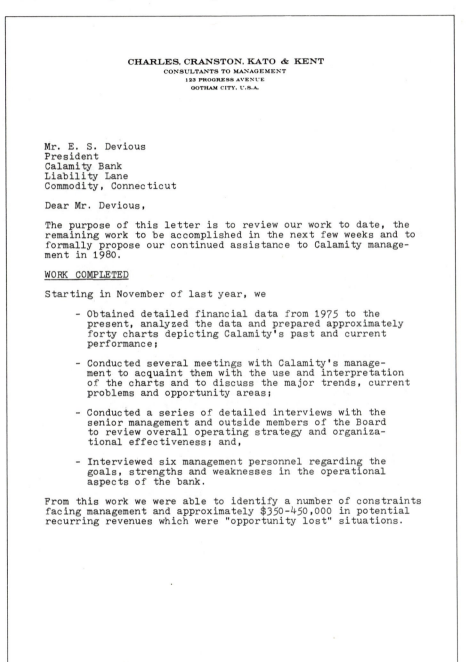

CHARLES, CRANSTON, KATO & KENT
CONSULTANTS TO MANAGEMENT
123 PROGRESS AVENUE
GOTHAM CITY, U.S.A.

Mr. E. S. Devious
President
Calamity Bank
Liability Lane
Commodity, Connecticut

Dear Mr. Devious,

The purpose of this letter is to review our work to date, the
remaining work to be accomplished in the next few weeks and to
formally propose our continued assistance to Calamity management in 1980.

WORK COMPLETED

Starting in November of last year, we

- Obtained detailed financial data from 1975 to the
  present, analyzed the data and prepared approximately
  forty charts depicting Calamity's past and current
  performance;

- Conducted several meetings with Calamity's management to acquaint them with the use and interpretation
  of the charts and to discuss the major trends, current
  problems and opportunity areas;

- Conducted a series of detailed interviews with the
  senior management and outside members of the Board
  to review overall operating strategy and organizational effectiveness; and,

- Interviewed six management personnel regarding the
  goals, strengths and weaknesses in the operational
  aspects of the bank.

From this work we were able to identify a number of constraints
facing management and approximately $350-450,000 in potential
recurring revenues which were "opportunity lost" situations.

EXHIBIT 15-1   (cont'd)

Mr. E. S. Devious   Page 2

We have already provided you with our recommendations in the form of a 10 page written report with respect to alleviating the constraints in the areas of sources and uses of funds, organization, personnel, compensation and the opportunities to generate the revenue from the "opportunity lost" situations.

Just last week, in reviewing the loan interest amortization problem as depicted on the charts, the accountants were able to pinpoint some $17,000 of loan interest which would not have been booked in 1980.

In summary, the work performed to date has not only been cost justified but it also has clarified the major issues to be addressed and resolved in 1980.

WORK IN PROGRESS

On January 26, 27 and 28 we will meet with your management team to conduct an intensive Profit Planning Retreat. The results of this Retreat will be:

- The development of overall long range goals;

- The development of a Profit Plan for 1980, the first year of the longer range plan;

- The identification of major constraints to the managers responsible for implementing that Profit Plan; and,

- The development of specific overall and detailed strategies to overcome those constraints and achieve the 1980 Plan.

Our work will be finished with a presentation to the Board of the finalized 1980 Profit Plan at the February Board meeting.

ADDITIONAL WORK PROPOSED

As we have discussed, the key to Calamity's success in 1980 and in the ensuing years will depend upon the ability of the management team to:

- Develop a methodology and the required systems and information to monitor its performance monthly against its quarterly and annual Profit Plans and to take action quickly to resolve deviations from the Plan;

EXHIBIT 15-1 (cont'd)

Mr. E. S. Devious   Page 3

- Offset the high cost of the branch plant and personnel through the development of a branch management team which will aggressively solicit deposits in a way whereby the sources of funds for lending and cash management can be more predictable and the costs projected and better controlled;

- Develop some marketing support to this branch effort through the development of products and services which attract and tend to retain low cost, stable deposits and promote greater branch traffic and overall awareness of Calamity in its branch market areas;

- Rapidly expand its lending activities to include Consumer Loans and greater involvement in commercial markets, both in Connecticut and in secondary markets;

- Develop a knowledge of and a systematic planning for sources and uses of funds between asset categories to maximize revenues;

- Develop a management compensation and fringe benefits structure, and meaningful performance review and career planning systems which will attract and retain the best people available in the market place;

- Develop and refine a longer range planning capability which provides management and the Board with a meaningful five year plan and the ability to achieve that plan;

- Develop an overall team approach among the managers so that the authority and responsibility required to effectively manage an even larger organization is delegated properly and a second line of management can be built, one that can be relied upon and which will become the senior management of the 1990's.

We believe that to achieve much of this in 1980 we can and should assist you as you decide upon the priorities for each of these tasks. Our experience in lending strategy, marketing, organization, compensation and planning can add an element of expertise which is yet to be developed at Calamity.

Therefore, we propose to meet with you monthly starting in February for two days each month. During these visits, we will review with you and your management team the financial charts which have been developed and assist you in analyzing actual versus planned profitability.

EXHIBIT 15-1 (cont'd)

Mr. E. S. Devious   Page 4

We would also devote our time to the specific projects listed above and would assist you and your managers in their accomplishment in 1980.

And, obviously, we would update the financial charts each month for you.

<u>FEES</u>

Our professional fees for this week, including the monthly update of the charts, will be $2,500 per month for a total of $27,500 through year end 1980.

Additionally, we will bill you for our out-of-pocket expenses at cost, and based on the experience from our previous trips to Connecticut, this would be approximately 13% of professional fees. As in the past, both professional fees and expenses are billed and are payable monthly.

<u>BENEFITS</u>

The cost benefits of this proposed work are clear. Just as was the recent experience with the loan interest accrual problem which more than offset our fees for the present work, we believe we can be instrumental in assisting Calamity to achieve much of its present "opportunity lost" revenue in 1980 which should amount to several hundred thousand dollars.

We look forward to the opportunity to continue assisting Calamity's management and to the challenges facing the bank in 1980.

                    Sincerely,

                    Nick Charles

                    Nick Charles
                    for CHARLES, CRANSTON, KATO & KENT

16

The Uniqueness
of Each Client

The longer one consults, the greater is one's experience with a variety of clientele. You learn slowly that rigid generalizations about consulting are suspect because each client possesses unique features that constantly surprise and challenge your skills. So it is with this book—an important caveat to all our generalizations thus far is that there are *no* immutable laws to consulting. There are only "rules of thumb" and a variety of techniques to be kept locked in your briefcase unless applicable to the peculiarities of each client's situation. If you try to shoehorn a client into a "tried and true" solution, be prepared for a disturbing reaction—clients resist universal panaceas, and for good reason!

This chapter calls attention to some of the unique client characteristics requiring a finely tuned sensitivity on the part of every consultant. Major multinational corporations differ enormously in their problems and management styles from small family businesses. Profit-making companies have market economics to guide them, whereas government agencies have their capricious legislatures. To prepare a proposal for a "Mom and Pop" operation that is geared more to an ITT is as absurd as to offer recommendations to a museum that only an RCA could implement.

MAJOR BUSINESS
CORPORATIONS

Large publicly held companies tend to use "big-name" consulting firms for large projects on complex problems, thereby making it difficult for small local consultants to crack the *Fortune* 500. One reason is that consultants from "big-name" firms tend to circulate in the same circles as key executives from big business. Another cause for mutual attraction is "elitism"—big clients want only the "best," and they can afford it. It is easier for their CEOs to defend recommendations made by McKinsey than by two partners from Albuquerque. Finally, small consulting firms rarely possess sufficient personnel or the specialized skills required by a giant client.

The most common problems handed to consultants by large businesses are strategic planning for diverse product lines, decentralization of a cumbersome organization structure, design and implementation of management information systems, market research and testing for new products, antitrust litigation, management development programs, acquisition and divestment planning, and broad compensation studies that involve incentives, stock options, benefits, and pensions.

The consulting process in a large business can be quite different from working with a small entrepreneurial firm. Executives from a large enterprise are usually clearer about the type of consulting study they want. They are typically well-educated and experienced professional managers who have a sense of "the problem" but want confirmation for it, and they want to see recommendations that can be compared with their own contemplated actions. Moreover, they will have sophisticated staff experts who are prepared to match wits with the best consultants. Because of their immense size, the data-gathering process is time consuming due to the sheer number of interviews and amount of information required to comprehend the problem. Large firms tend to prefer implementing their own solutions, and consultants are usually more than willing to let this happen because of the complexities and politics involved.

INDUSTRY
DIFFERENCES

Big enterprises vary as much between themselves as they do from small business. To lump big business into a single gross category is a mistake that social critics can make, but not consultants.

One key difference is between manufacturing and service-oriented businesses. Clients in the aerospace industry face issues that are uncommon to travel agencies. Manufacturing firms require large capital investments in machinery, whereas service businesses are labor intensive. The former turns out a tangible product; the latter provides an intangible one. The marketing problems of pricing and selling airplanes are obviously not the same as promoting travel packages to Hawaii.

Another major difference stems from the legal environments inherent in different industries. Some companies are in highly regulated industries, such as utilities and railroads, a condition that puts severe constraints on solutions to consulting problems. An electric utility, for example, cannot raise its rates automatically, nor can a savings and loan firm acquire a commercial bank. Mining and chemical companies are particularly vulnerable to OSHA safety regulations, whereas pharmaceutical and food companies are scrutinized by the FDA for their product's health consequences.

Economics play a big role in distinguishing between the problems of one industry and another; for example, a new and rapidly growing industry, such as microprocessors, requires a heavy but risky investment in R&D, although the rewards for successful innovation can be sizable. On the other hand, a declining industry, such as steelmaking, requires cost cutting and diversification into more profitable fields. A paper company or an oil company depends on vertical integration into finished goods to support expensive plants that process raw materials.

For a consultant to be effective in different industries, he or she must intensively study and experience the nuances of each industry, based on the economic, marketing, legal, and technological differences. You will not be seen as credible by a client if you cannot "speak its language." Naïve utterances and recommendations that are outside their sphere of reality and influence will lose you a client rapidly. They are not paying you to go back to school.

PRIVATELY HELD COMPANIES

Companies owned by a few shareholders present a real challenge to consultants. These owners often make decisions more on the basis of personal and emotional reasons than from a desire to squeeze the last dollar out of the bottom line. They have worked together closely for years and tend to feel that their company is a plaything, which it is!

Many classic problems exist in owner-manager firms. The composition of the board of directors, if there is one, is usually based more on personal friendships than on qualifications. The CEO may have learned his position by sole virtue of being heir to the founder. Management practices frequently suffer from a lack of delegation and headstrong excesses in decision making by one or two people. There is a dearth of management talent stemming from an "up-from-within" promotion policy that has placed the former bookkeeper in charge of all administrative duties. These companies tend to be slow growers and obsessively attached to one or two products that brought them initial success. As old George, the CEO, would say, "if gold-plated widgets made this company, why fool around with silver widgets?"

The consultant's dilemma with closely held firms is that, while they desperately need consulting help, they are loath to admit it. It's a tough sale, often made out of personal friendships between client and consultant or through a third-party friend who acts as matchmaker. Once inside the firm, the client is typically unable to state "the problem," preferring instead that you work on some trivial issue that keeps you from causing trouble.

You will be challenged to establish a trusting relationship yet gain acceptance for the techniques of professional management. The ideal change program will usually have to be scaled down to match the client's limited capabilities and the entrenched personalities who cannot be fired or transferred easily.

THE FAMILY BUSINESS

Many of the same features pervading closely held firms also pertain to family-owned and -managed businesses. They, too, are more "personality centered" than are large publicly held firms. But an added complication is the sticky set of relationships existing among family members, where business and home life are indistinguishable.

As an example, the authors are acquainted with a floundering family firm where the youngest of three brothers is constantly complaining to his semiretired father about the incompetence of his older brothers. The father appointed the older brothers to senior positions based on age, but he now empathizes with his youngest son who is closer to him in entrepreneurial philosophy. However, the father cannot bring himself to confront the older sons; instead, he relays the youngest son's complaints to his wife, who then talks to the oldest son. Sounds like a soap opera, doesn't it? But hardly uncommon for family businesses.

A common ailment of family businesses is a tendency to operate more like a family than a real business. Family behavior patterns established years before are acted out daily in business decision making. Consequently, the consultant must become a rare combination of psychotherapist and business educator. The most sensitive and difficult problem facing a family business is one of management succession—

which son or daughter or in-law will be selected to run the business? And how will nonfamily employees view this decision?

Our approach to this problem, as well to many other problems of a family business, is to establish an attitude with the current CEO that professional management methods should supersede family politics—which in the long-run will be best for the family too. In essence, this means that no favoritism is shown—all family members must earn their way to establish themselves as professionally qualified for promotion. The promotion of incompetent family members will eventually destroy the business.

The greatest skill that a consultant can bring to a family business is the ability to facilitate communication among the family members—in a way that brings them to a common understanding about how best to run the business. Next, there are financial, legal, and tax skills to assure that the business will survive estate settlements and money grabs by greedy and dissident family members. Finally, there are the basic skills of business management, such as accounting systems and job descriptions; family businesses are usually too primitive to require sophisticated and specialized consulting services.

STATE, LOCAL, AND FEDERAL GOVERNMENT

Public agencies cannot be run as if they are General Motors. They are subject to an entirely different set of laws, resource constraints, decision-making processes, and customer demands. Recognizing these inherent differences is often difficult for a consultant who is weaned on private-sector clients.

The most obvious difference between public and private organizations is that they do not rise and fall with customer reaction. The marketplace for public agencies is legislative bodies that control their purse strings. Politicians and politics determine directly the budgets of civil servants, whereas citizens produce only an indirect effect through periodic elections. Another difference is the "monopoly" effect, since little competition exists among public agencies to supply the same service. Thus, there is little natural incentive to become efficient. Numerous laws also dictate the limits of executive action—for example, civil servants cannot be fired easily nor can they be promoted quickly over others with greater seniority. Finally, senior executives are usually appointees who come and go with each change of administration.

Public agencies are clearly a consultant's nightmare and challenge. Change is extremely difficult but not impossible. Occasionally, consultants are hired to improve the management practices of agencies, but the alternatives for action are severely restricted. Strategic planning and reorganization studies are virtually nonexistent, but information systems can be improved to enhance decision making, or management training can be given to increase supervisory skills. Consultants are also hired for projects that involve the design and implementation of a new public service, such as Medicare.

The proposal and contract process in government is more formal and rigid than in private business. Projects are put out for bid through an RFP (request for proposal), and contracts are written that prescribe certain actions and reports at numerous stages in a project. You will not be paid unless completion of each prescribed step is performed and documented and submitted on an approved form, and even then payment may be weeks in coming.

NONPROFIT ORGANIZATIONS

Still different from government and private business are not-for-profit organizations, such as hospitals, charities, museums, churches, and universities. Professional management is seldom their forte as people who are appointed to administrative positions are either volunteers or are trained in technical fields. It is difficult to attract professional managers because salaries tend to be low, and managers recruited from the outside are seldom acquainted with the unique practices and problems of these special organizations. Financial limitations also make it difficult to afford large consulting contracts.

The major problems facing nonprofit organizations center on financial issues. Most critical is the attraction of funds: how to win government grants, appeal to wealthy donors, or attract more paying customers. This solicitation problem frequently involves marketing studies to identify potential clientele and then design communications to reach these targeted people.

Another financial problem focuses on cost containment, which requires effective accounting and information systems to keep expenses from outrunning uncertain revenues. Finally, training programs are needed to better equip neophyte supervisors with the tools of professional management. Effective human relations skills are particularly useful for motivating employees because pay and hierarchical advancement are seldom attractive inducements in not-for-profit organizations.

SPECIAL CLIENTELE

Consultants who earn themselves an outstanding reputation in a special field of expertise, such as labor relations or antitrust litigation, are attractive to "special clientele." This can mean a trip to Washington for consultation to key members of government, or the expert consultant may be asked to provide testimony in court cases involving alleged corporate wrongdoing, antitrust suits, and bankruptcy petitions. A national reputation can also bring paid speaking invitations to trade associations or corporate conferences.

These engagements require in-depth research on the client's needs as well as effective writing and speaking skills. Because of the depth of knowledge required, such consultants usually possess advanced degrees in law, accounting, management, or economics. The result can be not only high fees for a single engagement (up to $5,000 per day) but a welcomed break from the daily routine of consulting. An outstanding reputation and the demonstration of knowledgeable skills before a concerned audience can also be an indirect marketing technique for attracting new clients.

THE CULTURAL IMPERATIVE

Just as societies possess different cultures, so do organizations. Even with companies of similar size in the same industry, you will find disparate climates that make one look quite foreign to the other. A General Motors assembly plant will have managers with coats off and sleeves rolled up; a Ford plant will look like a fashion show of three-piece suits.

Consultants do not have to "join" the company culture, but they should understand it and work within its boundaries. Important to focus upon are the values and aspirations of senior management. What are their hidden aims? Do they want to be the biggest company in terms of sales or are they content with staying small? Do they favor executives with sales experience, or are they biased toward financial training? Are they numbers oriented, or do they play their hunches?

It will pay off for you to decipher the norms of the organization. What are the "shoulds" and "should nots" that seem to guide the behavior of many employees? For example, some organizations place a great emphasis on friendly cooperation; others stress fierce individual competition. Some like a positive upbeat atmosphere that is casual and free; others subscribe to a more formal and regimented climate. Employees who accept these "norms" are regular members; those who resist are deviants.

Knowing these norms will greatly color the kinds of recommendations you make to the client. A very formal culture will obviously be more receptive to formal presentations and written reports; an informal company will be amused by a stuffed-shirt consultant.

View yourself as an alien whenever you enter a new client relationship. People will try to find out how different from or similar to them you are. They will test you to see if you respect their way of life. While it would be phoney for you to acquire their habits and language suddenly, you don't have to frown upon their idiosyncracies or flout their rules. Little things to you may make a great difference to them. For example, one of the authors was reprimanded by a senior client executive after being late to a single interview appointment—that organization had a norm of punctuality!

UNIQUENESS AS A VALUE

Sameness is the pitfall of ineffective consultants. To apply the same approach and the same solutions repeatedly will stunt the growth of clients and the consultant as well.

Each client differs from its competitors, from its suppliers, from its customers, from its consultant, and even from itself five years before. Uniqueness exists at the board level, within the personalities of senior management, within the processes, products, and services it produces, and within the technology and workers who make and sell the final product.

The effective consultant will make every effort to identify, understand, and appreciate the uniqueness of each client, not only to secure acceptance for his or her proposal and to provide the best possible advice, but also to harvest a source of learning that will occur only once. No future client will be exactly the same as the last client.

RECOMMENDED READINGS

ABRAHAM, STANLEY CHARLES, *The Public Accounting Profession*. Lexington, Mass.: D.C. Heath & Co., 1978.

KENT, CALVIN A.; DONALD L. SEXTON; and KARL H. VESPER, eds., *Encyclopedia of Entrepreneurship*. Englewood Cliffs, N.J.: Prentice-Hall, Inc., 1982.

LEVINSON, HARRY, "Conflicts That Plague Family Businesses," *Harvard Business Review*, March/April 1971.

LEVINSON, ROBERT E., "What To Do About Relatives on Your Payroll," *Nation's Business,* vol. 64, no. 10 (October 1976).

METZGER, ROBERT O., "Productivity in Banking—And How To Improve It," *The Bankers Magazine,* vol. 164, no. 3 (May/June 1981).

ROSENBLUM, ROBERT, and DANIEL MCGILLIS, "Observations on the Role of Consultants in the Public Sector," *Public Administration Review,* vol. 39, no. 3 (May/June 1979).

WARWICK, DONALD P., *A Theory of Public Bureaucracy.* Cambridge, Mass.: Harvard University Press, 1975.

ZIMMERMAN, JOHN W., and PETER M. TOBIA, "Programming Your Outside Consultants for Success," *Training & Development Journal,* vol. 32, no. 12 (December 1978).

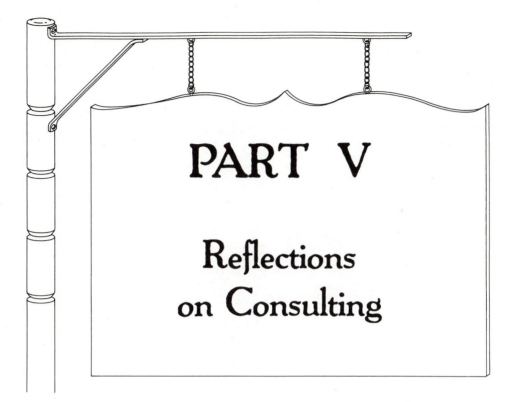

PART V

Reflections on Consulting

What is life really like as a consultant? How do consultants manage their firms and their lives? What constitutes ethical or unethical behavior in the profession? Why would anyone really want to be a consultant? The final part of this book covers those issues and a lot more, gleaned mostly from our own experiences. For all the triumphs and trips to the bank, there are also many defeats in this business. It's a tough, challenging career, one not at all for the faint of heart or the inflated ego. We hope, through these final chapters, to give the reader the benefit of our experience and insight and, then if the spirit is willing, to encourage the reader to pursue a successful consulting career.

17

Resolving Ethical Issues
You Can't Avoid Them

Consulting is filled with ethical dilemmas that you will need to resolve or else pay serious consequences. Too often the consultant has not anticipated these troublesome issues; then suddenly he or she is confronted with them before forming an opinion. Many consultants don't know that there are ethical issues or prefer to believe that ethics are reserved for theologians. As a result, they act out of what they "think" is common practice or out of self-serving values that may not be viewed as ethical by other consultants or clients.

This raises the question of why professions, such as consulting, should have ethical standards in the first place? Very simply, high standards are necessary if the profession is to remain reputable in the eyes of clients. Such high standards fall upon consultants because you are playing a high-stakes game with other people's money, lives, and careers. The responsibility to do a competent job without causing harm is very great.

Ethics are a difficult subject to discuss without lofty pontification or lengthy sermons. Where do you go for an "answer"? ACME has a set of ethics, to which we subscribe; these principles are described in Exhibit

17-1. At the same time, you may view such standards as too abstract or absolute for encompassing all consulting situations. Moreover, ACME has very limited powers for policing its member consulting firms and none for nonmembers.

Our position is that each consultant should search out his or her values and then act as a self-policing force. Other consultants and clients will police you informally, especially if you act consistently outside the norms of what they consider to be ethical behavior. Rest assured that the word will eventually get around if you are a black sheep. But why take chances or wait until you have botched a job? Standards must come from within yourself.

As a starting point for your own reflection and self-examination, we are writing this chapter around 14 issues of ethics that we have encountered. These issues go beyond ones we have already discussed in previous chapters, such as setting contingent fees for results, making disparaging comments about competitors, selling more than you can deliver, or staying on to milk the client.

While we identified the 14 issues jointly, we decided to each write a separate response without seeing the other's comments. You will observe that, for the most part, we are in agreement, although we do have differences. Even when in agreement, our reasons frequently vary. Before reading our answers to each situation, ask yourself what your response would be.

WHICH HEAD TO HUNT?

Q1:   You are new in the executive search business when an "old hand" tells you that the best way to find competent candidates for your search is to call up a satisfied, contented executive in another firm and try to lure that person away. He points out that "only less effective executives are out of work and looking for jobs." Would you do it?

G: No, I'm opposed to this practice of soliciting, even though it may be common practice. There are more responsible ways of building a pool of competent, available executives. First, you should create a favorable public image so that they come to you. Second, you can place selected ads describing the position. And, third, you can write letters to a mailing list of executives who know you. They will refer people to you—and maybe even themselves. I also take exception to the assumption that only good executives are currently employed. Many outstanding executives choose to quit and then search, and being fired may say more about the employer than about the employee.

M: Many major executive search firms do this, and it is exactly how they gained their reputations as "head hunters." While we have never made a practice of this methodology in our firm, if I knew of a particular executive with extremely narrow, specialized talents and felt that he or she was one of only a few people in the entire country who could meet a client's search needs, I probably would make contact. For the most part, a well-worded ad in *The Wall Street Journal* and other professional publications will attract a large number of qualified candidates for any job in question.

BITING THE HAND
THAT FEEDS YOU

Q2: You are contemplating leaving your present firm, where you are a junior partner, to start your own consulting business. You have the opportunity to take $250,000 in billing (a quarter of the firm's business) with you, because the client knows you well and is quite satisfied with your work. Should you proselytize the client?

G: Even if it were a million dollars, I would not "steal" the billing because they were generated while I was under my present employer, who did not employ me to destroy his business. If I leave and the client comes to me with a new project, that is okay. Or I can solicit the client later for a new project. But I would wait for a while until I had a separate image from that of my last employer. If you're going to survive on your own, you need to accept the challenge of building your own client base without trading off the past.

M: Ethically it would be wrong to solicit the client aggressively. However, if you have been the principal contact for that client with your firm and you announce, as a matter of course, that you will be leaving to start your own practice, then if the client approaches you on its own initiative to continue working with you, you have yourself a client without raising a question of ethics or exposing yourself to a possible lawsuit. The key is that the initiative must come from the client, not from you.

CASE OF THE AMOROUS
CONSULTANT

Q3: You discover that one of your consulting staff is sleeping with an executive in a major client firm. To make it more complicated, the executive is so senior that she has the power to cancel your contract with the company and cause you the loss of a major client. What would you do, if anything?

G: This happened to me once, and my first inclination was to fire the consultant. But then I decided that I might not have the whole story—also, firing could ruin the consultant's career. So I did what I still advocate—I confronted the person about the affair and discussed its consequences. When I did, the person denied it, and I still don't know whether it was a lie or the truth. Nevertheless, I went on to explain that the entire project could be lost if the affair became gossip in the firm. I requested that the consultant withdraw from the relationship until the project was completed, after which the consultant's private life was his own concern. The consultant stayed on the project, and I never heard anything afterwards.

M: In this day and age, this is not a moral issue, but rather a question of the consultant's ability to continue performing for that client objectively. I would bring the matter up directly, but with as much sensitivity as possible, to the executive in the client firm and suggest that, should there be a continued social relationship, the consultant in question would not be allowed to continue on the client account. If the client executive resisted this strongly, then I would probably acquiesce and continue to keep the consultant on the assignment but make certain that he was relegated to a minor role; also, I would make every effort to control the quality and objectivity of that consultant's work.

WHOSE PROFIT IS IT?

Q4: You complete a job for a client and find that it cost only 75% of what you bid originally in the proposal. Do you keep the difference or give back the professional fees over and above the work actually performed? What if the reverse occurs and you overrun the cost of the work proposed by 25%?

G: It depends on the quality of work delivered at a lower cost. If the project was 25% underbid, I would wonder what is wrong with our planning system or doubt that we did an adequate job. Should a review indicate that the job was shortchanged, I would tell the client and either make a refund or perform the additional work. But if the promised quality was delivered at a lower cost, then the added profit should be retained. If you overrun by 25%, that is tough luck and has to be absorbed. However, if the additional cost resulted from extra work requested by the client, then you should bill the client for work not covered in the original contract.

M: In the first instance, it is the policy of my firm to bill clients on a monthly basis for the actual professional fees incurred to date. Therefore, if we are able to finish a job for a client at only 75% of the fees originally quoted, the client will not pay more than that. In the second instance, it is extremely important that any work requested by the client or any tangents that the work leads you off on are documented clearly to the client so that, in the event of a cost overrun, additional costs can and will be billed and justified. In the rare circumstance where a job is managed or planned poorly and thus runs over, even while remaining within the parameters of the work proposed, my opinion is that the firm would eat the extra cost.

SHOULD EVERYONE
HAVE A PRICE?

Q5: You discover that your client's firm is going to double its profits compared with last year. Its stock is listed on the New York Stock Exchange and the market doesn't know about the earning gains yet. Do you rush out and buy stock? Tell your friends?

G: This is a definite "no-no" for me. I do not capitalize on "insider" information until it becomes public, and going public doesn't mean letting my friends know in advance. Once the increase in profits is made public, then I suppose it is alright to invest, although I prefer never to invest in a client until a project is completed. My job is to remain objective, and any financial link with the client raises the aura of "conflict of interest." Yet I know of one consulting firm that takes a position in each client's stock, because it believes that this investment provides added incentive to do a good job.

M: While the chances of your being discovered publicly for having purchased $1,000 or even $5,000 of the company's stock with "insider" information are quite small, the risk is always there and must be weighed against your professional reputation and the image of your consulting firm. I would not take advantage of such a situation; however, as most of my money is tied up in real estate, I have never been faced with such a dilemma!

GETTING YOUR LOYALTIES STRAIGHT

Q6: You discover that a senior vice president within your client's firm is planning a coup d'état to get rid of the president by embarrassing him with some scandalous information about his drinking problem. The president is the one who hired you. Do you tell him? What if the senior vice president hired you? Do you tell the president?

G: I would confront the senior vice president in both instances. "Telling stories out of school" can ruin a consultant. So I would try to find out the reasons and evidence from the senior vice president. If it appears that he has flimsy evidence and is just using it to cause mischief, I would go to the president. On the other hand, if the evidence is substantial to the point that the firm is being harmed, I would explore more constructive alternatives than a coup, which could easily backfire on the instigators. Remember that the client is not just an individual but also the entire firm, the latter being even more important as a source of your responsibility.

M: Much of my actions in this instance would revolve around the attitude of my client, the president. First, I would attempt to determine the extent to which his drinking problem was, in fact, a problem for the company. While they are rare, "palace revolts" are often built up around spurious issues in the rhetoric of the revolutionaries. If the drinking problem were real and harming the company, then I would confront the president to determine if he was aware just how much impact his problem had on the company. If he denied the problem or refused to do anything about it, then I would talk to the board about *their* problem and the effects it was having on the company and suggest ways in which to achieve a peaceful transition. I would also talk with the senior vice president about the implications of a "palace revolt" and try to get him to wait for the board to take action. In any event, while the president may be approving our bills, the client is the company, and its welfare, not the president's, comes first.

THE TRUTH ALWAYS HURTS

Q7: Your client asks you to give an informal appraisal of the competence of a senior executive whom you have interviewed and about whom you have a good deal of knowledge through subordinate interviews. His subordinates are very critical of his performance. This task was not part of the contract, but the question comes up in subsequent conversations with the client. Would you give the requested informal appraisal?

G: My position is never to reveal assessments of personnel unless that is a part of the contract. Clients have always appreciated this position, even after they have been refused an evaluation. I will discuss the individual's job in terms of what it requires in the way of skills and experience. Also, I will discuss the criteria for evaluating the performance of the incumbent. However, the actual assessment of an individual must remain with the concerned client. He or she must live with the decision, not the consultant.

M: It is my opinion that merely interviewing a person and his or her subordinate or superiors does not give a consultant sufficient information to pass judgment on the technical competence of a manager. Actually, clients raise these questions because they are unwilling to face the issue of performing good evaluations of their people. They abrogate that responsibility, or hope to, to the consultant. My response would be to prepare a solid, complete, and functional position description for that individual's job and then force the client to decide that the individual in question is performing that job adequately, is not performing it adequately but is displaying the ability to grow further in the job, or is not performing the job adequately and exhibits no evidence of any ability to grow in the job. At that point the client has taken on the appropriate responsibility for making a decision as to the competence of the manager in question.

THE SCIENTIFIC SPY

Q8: A consulting colleague suggests to you that a good way in which to gather data on a market research assignment would be to shop at the client's stores posing as a customer; then, take a sale all the way up to its conclusion before backing out. This would permit an evaluation of the effectiveness of that particular store's sales capability. Would you do it?

G: No! I don't believe in playing tricks on client employees. You will lose the respect and confidence of the employees if they learn about your subterfuge. Besides, all the information you need can be gathered openly through observations, interviews with customers, and sales performance data. I try to let the client and all employees know about my methods for gathering data. Everything is "above board."

M: There is nothing wrong with this approach. In fact, many of our retail customers routinely engage companies to shop their stores and test the product knowledge of their employees without anyone in the stores knowing. It is a very effective way of evaluating a number of retail marketing issues, including the competence and product knowledge of the sales force.

A SHADOW OF DOUBT

Q9: A client executive has hired you and you subsequently develop a feeling, based on his past behavior, that he may not be a very ethical or trustworthy person. You are therefore concerned about what he may do with sensitive data that you feed back to him. What should you do?

G: Tread very carefully, making sure that all plans are reviewed carefully with the client and that we have a clear agreement on how to proceed. If anything pops up that is questionable, confront the client with the evidence. Also, be prepared to terminate the relationship at any time, or seek another senior executive in the client firm who will serve as your contact. However, since these situations rarely go well, I try to stay away from them in the beginning. Better a client never gained than a tarnished reputation.

M: The first thing I would do is confront the client with the fact that he is giving me such an impression. I would ask him if he thinks that other people who deal with him might also have this impression. If the client does not respond or show concern, then I will be extremely guarded in protecting the sensitivity of material I share with the client. I would do everything possible to present my findings and recommendations without jeopardizing any of his employees.

CUTTING THE PROFIT PIE

Q10: Your consulting firm made $100,000 more in net profits than anticipated. What do you do with the additional profit? Divide it up exclusively with your other two partners, or share some of it with the nonpartners?

G: My preference is for some distribution to the nonpartners. Although the partners, in a strict sense, are the legal owners and are entitled to all the net profits, this is not the best motivational scheme. The success of consulting firms depends not only on the partners but also on the hard and competent work of the staff. This issue should not arise if a compensation formula has been designed in advance, and this should include a share for the nonpartners.

M: This is a difficult question because it does not explain how the extra profits were generated. I would make an analysis to determine if the entire profit came from one particular account, in which case, I would share a portion of the extra earnings with the nonpartner managing the client account, or the activities of a particular consultant versus overall operations due to sound administrative management on the part of all partners. In the latter case, where the profits are generated by the partners for the partners, I would divide the profits among the partners only.

PIRATING IN A PINCH

Q11: During a client assignment, you come upon an outstanding employee extremely skilled in computer hardware/software—just the employee for whom your consulting firm has been looking to join its staff. Moreover, she has approached you about a position in your firm. Do you make an offer?

G: It would be okay to make an offer, but only after the project is over. The client may still be suspicious even if the employee has come to you on her own initiative. So, as a matter of courtesy, you should notify the client once you have negotiated the contract. Never attempt to solicit directly a client's employees during a project. I would wait even a couple of years after a project before approaching anyone—thereby assuring the client that my hiring effort is unrelated to the previous project. Clients with a positive impression of you can become your clients again. Better yet, they can remain your friends.

M: I would not make a direct offer to the employee. If the employee wants to resign and, in fact, does leave her present position and subsequently approaches me, I would certainly give her consideration. However, I do not believe it ethical to recruit employees from currently active clients.

WAGGING OR BITING YOUR TONGUE

Q12: You are performing an executive search for a client and, in response to your ad in *The Wall Street Journal*, three senior executives from a competitor to your client apply for the position. Would you use this information to approach the president of the competitor to inform him that there is potentially something awry with his senior management group and then proceed to offer your services to help him determine the problem and take corrective action? Would you tell the president of your present client about the possible demise of a competitor?

G: While this situation seems a bit absurd, I know of a similar case where a consultant did indeed approach the president of a company with fleeing executives. But he was not in the search business and had heard about the situation from an executive working in the company. That is okay, although it is really aggressive marketing. I would definitely not do it if my lead was through a search ad. Nor would I say anything to my present client about the three key executives leaving the competitor. Consultants should not be gossips.

M: Under no circumstances would I use highly confidential information obtained in a candidate's application for another job to approach an employer as a prospective client. Nor would I tell my current client of the situation, except after screening interviews indicated that one of them was a viable candidate. However, if there is a way, at a later date, to be introduced to that employer, I might explore the problem without specifically mentioning my having learned that three of his key people wanted to leave.

OPPORTUNITY KNOCKS TWICE

Q13: You are in the midst of a marketing study for a client when you are approached by the client's fiercest competitor to take on a financial analysis project for them. Do you accept? Do you tell your client?

G: I would not take on the project or even submit a proposal until checking with my present client. Although the new project is different, there is still a risk of misunderstanding with the present client. That client could give you a lot more business in the future, and you haven't won the new proposal yet. If the present client says "no," I would not approach the new prospect. Sometimes a client will require that you not consult for a competitor for a one- or two-year period following the completion of a project. I find this too restrictive and would not agree to it. However, it signifies an ethical imperative that consultants not share knowledge of a former client with a new client, whether in the same industry or not.

M: Many consultants brush this issue off by stating that the major accounting firms do it all the time in the course of their audit work. But this is a false argument. Providing a company with an audit in no way involves the accountant in issues of strategy, policy, organization, or marketing. Consulting usually does. In my work with banks, especially in the Midwest where there are only two or three major competitors per state, I have always had an undocumented, gentlemen's agreement that, so long as I was working for bank A, I would not accept any assignment from any other bank in the state. In major metropolitan areas where there are dozens of big banks trying to outfox each other daily, I would ask my client if he or she had any objection, while stressing the point that we would assign different people to the competitor's account and do everything possible to assure that there was no sharing of data between the two teams. If the client was emphatically against the idea, then we would turn down the competitor's request for work.

TO Ph.D. OR NOT TO BE

Q14: You are one of two partners in a five-person firm. You have been asked to submit a proposal on a $100,000 strategic planning job to a large steel company that is accustomed to dealing with major consulting firms. It is important that the people on the assignment are specialists in strategic planning, even Ph.D.s, in that discipline, and the client has indicated that the consulting team would have to be experienced in the steel industry and large enough to do the job quickly. Your situation is that, while you have much experience and an outstanding reputation in strategic planning, there are no Ph.D.s on your staff, only one has experience in the steel industry, and only three staff members are available for what is a five-person job. To get the assignment, do you present yourself as a Ph.D.? Do you indicate that you have substantial experience in the steel industry? Do you tell the prospect that you are a ten-person company, or do you "fess up" that you will probably have to subcontract part of the job to other colleagues outside your firm?

G: It is suicidal to misrepresent yourself—lies will entrap you sooner or later. Besides, you have strengths to sell even if you don't meet all the criteria of the client. You are expert in the strategic planning topic, which is probably the foremost concern of the client. Next, you do have some experience with the steel industry, which could be sufficient in the eyes of the client. Lack of staff and Ph.D.s can be supplied easily by a part-time subcontract to a local university professor and an independent consultant with whom you've worked previously. All these facts should be acknowledged to the client. Finally, you can stress the emphasis and attention that your small firm will give to the project, which may not be the case with a large firm stretching itself across many clients.

M: Never, ever, would I present myself or my background as something more than what I am. While nine out of ten clients are sold based on the proposal and the rapport with the consultant and, thus, do not even bother to check with the references you give them, there is always the one in ten that does check, all the way back to your undergraduate degree. To be caught in a bold-faced lie about your credentials is unforgivable and dishonest. If you are an expert in the field in question, but don't have a Ph.D., stress your experience and sell it as something better than an academic expertise. And don't be ashamed to admit that you are a small company. By being small, you can provide your clients with partner-level involvement at less cost than larger consulting firms can. You can stress the benefit that your subcontractors are selected based on their experience in the field. Small firms have many attributes that permit them to be more competitive in many instances than the major consulting firms. Learn how to sell those points well rather than say you are something you are not.

RECOMMENDED READINGS

KENNEDY, JAMES H., "Management Consultants and Conflict of Interest," *Dun's Review,* vol. 111, no. 3 (March 1978).
RUDELIUS, WILLIAM, and ROGENE A. BUCHHOLZ, "Ethical Problems of Purchasing Managers" *Harvard Business Review,* March/April 1979.
"Should CPA's Be Management Consultants?" *Business Week,* no. 24, April 18, 1977
WARWICK, DONALD P., and HERBERT C. KELMAN, "Ethical Issues in Social Intervention," In *Processes and Phenomena of Social Change,* ed. Gerald Zaltman. New York: John Wiley & Sons, 1973.

EXHIBIT 17-1

ASSOCIATION OF CONSULTING MANAGEMENT ENGINEERS
(ACME)

Standards of Professional Conduct and Practice

1. Basic Client Responsibilities

   1.1 We will at all times place the interests of clients
ahead of our own and serve them with integrity, competence, and
independence.

We will assume an independent position with the client, making
certain that our advice to clients is based on impartial consideration of all pertinent facts and responsible opinions.

   1.2 We will guard as confidential all information concerning
the affairs of clients that we gather during the course of professional engagements; and we will not take personal, financial,
or other advantage of material or inside information coming to
our attention as a result of our professional relationship with
clients; nor will we provide the basis on which others might
take such advantage. Observance of the ethical obligation of
the management consulting firm to hold inviolate the confidence
of its clients not only facilitates the full development of
facts essential to effective solution of the problem but also
encourages clients to seek needed help on sensitive problems.

   1.3 We will serve two or more competing clients on sensitive
problems only with their knowledge.

   1.4 We will inform clients of any relationships, circumstances, or interest that might influence our judgment or the
objectivity of our services.

2. Client Arrangements

   2.1 We will present our qualifications for serving a client
solely in terms of our competence, experience, and standing, and
we will not guarantee any specific result, such as amount of cost
reduction or profit increase.

   2.2 We will accept only those engagements we are qualified
to undertake and which we believe will provide real benefits to
clients. We will assign personnel qualified by knowledge,
experience, and character to give effective service in analyzing
and solving the particular problem or problems involved. We will
carry out each engagement under the direction of a principal
of the firm who is responsible for its successful completion.

   2.3 We will not accept an engagement of such limited scope
that we cannot serve the client effectively.

Source: ACME, Inc.—The association of management consulting firms; New York

EXHIBIT 17-1   (cont'd)

2.4 We will, before accepting an engagement, confer with the client or prospective client in sufficient detail and gather sufficient facts to gain an adequate understanding of the problem, the scope of study needed to solve it, and the possible benefits that may accrue to the client. The preliminary exploration will be conducted confidentially on terms and conditions agreed upon by the member and the prospective client.

2.5 We will, except for those cases where special client relationships make it unnecessary, make certain that the client receives a written proposal that outlines the objectives, scope, and, where possible, the estimated fee or fee basis for the proposed service or engagement. We will discuss with the client any important changes in the nature, scope, timing, or other aspects of the engagement and obtain the client's agreement to such changes before taking action on them - and unless the circumstances make it unnecessary, we will confirm these changes in writing.

2.6 We will perform each engagement on an individualized basis and develop recommendations designed specifically to meet the particular requirements of the client situation. Our objective in each client engagement is to develop solutions that are realistic and practical and that can be implemented promptly and economically. Our professional staffs are prepared to assist, to whatever extent desired, with the implementation of approved recommendations.

2.7 We will not serve a client under terms or conditions that might inpair our objectivity, independence, or integrity; and we will reserve the right to withdraw if conditions beyond our control develop to interfere with the successful conduct of the engagement.

2.8 We will acquaint client personnel with the principles, methods, and techniques applied, so that the improvements suggested or installed may be properly managed and continued after completion of the engagement.

2.9 We will maintain continuity of understanding and knowledge of clients' problems and the work that has been done to solve them by maintaining appropriate files of reports submitted to clients. These are protected against unauthorized access and supported by files of working papers, consultants' log-books, and similar recorded data.

2.10 We will not accept an engagement for a client while another management consulting firm is serving that client unless we are assured that any conflict between the two engagements is recognized by, and has the consent of, the client. We will not endeavor to displace another management consulting firm or individual consultant once we have knowledge that the client has made a commitment to the other consultant, unless we are assured that the client is aware of any conflict between the two commitments.

EXHIBIT 17-1   (cont'd)

2.11 We will review the work of another management consulting firm or individual consultant for the same client, only with the knowledge of such consultant, unless such consultant's work which is subject to review has been finished or terminated. However, even though the other consultant's work has been finished or terminated, it is a matter of common courtesy to let the consulting firm or individual know that the work is being reviewed, provided that the client consents to such disclosures.

3. Client Fees

3.1 We will charge reasonable fees which are commensurate with the nature of services performed and the responsibility assumed. An excessive charge abuses the professional relationship and discourages the public from utilizing the services of management consultants. On the other hand, adequate compensation is necessary in order to enable the management consulting firm to serve clients effectively and to preserve the integrity and independence of the profession. Determination of the reasonableness of a fee requires consideration of many factors, including the nature of the services performed; the time required, the consulting firm's experience, ability, and reputation; the degree of responsibility assumed; and the benefits that accrue to the client. Wherever feasible, we will agree with the client in advance on the fee or fee basis.

3.2 We will neither accept nor pay fees or commissions to others for client referrals, or enter into any arrangement for franchising our practice to others; provided, however, that two or more consulting firms or individuals may agree as to sharing of any fee or commission on a basis reasonably commensurate with the relative values of the services performed for the client. Nor will we accept fees, commissions, or other valuable consideration from individuals or organizations for recommending equipment, supplies, or services in the course of our service to clients.

Professional Practices

In order to promote highest quality of performance in the practice of management consulting, ACME has developed the following standards of good practice for the guidance of the profession. Member firms subscribe to these practices because they make for equitable and satisfactory client relationships and contribute to success in management consulting.

1. We will strive continually to advance and protect the standards of the management consulting profession. We will strive continually to improve our knowledge, skills, and techniques, and will make available to our clients the benefits of our professional attainments.

EXHIBIT 17-1 (cont'd)

2. We recognize our responsibilities to the public interest and
    to our profession to contribute to the development and under-
    standing of better ways to manage the various formal institu-
    tions in our society. By reason of education, experience,
    and broad contact with management problems in a variety of
    institutions, management consultants are especially qualified
    to recognize opportunities for improving managerial and
    operating processes; and they have an obligation to share
    their knowledge with managers and their colleagues in the
    profession.

3. We recognize our responsibility to the profession to share
    with our colleagues the methods and techniques we utilize
    in serving clients. But we will now knowingly, without
    their permission, use proprietary data, procedures, materials,
    or techniques that other management consultants have developed
    but not released for public use.

4. We will not make offers of employment to consultants on the
    staffs of other consulting firms without first informing
    them. We will not engage in wholesale or mass recruiting of
    consultants from other consulting firms. If we are approached
    by consultants of other consulting firms regarding employment
    in our firm or in that of a client, we will handle each
    situation in a way that will be fair to the consultant, the
    firm, and the client.

5. We will not solicit employees of clients for employment by
    us or by others, except with the consent of the client. If
    we are approached by employees of clients regarding employ-
    ment in our firm or in that of another client, we will make
    certain that we have our clients' consent before entering
    into any negotiations with employees.

6. We will continually evaluate the quality of the work done by
    our staff to insure, insofar as is possible, that all of our
    engagements are conducted in a competent manner.

7. We will endeavor to provide opportunity for the professional
    development of those who enter the profession, by assisting
    them to acquire a full understanding of the functions,
    duties, and responsibilities of management consultants, and
    to keep up with significant advances in their areas of
    practice.

8. We will administer the internal and external affairs of our
    firm in the best interest of the profession at all times.

9. We will not advertise our services in self-laudatory language
    or in any other manner derogatory to the dignity of the
    profession.

10. We will respect the professional reputation and practice of
    other management consultants. This does not remove the
    moral obligation to expose unethical conduct of fellow mem-
    bers of the profession to the proper authorities.

EXHIBIT 17-1   (cont'd)

11. We will strive to broaden public understanding and enhance
     public regard and confidence in the management consulting
     profession, so that management consultants can perform their
     proper function in society effectively. We will conduct
     ourselves so as to reflect credit on the profession and to
     inspire the confidence, respect, and trust of clients and the
     public. In the course of our practice, we will strive to
     maintain a wholly professional attitude toward those we serve,
     toward those who assist us in our practice, toward our fellow
     consultants, toward the members of other professions, and the
     practitioners of allied arts and sciences.

                                        Adopted February 1, 1972
                                        Amended September 19, 1978

18

Stepping Back
How To Stay Sane and Avoid Burnout

We have some bad news: consulting is one of the most intense, frustrating, fatiguing, and damnable professions one can choose. Six-day weeks are not uncommon, with some days running up to 12 hours. If the reader is already managing a successful practice, he or she knows all about spending Monday to Friday with Client Jones and then reserving the weekend to prepare for Client Smith in the upcoming week. You are likely to spend 50% of your time on the road, and just when you plan to sneak out of a client's office for a quiet dinner alone, ole' Smedley grabs you to insist on dinner where he can share his life story with you. Being "out of control" is a frequent complaint of consultants.

Consultants are vulnerable to personal self-neglect because the job environment provides little stability or free time. You cannot count on jogging around your neighborhood every morning at six o'clock. Yet, if you don't look after yourself, it is easy to fall prey to all the physical and emotional ailments associated with stress. You won't survive in consulting very long without lots of personal care.

How do you keep your sanity and health in the face of intense pressure and long days? Foremost is for you to acknowledge that consulting is not the romantic profession popularized in fiction where you fly into Paris on the CEO's private plane to spend a few hours of work in return for a generous fee, a gourmet dinner, and a night at the Ritz. The town will more likely be Paris, Indiana; the plane a puddle-jumper out of Chicago; the restaurant a nearby greasy spoon; and the sleeping quarters a plastic motel.

Once you have accepted the discomforting realities of consulting, you are ready to draw up a personal plan and fortify it with lots of self-discipline. This chapter identifies the principal sources of stress, and for each source we suggest some remedies that have proven useful to us in our experience. While our solutions may not be exactly appropriate for you, you can easily find lots of substitutes once you have anticipated the diseases that will be lurking ahead. For example, the "fatigue factor" requires that you keep physically fit, but that could be solved by jogging for some or swimming for others.

FATIGUE AND STAYING FIT

Consulting places a heavy physical demand on the human anatomy. There are hours and hours of sedentary life in planes, airports, cars, client meetings, restaurants, and report writing. Your once-youthful figure sinks rapidly to the bottom. To top it off, there are long flights, rough flights, close connections, lost luggage, poorly maintained rental cars, high-sodium and -cholesterol food, filthy hotel rooms, and extreme climatic changes that play Handel's *Messiah* on your sinus cavities. Warning: consulting may be harmful to your health!

We strongly believe in traveling first class whenever possible—not because you are a jet-setter but because you need to preserve your strength. Short airplane trips can be made on economy rates, but long hauls require more space to stretch out and even space and privacy to study your notes. Hotels don't have to be the Pierre in New York or the Beverly Wilshire in Los Angeles, but they should be comfortable and convenient to the client and provide a nutritious kitchen fare. Bargain rates on rental cars aren't worth the maintenance breakdown on the freeway, and taxis relax you more than do crowded airport buses.

Avoid creating your own aggravations—there are enough without you personally adding to the frustration level. Take only the clothes that you can carry on the plane; never check your luggage. It's a well-known fact that airlines can spot a consultant's bag and promptly lose it. Don't plan your flight connections so closely that you have to emulate O.J.

Simpson. Be aware of alternate flights, just in case. Occasionally, if it's only 200 miles to a client and the flying weather looks bad, rent a car and relax with a leisurely drive.

Excessive eating and drinking are constant temptations for consultants. Restaurant menus contain more calories than needed, and clients push drinks at you before, during, and after meals. We try to remember the old axiom, "Breakfast like a king, lunch like a prince, and dine like a pauper!" Too many heavy evening meals can add pounds and lose hours of sleep, while a good breakfast can make you a terror to behold. Stay away from booze, discos, and junk food—just because you are away from home, you don't have to behave like an adolescent. Most important is a good night's rest on a king-sized bed away from traffic noise and flashing neon lights. We like to rise early, order a room service breakfast, and take our time in preparing for the day ahead.

An exercise program is a must, not only to take off calories but to give you added energy for late in the day. Exercise on the road is difficult but still possible if you plan ahead and adapt to the environs. Ask your client if he can put you up at the local athletic club where you can take a swim or workout after work. Or arrange for a hotel next to a park where you can take an early-morning jog. Even in your hotel room you can begin and end the day with twenty sit-ups and ten push-ups. Sometimes you can learn more from your client on the golf course or tennis court than in a busy office environment interrupted by phone calls.

Back at home our admonitions about eating, sleeping, and exercising go double. This is your safe haven where you recuperate and replenish yourself for the next draining adventure. A thorough annual physical exam, which requires more than a 30-minute "let me listen to your heart" checkup, is essential. Tests that "look inside you" are much more revealing, such as blood analysis, urine specimen, stress EKG, and that marvelous proctoscopic.

Finally, take a vacation—and make it one that does not resemble your usual travel routine of one hotel, city, and restaurant after another. We know too many consultants who rarely take a vacation, and they look it! August is a good time for vacations; this is when the clients are away too.

RESPONSIBILITY AND MAINTAINING PERSPECTIVE

The consulting profession carries with it awesome responsibilities—of making the right recommendations, of being certain of the facts, and of staying within budget. Not only does the client expect you to furnish an expert diagnosis of the problem, but the client expects you to be helpful in solving it too. Many people are depending upon you—your client, the client's employees, the shareholders, and your consulting staff.

This is a frustrating profession. Clients can be whimsical about your recommendations, your time schedule, and your priorities. You can easily become exasperated at the incredible incompetence of client executives who are managing major companies and being paid small fortunes for messing them up. There are also the unethical competitors who are telling people that you went out of business or got fired from your last job. And there's the major proposal you made, which took weeks of research, only to be lost to the last competitor in the door and freshest in the client's mind.

Just when you experience moments of relief following a job well done for a satisfied client, you are whipsawed by the nagging anxiety of finding a new client to replace the old one left behind. Even when you do a good job for a client, there can be the screaming silence and insensitivity from clients who never write to say "thank you," who pay their bills begrudgingly, and who make an extra million or two from your recommendations and then tell their boards about the brilliant solutions that they've created.

If you are to avoid an emotional breakdown, we urge upon you a contradiction—never take yourself or your clients too seriously! A sane consultant will maintain perspective, recognizing that all humans, including consultants, are not omnipotent, in fact, that aura of fallibility is what makes the consulting game so interesting and challenging. Clients, just like spouses, lovers, relatives, and friends, often do things for their own selfish reasons, not yours.

So relax and try to stay calm, even to the point of being able to smile at the craziness you will encounter. Clients may reject your recommendations for nothing to do with your competence; rather, it may be the obstinate chairman of the board who wants to hang onto his toy corporation. Even when you make a mistake, which will happen often enough, regard it as a learning experience instead of a haunting nightmare.

Relaxation techniques are not the sole possession of mystics. You should find ways to relieve tension—from meditation to stamp collecting. Be alert to signs of stress—headaches, rapid heartbeat, tight muscles, backache, and temper outbursts. Both of us practice relaxation techniques in the office or on the road for a few minutes each day—and it is simple as you learn to move your relaxation attention from toes up through your body to your forehead. Physical exercise, which we discussed in the previous section, is also an ideal way to drown out evil spirits.

Simply "getting organized" will contribute a lot to your mental state. Too many of us suffer from the hypocrisy of helping to organize our clients but neglecting to organize ourselves. Plan your schedule as far in advance as you can with any certainty. If you are managing two or three client jobs at the same time, and that is about the maximum work load, you should be able to project your time out at least three months to the point of being able to know where you will be and what you will be doing every week of that period. If you have that foresight, there shouldn't be too many weekend crises or report-writing deadlines sneaking up on you.

Plan your daily work so that you are able to put in eight or nine very effective hours and then quit at a reasonable hour. Overly long days are a clear sign of poor time management. On the road, be firm with possessive clients who may feel obliged to entertain you. A polite turndown with "I'm sure you have seen enough of me today" will probably be secretly welcomed by the client too. Some quiet time alone in your hotel with a good book or your favorite TV program will do more good for you than will a thick steak and three gins. Get a pocket dictaphone recorder for correspondence and report writing while you are away from home. Check in with your office daily to receive messages. Use your waiting time efficiently to return calls. Above all, stay ahead of deadlines, which are daily, not monthly, in this hectic business.

Even if you do a good job of planning and organizing your schedule, you will still need an outstanding secretary to take care of the many details—as well as to remind you of your scheduled deadlines. He or she can assume much responsibility for travel arrangements, dealing tactfully with frustrated clients, editing reports, recording expenses, and billing clients. Consultants who become their own secretaries are raising their blood pressures needlessly.

OBSOLESCENCE
AND KEEPING UP

So far we have stressed the physical and emotional pressures of consulting, but there also is the heart to all successful consultants—their minds. Consulting requires its practitioners to be in the forefront of knowledge. To fall behind your clients in knowledge is to become useless to them.

But how do you keep up when you are so busy in your daily work? The other pressures we have discussed take such a toll that it leaves little time or energy to remain a knowledge leader in the field. Technical obsolescence is a constant hazard.

Any consulting office, no matter how small, should have an up-to-date reference library. You can place yourself on the mailing lists of all major publishers of the management literature. When you or your colleagues spot an interesting book, buy it. Also you should subscribe to and read regularly the following periodicals: *Harvard Business Review, For-*

tune, Business Week, Forbes, and, of course, *The Wall Street Journal.* If that isn't enough, then subscribe to the *Sloan Management Review, California Management Review, Business Horizons, Columbia Journal of World Business,* and the *Administrative Science Quarterly.*

The best way in which to keep up with your reading is on planes, in hotels, and on vacation. Remember to keep copies in your briefcase. Ask colleagues to refer interesting articles to you, and reciprocate. The key is to establish a regular habit of reading, even if only skimming the index of journals for interesting titles. Cull out the gems for more thoughtful study.

A less frequent but useful source of ideas and techniques is to attend short executive seminars sponsored by leading business schools and professional associations. You should also belong to a scholarly association that matches your special field of expertise, such as the American Marketing Association, the Academy of Management, or the American Society for Training and Development. These groups hold annual meetings where scholars present their latest research findings. All these learning activities require you to block out a few days on your calendar long in advance; then you won't have a last-minute excuse for not attending.

Finally, and not to be overlooked, is the most immediately available source of learning, which occurs from a careful debriefing of each consulting project. Search through it with colleagues to determine what went right and wrong. Making the same mistakes again is too costly in dollars and emotions. Keep well-documented files on each project, so that, when you encounter a similar problem in the future, you can look back for helpful hints.

Underlying all these avenues to learning and updating is the need for you to determine those particular areas of management consulting that will be your special field of expertise. You can't be a simultaneous whiz at finance, marketing, and planning unless you're a good actor and dilettante. Knowledge is growing and changing too rapidly to excel on all fronts.

AND NOW FOR
THE GOOD NEWS

If our admonitions about the high degree of anxiety, tension, and responsibility inherent in consulting have suppressed your enthusiasm for the profession or made you question why you are now a consultant, read on. There is hope!

To begin, most people who enter consulting rarely make it a lifelong career. They regard consulting as a "stepping stone" from one career to still another. The vast majority, perhaps as high as 60%, remain as consultants for only three to six years to gain the necessary experience, expertise, and exposure before moving on to that choice job of planning director at International Widgets. Another 30% realize that they are doing better financially than in private industry and stick it out for up to ten years until they, too, leave for International Widgets as vice president of personnel. The remaining 10% are either faculty at universities who consult part-time forever, or they are senior partners in consulting firms who find that they are consulting less, administrating more, and earning in excess of $150,000 per year.

The major attractions of consulting, even if it carries with it a lot of wear and tear for a short time, are those of tremendous challenge, independence from close supervision, and significant rewards in learning and money. You would need to be CEO of a multinational corporation to experience the variety of problems faced by consultants on a daily basis. Successful consultants earn as much money as many CEOs, and they deserve it—for their investigative research, their creativity, and most of all their ability to implement change with no real authority to do so. Consultants enrich the lives of their clients and, in so doing, enrich their own lives.

So pack up your carry-on luggage, tuck that hot proposal under your arm, don't forget the double roll of antacid pills, and come with us . . . we're now going to show you how to set up and manage your own consulting practice.

RECOMMENDED READINGS

BENSON, HERBERT, and ROBERT L. ALLEN, "How Much Stress Is Too Much," *Harvard Business Review*, September/October 1980.

EDELWICH, GARRY, and ARCHIE BRODSKY. *Burn-Out Stages of Disillusionment in the Helping Professions,* New York: Human Science Press, 1980.

FREUDENBERGER, HERBERT J., *Burn-Out.* New York: Anchor Press, Doubleday, 1980.

FREUDENBERGER, HERBERT J., "The Staff Burn-Out Syndrome in Alternative Institutions," *Psychotherapy: Theory, Research and Practices*, vol. 12, no. 1 (Spring 1975) 73-82.

LEVINSON, HARRY, "When Executives Burn Out," *Harvard Business Review*, May/June 1981.

McLEAN, ALAN A., *Work Stress*. Reading, Mass.: Addison-Wesley, 1979.

PETERS, RUANNE K., and HERBERT BENSON, "Time Out from Tension," *Harvard Business Review*, January/February 1978.

SELYE, HANS, *Stress Without Distress*. New York: H.B. Lippincott, 1974.

"Should a Consultant Sit in the President's Seat?" *New England Business,* vol. 2, no.7 (April 6, 1980).

19

Managing Your Own Firm
Clues to Success

One assumption made frequently by consultants is that, by simply doing a good job for the client, their firms will reap a handsome profit. Unfortunately, this is a myth. While they are out helping major corporations to introduce sophisticated new systems, the consulting firm back home may be burning. Consulting firms don't run by themselves simply because they are populated with learned professionals. Management consultants must also practice what they preach. The consulting firm itself must be managed carefully and skillfully if costs are to be controlled and growth targets are to be reached.

Consulting is a unique business. It is labor intensive with expensive professionals who provide a nebulous service to a capricious marketplace. Selecting competent professionals and motivating their delicate egos is a perplexing challenge. Maintaining control over a variety of projects taking place miles away is never ending. Assuring that clients are billed properly and invoices collected on time is forever frustrating. Much can go wrong at every turn, and often you don't know until it's too late.

The management problems of any professional service have many similarities for both smaller and larger firms, although the solutions vary at a particular stage in the growth cycle. So in this chapter we will begin with a small consulting firm as it gets off the ground, survives, and then proceeds along a path of growth to encounter the spectrum of problems facing all successful firms.

SELECTING THE
RIGHT PARTNER

Establishing your own consulting practice is rarely easy unless you are breaking away from an existing organization and are certain to carry with you some of your current clients. If you can do that without legal entanglements with your former employer, you are one of the lucky ones. More common is the aspiring individual with no clients but a few solid contacts who decides to set sail from scratch and build a firm.

However, it is very lonely out there with no peers to complement your technical expertise and to share your business development efforts. When you devote time to marketing, you are not generating income, and when you are working on a client assignment, you neglect marketing. This creates severe swings in earnings and an unstable climate in which to plan or control your business, social, and family commitments.

Many independent consultants try this solitary and masochistic life-style for a year or so, only to decide to "come in from the cold." What might have been a successful practice ends up as a retreat to corporate life or a seven-year wait for partnership behind an anonymous desk in a large consulting firm. Partnerships have a much greater chance of success than do solitary consultants. Not a month goes by that we do not interview some very capable consultant who tried it alone and failed or who has grown weary of the struggle and thrown in the towel.

Therefore, we recommend the selection of a partner. Try to choose a professionally competent person with similar career and financial objectives, preferably someone whose technical expertise complements your own. If you are a whiz at finance, planning, and organization, then find a partner whose forte is compensation, communications, management development, and training. Between the two of you, the partnership will be able to handle most client needs.

Another advantage of partnership is economic stability. When one partner is working for a client, the other is marketing. It smooths out the earnings curve. Also the earning power of two can better afford the price of an office and a competent secretary, whereas a loner often ends up working out of his or her house and using part-time, undependable clerical support. Choosing the right partner may not be easy, but it is a substantial step in the right direction to reduce the risk of failure.

LEGALITIES, BOOKKEEPING, AND OFFICE SPACE

Once you have found a partner, or if you have self-destructive tendencies for going it alone, choose a good lawyer to help you with the paperwork. You will need an employer I.D. number for tax purposes, company bank accounts, stock certificates, and a company seal if you decide to incorporate or a partnership agreement that addresses the responsibilities of the survivor in the event that a tragedy befalls one of you; you may even want to copyright your marketing material.

Another nagging reality is the need for a good but reasonably priced accounting firm to do your books and calculate your payroll taxes. It is not an effective use of professional time to keep the books yourself; nor is it efficient to hire a high-priced executive secretary who also knows a bit of accounting. That leaves you with half a bookkeeper and half a secretary when you really need a full-time secretary.

A small CPA firm can put your general ledger on a computer for a couple hundred dollars a month or less, which will give you a monthly P&L statement and balance sheet, together with a *sources and applications of funds report*. If your firm ever needs interim financing, it is a lot easier to get a short-term line of credit at the bank if your books are kept by an independent CPA than if you are keeping the books yourself in the garage. Also, if your CPA is handling your company's books, you will probably get a break on fees for your personal tax work at year-end.

You should not overlook insurance needs either. As your firm grows, you will accumulate irreplaceable client files and notes. And, if you are leasing any furniture or office equipment, you are liable to IBM, Xerox, or whomever in the event of theft or fire. Find an insurance agent willing to work with you to provide appropriate liability coverage. Workmen's compensation insurance is mandatory in most states. You and your partner may even want to take out "key executive" life insurance in the event that something happens to one of you.

Finally, you need to locate and lease an office. Try not to let your ego or social needs make this decision for you. As a beginning consultant, it will be a long time before your clients visit you or unsolicited prospects pound on your door. You will be out after them. It is pointless to occupy a vacant space in the heart of the financial district. Your downtown ego means nothing until your billings are up to $500,000 a year.

So look around, preferably near your home or near an airport if you plan to be a regional or national practice. With what you will save in rent by avoiding downtown space, you will be able to afford a larger, more comfortable office, better parking facilities, plus additional room for expansion. If you do not plan your space ahead, and you are successful, you will end up moving every six months to accommodate a growing staff. That not only looks funny to clients, but it raises havoc with printing costs for new calling cards, stationery, and marketing material.

CHOOSING A NAME

Consulting firms have traditionally taken the same approach as legal and accounting firms by using the founding partners' names. If you have a conservative bent or intend to consult with "the establishment," this form of narcissism is probably appropriate, unless of course your names are Bill Kiss and William Tell, III.

However, there are many fine and successful consulting firms today that have broken with tradition by adopting anagrams for names. MAC (Management Analysis Center in Cambridge) is known throughout the United States, as are SRI (formerly the Stanford Research Institute) and ADL (Arthur D. Little).

Many firms have decided against the use of partners' names due mainly to today's bright young consultants who need and demand recognition of their own, as well as preferring an environment where everyone receives credit for work well done, not just the founding partners.

Try to select a name that in some way signifies what it is that your firm does or that specifies the field of your expertise. For example, it could be SPA, which stands for Strategic Planning Associates. Make sure that no one else is using the same name or anagram, and then register it with your state's secretary of state. The filing fee is only $5.00–15.00.

TO GROW OR
NOT TO GROW

If you are successful, there will come a critical point at which you have to decide on the size and kind of firm you want to have for the longer term. It is the authors' experience that partnerships with just two or three people working at maximum billing rates can be extraordinarily profitable for two or three years. The price for this intensity, however, is continuous travel and long hours, followed by physical and emotional burnout.

If money is your initial motivation, then you should stay small for a while. A good consulting staff is very expensive, and a small, relatively unknown firm pays dearly for expensive fringe and bonus plans to attract the best consultants from larger, more prestigious consulting firms. However, if you and your partner find that you have "cracked the market" and have more business than you can handle on your own, it is time to think expansion.

Whatever you decide, try to avoid the pendulum management style that this industry calls *the Jesus Christ syndrome*, which describes the consulting firm that is totally out of control—where one partner or another is constantly reaching one of two conclusions, beginning with "Jesus Christ, we've got to get some business in here to make the payroll!" followed shortly thereafter by "Jesus Christ, look at all this business! We've got to hire some people quickly to get the work done!" This same scenario is repeated a few months later and continues until the partners become unraveled.

Plan your work load every month. When you find that you have more clients than you can handle at one time, try to get a client to agree to a delay or renegotiate the timing of the project. Infrequent surges in work can also be met with a subcontract to outside independent consultants who you know well and with whom you have dealt on past assignments. In this way you will be in a better position to maximize everyone's billed time while avoiding the crisis of "Jesus Christ" management. When you do find that you have lined up a solid backlog in excess of your firm's available man-hours, then and only then is it time to hire another professional.

PROFITABILITY: THE
ART OF LEVERAGE

If you plan your work well up front and have mastered the art of selling, you are going to make money in this profession. There are several ways of doing so, depending on how you want to spend your time and energy.

If you are a hard worker enjoying a small partnership organization, keeping your expenses and overhead down, and having budgeted your proposals well, you can easily earn $100,000 a year. If you and your partner are at least 50% billable during the year, then between both of you at a rate of $85 an hour each, you should generate about $150,000 a year in revenues. If you apportion most of your costs to bill back to your clients, then you will have few operating or payroll expenses. Add to these revenues the occasional job with a high profit margin, such as a two- to three-day planning retreat for $8,000–10,000 or a market research project for $10,000–15,000 that takes only $3,000–4,000 of your time, then $100,000 for each partner's income is not unrealistic. If you bill yourselves out at more than $85 an hour or if you are both more than 50% billable during the year, then your earnings will be proportionately greater.

For those of you who are builders and who have the ambition to develop a larger firm, the sky is the limit. Most of your energy will be split between business development and the time it takes to develop a competent staff to perform the actual work.

It is the "margin" over staff costs that leverages the firm to high profits. Let us assume, for example, that your firm hires a bright, young MBA with three to five years of business experience in a major corporation who is earning a salary of $30,000 a year plus a 5-10% bonus. If you can sell enough work to keep him or her 80% billable at $65 an hour, then you can afford to offer a salary of $35,000 a year and a 20% bonus. That works out to $42,000 plus, say, 20% for fringes and payroll taxes. The MBA is delighted and your cost for a good man or woman is about $50,400 a year. But at 80% billable time, he or she will generate 1,650 hours at $65 per hour for over $100,000 in revenue a year to the firm. With no more than a half-dozen or so of these bright, capable people, you have yourself a gold mine. The authors are aware of senior partners in major consulting firms who have personally banked as much as $500,000 in a good year (see Table 19-1).

All it takes is an incredible amount of very hard work in the early years and phenomenal judgment in people during the later years. It also helps to say a prayer and trust in luck.

JOB TITLES AND RESPONSIBILITIES

Consulting firms rarely generate lots of job titles. There are five basic professional jobs to be performed, as described in the paragraphs that follow. Smaller firms will often combine these into two or three functions because of limited staff. Larger firms will build a hierarchy to include all five functions and their equivalent titles.

Founding Principals

These are the entrepreneurs who began the enterprise, invested and risked their personal capital, and brought with them or developed the business that launched the firm. Their responsibilities are to develop and set firm policy, to obtain new business, and to explore new markets as well as to assure quality services to all accounts and to manage the overall business. They have the final say, for they are the owners.

Principals

These individuals have been awarded shares or partnerships in the firm through developing significant amounts of new business. They have also proven their technical and management skills in handling the business they have sold. Their responsibilities are to assist and advise

TABLE 19-1 Consultant Costs and Billing Rates

CONSULTANT'S ANNUAL BASE SALARY	+ FRINGES AND TAXES (@ 30%)	= TOTAL CONSULTANT COST	PERCENTAGE OF TOTAL HOURS (1,864) BILLABLE AND ACTUAL NO. HOURS				
			40% (750 hr)	50% (940 hr)	60% (1.125 hr)	70% (1.315%)	80% (1.500 hr)
$ 25,000	$ 7,500	$ 32,500	$ 43/hr	$ 35/hr	$ 29/hr	$25/hr	$22/hr
30,000	9,000	39,000	52/hr	42/hr	35/hr	30/hr	26/hr
35,000	10,500	45,500	61/hr	48/hr	40/hr	35/hr	30/hr
40,000	12,000	52,000	70/hr	55/hr	46/hr	40/hr	35/hr
45,000	13,500	58,500	78/hr	62/hr	52/hr	44/hr	39/hr
50,000	15,000	65,000	87/hr	69/hr	58/hr	49/hr	43/hr
55,000	16,500	71,500	95/hr	76/hr	64/hr	54/hr	47/hr
60,000	18,000	78,000	104/hr	83/hr	70/hr	59/hr	52/hr
65,000	19,500	84,000	112/hr	89/hr	75/hr	64/hr	56/hr
70,000	21,000	91,000	121/hr	97/hr	81/hr	69/hr	60/hr
75,000	22,500	97,500	130/hr	104/hr	87/hr	74/hr	65/hr
80,000	24,000	104,000	138/hr	111/hr	92/hr	79/hr	69/hr
100,000	30,000	130,000	173/hr	138/hr	115/hr	99/hr	87/hr

Example: Mr. Kato receives a base salary of $50,000 per annum. Historically, he has been 50% billable to clients. Therefore for the firm *to break even* on Kato it must bill him out at $69 per hour. To make money on Kato, he must bill out at more than this, say, $80 per hour.

Base calculation of hours:

One year = 365 days − 104 days (52 weekends)
        = 261 days −   8 days (holidays)
        = 253 days − 10 days (sick leave)
        = 243 days − 10 days (vacation)
        = 233 days × 8 hr/day
        = 1,864 hr/yr − 20% (travel, training, administration)
        = approx. 1,500 hr/yr maximum available for billing

the founding principals in the development of policy and planning, to secure new business, to assure quality service on accounts they manage, and to supervise senior consultants. Through minority ownership, they have a say in how the company is managed.

Senior Consultants

These advanced consultants have worked hard and successfully and are likely, at some future date, to accumulate enough new business volume to qualify for partnership. They have demonstrated both their technical skill and their ability to manage a client account at the CEO level as well as to train and manage other professional associates and staff on client accounts. Their responsibilities are to manage existing client accounts, to train professional associates and junior staff, and to expand their personal areas of expertise. They are measured on the basis of client satisfaction, new business from existing clients, their ability to meet budgets and schedules, and their skill in building an effective project team of junior consultants.

Consultants

These individuals have joined the firm with specific fields of expertise or business experience and are assigned to work on tasks by the senior consultants. Their responsibilities are to provide direct professional support on each project, to prove their advancement in the practice of their particular field of expertise, and to demonstrate new skills with clients. Consultants are measured on the quality of their data gathering and analytical work, their skill in writing reports, their ability to be a team player, and, if they choose to develop business, the quality and volume of new accounts.

Researchers

These individuals have little, if any, consulting experience or depth of personal skills and have been hired to learn the business and provide staff support. Their primary role is to do library research, to edit reports, to prepare presentation materials, and generally to assist on each project. They engage in little, if any, client contact initially. Their responsibility is to work on tasks assigned to them by consultants and senior consultants. They are measured on the quality of their research reports, their ability to learn and grow, and their support for the client team.

FINANCIAL CONTROLS

While the primary reason for failure in consulting firms is lack of clients, the second most common reason is lack of financial control. You must know how to develop time and expense reports quickly at the end of the month so that invoices are sent out immediately. You also need a tracking system to know what your accounts receivable are at any given time; and most critical of all, you need to prepare an effective cash flow forecast to pay your staff. Without such controls, you're shooting craps, not running a business.

At least once a month, the *cash flow forecast* should be put together (see Exhibit 19-1). One part of the cash flow forecast projects actual billings and receipts from work-in-progress; the other part is a realistic assessment of forthcoming business from serious prospects. This "guess-timate" can be quantified, based on the probability of work being realized and the timing of each prospect's final decision. For example, we have developed a system whereby proposed fees for "hot" prospect proposals are factored at 60%, "warm" prospects at 30%, and "cool" prospects at 10%. Cash flow forecasting is more an art than a financial skill. It takes some experience and judgment to sense the probabilities of when receipts will arrive and which prospects will actually become new clients.

The cash flow forecast is projected ahead at least six months with the realization that beyond three months everything is basically a wild guess. Long-term uncertainty is due to "hot" prospects who may decide not to accept a proposal and "cool" prospects who may say "yes" when you least expect it. Even work-in-progress, while sold, may be delayed or rescheduled, based on changing client priorities.

The cash flow forecast is the principal document for avoiding all the uncertainties of managing a consulting practice, determining how your firm is doing against its financial plan, and seeing whether you can meet your financial commitments. Without it, you are flying blind!

Second, an effective *time and expense report* is mandatory. Each consultant logs in daily the hours spent on a particular client account, on business development, on training, and on administrative matters (see Exhibit 19-2). This report should be submitted at two-week intervals so that the office manager can keep client files up-to-date in preparation for month-end billings. The time and expense report is also necessary to assure that consultants are reimbursed for out-of-pocket expenses and to ascertain that clients are charged back for direct costs incurred.

Third, each client file requires a *billing worksheet* (see Exhibit 19-3), which contains a summary of client charges from the time and expense report. The billing worksheet is the foundation for preparing each client's invoice at month-end. It is also used by the client director to manage each client's profitability through comparing fees and expenses billed versus work-in-progress.

The fourth form needed to manage your business is a *personnel planning sheet*, which is prepared by the managing partner every month to identify work assigned to each consultant (see Exhibit 19-4). Its purpose is to identify those consultants who are overloaded and those who have hours available for reassignment. You cannot afford to leave expensive consultants sitting around the office. Their time must be close to 80% billable or profits slip dramatically.

Together, these four forms allow you to plan and control your practice and ultimately to provide your clients with the best possible professional support.

RECRUITING, TRAINING, AND CAREER DEVELOPMENT

Two vastly different hiring strategies prevail in the consulting industry. One, which is pursued more by larger firms, is to hire bright young people out of MBA programs from the same leading business schools attended by the firm's partners. The second approach, followed more by smaller firms, is to seek older, more experienced people from large consulting firms or from corporations. Each strategy has very different consequences for recruitment, training, and career development.

The larger firm knows where to go directly for its prospects: to Harvard, Stanford, Dartmouth, and Wharton. They look mainly at the top 10% of each graduating class and offer them high starting salaries. These new recruits are then given narrow responsibility for performing specialized segments on large projects under the supervision of a hierarchy of project and client directors. Each year the recruits are weeded out by appraisal and self-selection until, at the end of seven to ten years, only about 5% remain for partner consideration.

While this "up or out" promotion strategy may seem heartless, it has numerous advantages for the large firm and even its recruits. For the firm, it polishes their "elitist" image and provides for low-risk foul-ups on client assignments. Little money is spent on training, because the recruits are supervised closely, and besides they already "think" like their partners based on similar educational backgrounds. Moreover, new blood is entering the firm continually, and malcontents are removed with ease.

For the recruits, it is fine on-the-job training enroute to a lucrative executive job with a client. They are able to skip the lengthy process of having to spend years climbing the corporate hierarchy. As future high-placed executives, they become "seeds" for returning later to hire their former colleagues as consultants to their corporations. This personnel policy of planned turnover, in essence, becomes a shrewd marketing strategy.

Conversely, the small firm should look more for consultants with business experience. It takes too long to assimilate an inexperienced graduate; the risk in letting loose a new recruit to deal directly with a client on a broadly defined project is too great. Clients look for their primary consultant to have a few gray hairs. But if you are the only silver fox in a small firm filled with precocious kids, then prepare yourself for a nervous breakdown. Your conservative clients will expect you to do all the work.

Where does the small firm go for its new recruits? Most often it goes to larger consulting firms for those individuals who like consulting but can't stand the monolithic structure. Or it goes to corporations where executives or specialists are ready for a change. Leads for new hires may occur through friends or previous clients, although it is important to advertise to be sure that all the available talent has been reached. Hiring only your friends or friends of friends can get sticky.

The small firm must screen and test prospects more carefully than does a large firm. A bad decision can be quite costly, not only in terms of salary, but also because that one "bad apple" in a small firm can wreak havoc. If possible, try to evaluate candidates on a "temporary" basis through part-time assignments on current projects. That way you are able to tell if the "chemistry" is right. Another alternative is to negotiate a one-year contract, which allows for a mutual evaluation with better data.

Being short on personnel for a project is no reason to hire a permanent employee. A new hire should occur only when you are certain that there is enough future work to guarantee at least one year's employment. Hiring someone just to complete a project and letting him or her go six months later is downright unprofessional; you cannot play roulette with other people's lives. The new hire in a small firm is expecting a longer-term career with an opportunity to become a partner. The high-turnover philosophy of larger firms is inappropriate for small consulting firms.

Another source of valuable part-time help for the small firm can be professors at local universities. They are particularly useful on difficult or esoteric assignments where the academic's knowledge can provide the right novelty to untie a Gordian knot. Professors may also be a source of client referrals and they can add prestige needed to make "the big sale."

COMPENSATION

Remuneration in consulting firms occurs in the typical form of salaries, fringes, and bonuses. However, the manner of handling them is different from traditional manufacturing firms. Consulting firms employ and depend upon high-priced professionals whose sensitive egos expect "kid-glove treatment" in salary, incentives, and appraisals. Complicating that reality is the uncertainty of revenues where a few lost proposals can suddenly create a bad bottom line from which to support an expensive staff. Variations in pay schemes are also dictated between large and small consulting firms and between partnerships and corporations.

Salaries in all consulting firms are fixed each year for the staff, including the partners, although theoretically everyone's salary is a draw upon anticipated earnings. Base salaries should be set only so high as to attract and retain talent, but not so high as to risk laying someone off if revenues don't materialize. Instead of excessively high salaries, we prefer a profit-sharing plan. It creates an incentive to keep costs under control and makes the firm less vulnerable to downturns.

Fringe benefits should be comprehensive in terms of health and life insurance. Most insurance companies provide group plans that will meet your needs. However, retirement programs are more complicated. Some firms don't have them, preferring to pay their staffs well and let them plan their own retirement incomes. Other firms choose IRA (Investment Retirement Account) or Keogh plans, and some large firms manage their own investment funds.

By far the most important and challenging method of remuneration is the profit-sharing plan. How much do the partners take out? What will be reinvested in the future development of the firm? How much should be set aside for the staff? And what should be the evaluation procedure for deciding upon profit distribution?

The first place *not* to begin is with the partners' share of the pie. We have seen too many firms with greedy partners who drained the business and left everyone else with slim pickings. That practice leads to high turnover and no growth.

We favor setting aside up to 35% of staff salaries for incentive compensation, especially in small firms where everyone must pull his or her weight. This bonus pool is distributed according to year-end performance appraisals that will be discussed in the next section. Obviously, the professional staff is going to share more in the pool than is the administrative staff. Some firms will even award an extra profit share of up to 10% of everyone's salary in especially good years. This philosophy helps to maintain an atmosphere of "we're all in it together."

Next comes reinvestment in the future of the firm. If the firm is to grow, you will need to make new investments in office space, equipment, recruiting, training, research, and marketing. Progressive firms will give careful attention to planning for these needs, because doing so assures long-term profitability. Reinvestment often takes precedence over profit-sharing in small firms.

Finally, we get to the partners, or the principal stockholders. They are left with the very delicate problem of evaluating and assigning income to themselves. How can this be done without causing hard feelings? The easiest way is to distribute the remaining income equally, assuming that each partner deserves the same reward because all bear ultimate responsibility and liability for the success of the firm. Equal shares is a typical practice in small firms with two or three partners who are equal owners.

But when the firm grows to include "senior" and "junior" partners, it is faced with a more difficult equation. The most common practice is the creation of a share system whereby differential shares are held and rewarded on the basis of seniority and performance. A subcommittee of partners is assigned the task of assessing performance each year and awarding new shares. A uniform share value is calculated on the basis of dividing profits available for distribution by the total shares outstanding. Junior partners are often asked to buy new share awards out of their income, which provides an indirect source of reinvestment capital.

PERFORMANCE APPRAISAL

An effective performance appraisal scheme must underlie all distribution of income. It also serves as an indirect control mechanism during the year, as each partner and staff member gauges his or her actions toward the firm's performance criteria. All consulting firms tend to adhere basically to the same criteria for assessing performance.

Performance on Client Assignments

This involves an evaluation of each individual's contribution to each client assignment. Has he or she enhanced the quality of the work? Was the work completed on time? Were relationships with the clients managed well? Has he or she been a team player within the engagement team?

Management of Client Assignments

An assessment of executive qualities is necessary for those who are responsible for supervising assignments. Have they performed within budgets and schedules? Did they manage and appraise their subordinates well? Was each client satisfied with the product?

New Business Development

An evaluation is made of the marketing success of each individual. What was his or her volume of new business? How much did he or she generate from existing clients? Was this individual active in making new contacts? What was his or her contribution to proposal development?

Technical and Professional Development

This area focuses on the individual's improvement in the skills of being an effective consultant. In what substantive areas has this individual improved his or her expertise? Did he or she write any articles or make any public presentations? Is this individual active in professional organizations? What seminars did he or she attend?

Typically weights are placed on each of these four areas depending on the overall goals of the firm and on each individual's level within the firm. If the firm needs new business, then this will receive greater priority and weight overall. Generally partners will be assigned a higher weight for new business development than are senior consultants, who are held more accountable for their project management results. Junior members will be evaluated more on their technical skills and client relationships than on their management or marketing abilities.

Performance assessments are highly subjective, due to the complexity of consulting work and the high degree of teamwork required. It therefore helps to involve more than one person in making appraisals, including the appraisee. Professionals are often more self-critical than others; so don't attempt to play God. Because of sensitive egos, the focus of any appraisal should be on constructive improvement, unless you desire to "counsel" someone out of the firm.

We favor a modest management-by-objectives approach where, at the beginning of each year, the consultant submits and discusses his or her specific goals for the coming year in each of the four categories mentioned earlier. This approach encourages the consultant to "own" his or her goals, which results in better self-control during the year and aids in self-evaluation at the end of the year. We prefer that each consultant submit a file at year-end with a list of accomplishments and a self-critique.

OFFICE MANAGER
AND STAFF SUPPORT

When you become a firm of 15 to 20 professionals, you should consider the recruitment of a good *office manager*. The role of office manager is multifaceted and the pivotal point around which the firm's daily activities flow. A job description for an office manager might appear as follows:

- Manages all the firm's bank accounts, payroll taxes, and payables and is the principal interface with the firm's CPA firm to prepare and produce monthly and special financial reports.
- Collates all time and expense reports in preparation for monthly client billings.
- Prepares and sends out all client invoices and tracks accounts receivables.
- Manages all office supplies and purchasing and monitors and is the principal interface with all outside vendors.
- Administers all fringe benefits and is the principal contact with all insurance, pension, and other similar vendors.
- Types minutes of all partners' or principals' meetings, updates policy and procedure manuals, and maintains the firm's library of technical books, journals, notes, and client reports.

The following is a different analysis of management consultant personnel:

Managing Partner. Leaps tall buildings in a single bound; is more powerful than a locomotive; faster than a speeding bullet; walks on water; gives policy to God.

Partner. Leaps short buildings in a single bound; is more powerful than a switch engine; is just as fast as a speeding bullet; walks on water if the sea is calm; talks with God.

Lead Consultant. Leaps short buildings with a running start and favorable winds; is almost as powerful as a switch engine; faster than a speeding BB; walks on water in an indoor swimming pool; talks with God if special request is approved.

Junior Consultant. Barely clears a quonset hut; loses tug of war with locomotive; can fire a speeding bullet; swims well; is occasionally addressed by God.

Analyst. Makes high marks on the wall when trying to leap buildings; is run over by locomotives; can sometimes handle a gun without inflicting self-injury; dog paddles; talks to animals.

Junior Analyst. Runs into buildings; recognizes locomotives two out of three times; is not issued ammo; can stay afloat with a life jacket; talks to walls.

Management Trainee. Falls over the doorstep when trying to enter the building; says, "Look at the Choo Choo"; sprays himself with a water pistol; plays in mud puddles; mumbles to himself.

Office Manager. Lifts buildings and walks under them; kicks locomotives off the tracks; catches speeding bullets in her teeth and eats them; freezes water with a single glance; SHE IS GOD.

   Effective secretarial support becomes paramount to the firm's success. Consultants become angry and ineffective very quickly if their proposals are riddled with typographical errors, if their reports are not completed on time, if their telephone messages are not relayed properly, or if their travel arrangements are handled improperly.
   At the same time, it is not cost effective for each consultant to have his or her own full-time super executive secretary, if for no other reason than the fact that fully chargeble consultants are out of the office dealing with clients a good deal of the time, and when they are in the office, they give their secretaries enough work at one time for three people.
   To resolve this irregular work load, many firms use a "team" approach to secretarial support, for example, by requiring three consultants to share one secretary. This ratio works fine in a busy office, because the odds are that on any given day two of the three consultants will be out of the office.
   In periods of high activity, when one consultant has a major report to produce and the other is developing 50 copies of a training manual for a client's management seminar, one consultant negotiates informally with the other consultant to determine whose project has priority. If they are unable to balance the work load, then another secretary in the office may be used. In a large office, it helps to have one or two people assigned full time to typing and printing major reports.
   You cannot scrimp on secretarial salaries. Be very selective in recruiting secretaries who are excellent, detail-oriented typists, as this will be 70–80% of their work. They should also have friendly and cooperative personalities and be willing to work overtime or on Saturdays if a major project falls behind schedule. They also must be professional in dealing with clients on the telephone, as well as familiar with handling travel arrangements. In essence, you are not seeking an executive

"hands-off" secretary, but rather a highly organized, personable, and skilled typist-assistant. They are hard to find and, once found, are invaluable. Take good care of them!

ORGANIZATION AND PLANNING

As with your client's organization, one of the fundamental needs of your firm is planning its business strategy and organizing the work of others. If you decide on maintaining a small firm, much of this can be done by you personally. But if you have opted to grow and have visions of competing with the Big 8 and McKinsey someday, then your organization and planning must be delegated to other principals.

Basic choices must be made about how to organize for different market segments. The key choices are (1) Is responsibility to be assigned based largely on different products, such as for data-processing clients, or strategic planning jobs, or executive search assignments? or (2) Will it be a geographically based organization with a variety of offices in different cities? or (3) Is it to be an industry-oriented firm with assignments for real estate clients, utilities, banking, and so on?

Smaller firms will usually combine product, geography, and industry informally among two or three partners. They become "jacks of all trades" in a variety of products and industries. Larger firms will grow by concentrating more people exclusively on one or two of the choices. For example, one consultant might open another office; another might pursue the real estate industry; still another might become known for specialization in compensation studies.

The choice you make depends not only on the size of your firm, but also on the strengths and preferences of your personnel as well as on the market opportunities facing you. It may be that one partner wants to move his home to a "hot" new market, so you decide to grow geographically by opening another office. Or it may be that a successful client leads you to other clients in the same industry, so you decide to focus on that single industrial growth segment. The point is to be aware of alternative choices and organize appropriately. The basic segments become profit centers around which to plan, allocate resources, and measure performance.

Even after you make an organizational choice, the firm will have to be managed flexibly. Partners and senior consultants may be assigned responsibility for a single segment, but lower-level consultants must often remain as a "pool" to be "farmed out" across various segments. You have, in essence, a matrix organization, where junior consultants are reporting to two or three bosses at the same time. This requires skillful coordination among the senior partners who, if they are in continual conflict, will demoralize young consultants and possibly overrun costs on delayed projects.

To give guidance to the overall organizational structure, we suggest formation of either a *partners' executive committee* or a board of directors to act as a source of advice and accountability for the managing partner. This group should be a "working" committee, not a ceremonial association. It should meet at least quarterly to review and approve major plans and decisions facing the firm.

All of this brings us, finally and most importantly, to the planning process of the firm. Strategic choice provides the essence of all consulting firms, large or small. Without choice, the firm and its consultants remain adrift in a vast, highly competitive, and unpredictable marketplace. Choice is a "proactive" decision to take control and to aim the firm's energy toward a particular market niche. You cannot be all things to all clients. If you attempt to do so, you will be nothing.

What are the basic choices? To remain small or to grow? To provide a broadly based practice or to offer a specialized product? To concentrate on a few industries or to service many different ones? To remain local or to expand regionally or nationally? To be a partnership or a corporation?

These choices must be made in an interrelated fashion so that one decision does not contradict another. For example, you cannot be a national firm without obviously choosing to grow in size and geography. Another watchword is to keep your choices realistic in terms of the strengths and weaknesses of the firm—you cannot specialize in compensation studies unless you have a high degree of expertise in that field. Overall, you will have to update your plans constantly as the firm gains experience through success and failure in a dynamic marketplace. Strategic choice is validated only by the positive reactions of clients.

How do you go about formulating a plan in a consulting firm? You cannot plan in an autocratic fashion as if you are running an impersonal bureaucracy. Three important criteria to apply are openness, participation, and consensus. Openness is essential to confront natural differences in opinion inherent to a highly personalized business. Participation is required to tap valuable ideas and soothe professional egos. Consensus is vital for moving a diverse and autonomous staff in a coherent and coordinated direction.

We suggest a semiannual planning conference that is conducted away from the office and that includes all the key staff. This should be a "take off the gloves" session, where plans are critiqued thoroughly and reformulated. Preparation for the meeting is essential to give the discussion a clear focus, and it should concentrate on new issues and opportunities solicited from the firm's employees beforehand. This will put a constructive emphasis on creating new plans for the future, instead of defending the past. A side benefit from this "off-site" session is a more relaxed and personalized atmosphere that aids in rebuilding the *esprit de corps* among staff members who may rarely see each other, except in passing at airports.

MANAGING THE WORK LOAD

Assuming that you have followed our advice and have found a good partner, set up your own firm, generated a backlog of billings, hired additional staff, established a matrix organization, created a sound compensation program, and devised an overall strategy, there still remains the pragmatic operating question of how to manage the work load without doing everything yourself. As the managing principal, you must decide who to assign to which projects and in what capacities, how to control the work-in-progress on a given job, and how to motivate the bright people you have recruited.

The role of a managing principal is a complex one that attempts to orchestrate a variety of professional talents and personalities around a variety of constantly changing client needs. The key to performing such a role successfully rests, in our experience, on careful quality control of work-in-progress, while also assuring the ongoing training of the professional staff.

Each client should be the ultimate responsibility of one of the firm's principals, regardless of which member of the staff is appointed to be "client director" on the assignment. That principal, then, screens the initial proposal, attends business development meetings with the client, and guides the "client director" in selecting a team to do the work. Many of the factors leading to that decision will rest on the client's "personality." Different consultants will be selected if the client's environment consists of bright young people working in an informal structure, as compared with a highly structured client with older, conservative executives.

Once an engagement is underway, the *principal in charge*, better known as the PIC, should develop and rigorously use *status reports* on all client assignments. A status report is an informal memorandum for the client's file that reviews briefly each and every trip made to the client as well as any major telephone conversations. A good status report documents which consultants visited the client, for what purpose, who was contacted in the client's organization, and what was accomplished and gives a brief analysis of the client's situations, outlines the proposed next steps, and presents a schedule for future trips. A status report not only helps the client director to organize his or her thoughts, but it is a means whereby the PIC can stay in close touch and in control. If any member of the consulting team should fall ill or leave the firm, his or her replacement can be oriented quickly to the project through reading the status reports chronologically. The PIC also should ask to see the client director's detailed notes periodically to assure that the right issues are being addressed. (See Exhibit 19-5.)

Another method of project control for the PIC is informal debriefings. Just as the client director should be debriefed by his or her on-site team each evening back at the hotel through "dumping" information gathered during the day's work, so, too, should the PIC receive a debriefing from the client director upon returning from each visit to the client.

Further, each PIC should schedule at least one visit to the client in the middle of a project or at least once per quarter on lengthy projects to test the client's perception of how the job is progressing and to obtain feedback on how the client's employees are reacting to the consulting team and the client director.

Finally, the PIC should review all final reports and recommendations prepared for the client, attend all final presentations, and, most important, help sell more work.

Occasionally a bright, aggressive client director will chafe at the PIC's attempts at control, interpreting such behavior as a demonstration of lack of trust in the capability of the client director. Usually these misunderstandings can be resolved quickly by reminding the client director that, if the project, for any reason, is fouled up, the worst that can happen to the client director is loss of his or her job while the worst that can happen to the partner is loss of the firm.

One of the most difficult responsibilities of a managing principal is assuring the ongoing training of an already highly educated professional staff. In the consulting profession, however, formal training can be extraordinarily expensive. For example, with partners' billing up to $1,000-a-day and staff consultants up to $750-a-day, a one-day in-house training seminar for two partners and ten consultants can cost the firm almost $10,000 in lost revenues. To hold one day of in-house training each month equals $120,000 a year of lost revenues, assuming that the work has been sold and could have been performed. This realization has put off many consulting firms from developing in-house training and has influenced others to hold training programs exclusively on weekends so as not to compromise billable time. Neither approach is sound.

To avoid training for the purpose of sharing client experiences, knowledge, and problems is to shortchange both the professional development of the staff and the long-term growth of the firm. To insist that training days occur on weekends when everyone is tired from the previous week's travel can only lead to turnover, absenteeism, and a resistance to learn anything.

Our experience has been that it pays to schedule one day of training a month during the week to allow all professional people to discuss their projects with each other and to focus on unique client issues. These staff training sessions should be planned well enough in advance so that everyone is scheduled to be in town that day, say, a Monday or a Friday.

There are also other steps that a managing principal can take to encourage professional development. One is the creation of a *reading file*, which is a centrally located box for each client into which is placed a copy of everything—letters, status reports, proposals, final reports, inter-office memos, technical notes to the client. Everyone on the staff is encouraged to read the file whenever they have time, and every three months or so the file should be cleaned out so that a new file can build up. The result is a broadening awareness among all staff members for what is going on with all clients, thereby making it possible to share knowledge across projects.

The frequent interchange of staff communication can be facilitated by the supportive physical layout of office space. The offices of principals should be scattered among the staff instead of being cloistered in a single isolated area. As the firm grows and the partners can afford it, comfortable coffee rooms and libraries can be developed where space exists for professionals to meet and talk shop. The firm's internal library is a sound training source where consultants can read previous client research and specialized reports on compensation, organization, and market research. Surely, if a consultant has never worked on a compensation assignment before, it is imperative that the consultant go to the firm's library and read a copy of every compensation study performed by the firm in the past few years.

A further training ploy used by many of our colleagues is to put together different staff members with different skills on client assignments so that they can learn directly from each other. For example, a consultant needing to sharpen his or her skills in report writing might be paired with a client director who excels in that area while another consultant with a shy demeanor with clients can be paired with one of the more socially fearless client directors.

RECOMMENDED READINGS

ALTMAN, MARY ANN, and ROBERT I. WEIL, *Managing Your Accounting and Consulting Practice*. New York: Matthew Bender, 1978.

KELLEY, ROBERT E., Consulting: The Complete Guide to a Profitable Career. New York: Charles Scribner & Sons, 1981.

MARTIN, CHARLES C., *Project Management: How To Make It Work*. New York: AMACOM, 1976.

MANCUSO, JOSEPH R., "How To Name- and Not Name - a Business," *Harvard Business Review,* November/December 1978.

EXHIBIT 19-1 Sample Cash Flow Forecast

CHARLES, CRANSTON, KATO + KENT CASH FLOW FORECAST, MAY - DECEMBER

	MAY	JUNE	JULY	AUGUST	SEPT	OCT	NOV	DEC
RECEIPTS ($)								
CONTAMINATION CHEMICAL			1,500	1,000				
FLAMEOUT FEDERAL	1,500	250	250	250	250	250	250	250
ECI		500						
CALAMITY BANK		2000		4000	5000	5000	3000	3000
OTHER A						500		
B						2500	5000	5000
C							5000	5000
TOTAL RECEIPTS	1,500	2750	1,750	5250	5,250	8,250	13,250	13,250
EXPENSES ($)								
RENT	275	275	275	275	275	275	275	275
CARS	400	400	400	400	400	400	400	400
TELEPHONE	250	250	250	500	500	500	500	500
COPYING	100	100	100	100	100	100	100	100
PRINTING + OFFICE SUPPLIES	200	1,000		100		100		100
FURNITURE + FIXTURES		2,750						
POSTAGE	20	100	20	20	20	20	20	20
INSURANCE (GROUP MED)	400	400	400	400	400	400	400	400
INSURANCE (OTHER)		500	100	100	100			
LEGAL + ACCOUNTING	200	200	100	100	100	100	100	100
BUSINESS DEVELOPMENT				500	500	500	500	
PAYROLL	1,150	1,150	1,150	1,150	1,150	1,150	1,150	1,150
PAYROLL TAXES	250	250	250	250	250	250	250	250
MISC	150	150			100	100	100	100
TOTAL EXPENSES	3,195	7,525	2,945	3,795	3,795	3,895	3,795	3,395
CASH FLOW	(1,695)	(4,775)	(1,195)	1,455	1,455	4,355	9,455	9,855
BEGINNING BALANCE	10,000	8,305	3,530	2,335	3,790	5,245	9,600	19,055
ENDING BALANCE	8,305	3,530	2,335	3,790	5,245	9,600	19,055	28,910

EXHIBIT 19-2 Sample Time Sheet for All Employees

MONTHLY TIME ANALYSIS

CHARLES, CRANSTON, KATO & KENT

ENDING: APRIL 30, 1982

CLIENT	①/16	②/17	③/18	④/19	5/20	6/21	⑦/22	⑧/23	⑨/24	⑩/25	⑪/26	12/27	13/28	⑭/29	⑮/30	31	TOTAL HOURS
Contamination Chemical	8	8	8	10													34
Flameout Federal							5	8	8								21
Puerto Rico Power										8	8						16
Calamity Bank														8	8		16
TOTAL CHARGEABLE	8	8	8	10			5	8	8	8	8			8	8		87
TRAVEL																	
TRAINING																	
VACATION																	
HOLIDAY																	
BUS. DEVELOPMENT								2	2					2			6
OTHER/ADMIN.							3										3
ILLNESS																	
TOTAL NONCHAR.							3	2	2					2			9
TOTAL ALL TIME	8	8	8	10			8	10	10	8	8			10	8		96

Note: 96 HR ÷ 87 HR BILLED = 91% BILLABLE.

Lamont Cranston
Name

355

EXHIBIT 19-2 (cont'd) **Sample Expense Report**

CHARLES, CRANSTON, KATO & KENT

NAME: *Lamont Cranston*   PERIOD ENDING: *April 30, 1982*

PREPAID EXPENSES (CATEGORY A)

DATE	FROM	TO	CARRIER	CHARGE TO	AMOUNT
4/4	L.A.	Boston	AA	Contamination Chem.	725.00
4/21	L.A.	N.Y.C.	United	Calamity Bank	725.00

TOTAL PREPAID EXPENSE:	$1,450.00
TOTAL OUT–OF–POCKET EXPENSE:	932.50
TOTAL ALL EXPENSES:	$2,382.50
LESS PREPAID EXPENSE:	–1,450.00
LESS TRAVEL ADVANCES:	– 250.00
TOTAL REIMBURSABLE TO ME:	$ 682.50

TOTAL EXPENSE RECONSTRUCTION*

CLIENT ACCOUNT	TRAVEL (A)	HOTEL & MEALS (B)	OTHER EXPENSE (C)	(D)	TOTAL
Cont. Chem.	$851.70	$235.00			$1,086.70
Calamity Bank	901.50	262.50			1,164.00
Bus. Development		131.80			131.80
TOTAL:					$2,382.50

SIGNED: *Lamont Cranston*   DATE: *April 30, 1982*

*CATEGORY (A): ALL PLANE FARES, CAR RENTAL, PARKING, MILEAGE, TAXIS, ETC.
CATEGORY (B): ALL HOTEL, MEALS, AND ENTERTAINMENT EXPENSE, TIPS.
CATEGORY (C): TELEPHONE, POSTAGE, MISCELLANEOUS.
CATEGORY (D): FOR OFFICE USE ONLY.

EXHIBIT 19-3 Sample Billing Sheet

CHARLES, CRANSTON, KATO & KENT

MONTHLY RECAP

CLIENT: _CONTAMINATION CHEMICAL_   MONTH ENDING: _APRIL 1982_

Name	Time Period	Hours Number	Hours Charge	Prof. Fees	Travel	Lodging, Meals	Cartography Fees	Misc.
NICK	1–15	20	$100	$2,000	$600	$352.10	—	—
CHARLES	16–30	10	100	1,000				
LAMONT	1–15							
CRANSTON	16–30							
KATO	1–15	20	50	1,000	600			
	16–30	10	50	500				
CLARK KENT	1–15							
	16–30							
MILLARD	1–15							
FILLMORE	16–30							
JACK B.	1–15	15	30	450	600			
NIMBLE	16–30	15	30	450				
HARRIET	1–15	15	30	450	600			
PERT	16–30	15	30	450				
Total				$5,300	$2,400	$352.10		

Total Fees: $ 5,300

Name	Time Period	Hours Number	Hours Charge	Fees	Tel.	Copy	Postage, Freight	Cartography Supplies
PATIENCE	1–15	10	$15	$150	$72.50	$34.00	$10.00	—
	16–30	5	15	75				
PRUDENCE	1–15							
	16–30							
PUBERTY	1–15	20	15	300				
	16–30	20	15	300				
Total				$825	$72.50	$34.00	$10.00	

Total Expenses: $ 3,693.60

Grand Total: $ 8,993.60

EXHIBIT 19-4   Sample Work Planning Sheet

WORK PLANNING SHEET

CHARLES, CRANSTON, KATO & KENT

CLIENT: *Flameout Federal*   DATE: *15 April 1982*

   Nick Charles   JOB: *Org. Study*

   Partner in charge

CONSULTANT	TASK	TOTAL HOURS	RATE	ESTIMATED FEES
Charles	*Org. Dev. & Report*	*200*	*$100*	*$ 20,000*
Kato	*Research*	*400*	*50*	*20,000*
Pert	*Research*	*450*	*30*	*13,500*
TOTALS		*1,050*		*$53,500*

PLUS ESTIMATED EXPENSES: *@ 20% of fees*   *10,700*

TOTAL TO BE PROPOSED: $ *64,200*

ANTICIPATED BILLING:

	MONTH	*June*	*July*	*Aug.*	*Sept.*	*Oct.*		TOTALS *5 mos.*
	AMOUNT	*10,000*	*10,000*	*20,000*	*10,000*	*14,200*		*$64,200*

EXHIBIT 19-5   Example of a Status Report

STATUS REPORT

The Bank of Disintermediation

Denver

7 March 1981

NC and ABD traveled to Denver on 3 March to meet with George
Winless to review our recommendations with respect to the merged
organization of Disintermediation and the Seventy Second State
Bank of Colorado Springs.

As mentioned in earlier status reports, we believe that George's
insensitive and "macho" behavior is the major constraint to a
smooth, well accepted merger and we were quite direct in our
presentation of this point. George had a great deal of trouble
accepting this fact.   However, by the end of the 5 hour presentation, he began rationalizing the recommendation that he place an
EVP between himself and the organization. He also accepted our
advice to call in Frank Fearless from Colorado Springs to discuss
our proposal that he be appointed the first EVP.

For the most part, the functional organizational recommendations
were acceptable to Winless and, overall, the meeting seemed to
go well.

Merger Time Table

However, with respect to the timing of the merger, another bank in
Colorado Springs filed a protest on the proposed name of the
merged banks and a name change has been instituted by Winless and
his board.   This protest, though, will delay the final approval
of the merger by the authorities in Washington until late
September or October.   This pushes back our entire schedule of
support to the merger process and it is questionable if we will
have any more work to perform on this assignment after March until
July or August.

Marketing

In an effort to sell some product development and marketing work
to Disintermediation to fill in the gap of April, May and June,
NC met with Jim Joyfull on Wednesday, 5 March. We shared with him
our general approach to our work with Flameout Federal.   Joyfull
will get back to us.

EXHIBIT 19-5   (cont'd)

Frank Fearless

On Thursday, we orchestrated a meeting between Fearless and
Winless. The meeting went very well with both parties being very
candid with each other. The major points communicated from
Winless to Fearless were:

- We are doing everything possible here and in
  Washington to make the merger happen;

- We have paid a high price for your bank but
  part of that is for the people;

- There will be no EVP as of the first day of
  the merger but there will be one within six
  to nine months and you (Frank) have a good
  shot at it;

- I am very concerned if any of the younger
  officers in Colorado Springs misunderstood my
  statements - they are all valued by me.

Fearless' major points to Winless were:

- We, too, want the merger to be successful;

- My younger officers are behind you but they
  are a little nervous and immature - I will work
  to calm their fears;

- I feel I can contribute to the merged organization and want a chance at a high level to do so;

- I have not made up my mind to leave so don't
  believe any industry rumors to the contrary;

- I am prepared to move to Denver;

- Please understand, we still have a responsibility
  to our shareholders to have a contingency plan
  just in case the merger doesn't get approved, but
  please don't misinterpret our activity in this
  area to mean that we are not 100% behind the
  merger.

Modifications to Our Proposal

Winless, in general, is pleased and was very friendly to us as
we left for the airport. He would like us to expand our recommendations to include three organizations at different asset level
sizes, with no EVP, with one EVP and with two EVP's.

EXHIBIT 19-5 **(cont'd)**

<u>Next Steps</u>

We were able to speak to several new issues as they came up on Thursday. Each may generate additional business for us. They are as follows:

. Fearless and the Colorado Springs organization needs help in financial planning, training and NOW account development. We offered to send Frank a proposal and he was very positive to this idea;

. We stressed to George that to assure a smooth merger, he needs to give some organizational, personnel administration and training support to various parts of his present organization. George agreed and suggested we follow-up with him on this later in the month; and,

. We have outlined a marketing proposal to help Jim Joyfull. This, too, should be followed-up in a few weeks.

Our next steps are to make some modifications and additions to our organizational proposal and to follow-up with Winless on any modifications he and his management team may make in the coming weeks.

Index